The Enlightened Leader

With due recognition of the increasingly important role that female leaders play in corporate life, this book follows the convention of using male forms in cases where both genders are meant – 'mankind' has always included women – but where it could be done elegantly both forms were used. All cases presented here are true to life, yet modified sufficiently to preclude recognition of individuals or organisations discussed.

Legal Note

All 'Archetypes' presented are 'faction': pieces of fiction, inspired by actual events, but so fundamentally altered as to not reveal any living person's or any functioning organisation's identity. All characters named with first name and initial are composites, created by arranging aspects of a variety of living persons' personalities, similar to the manner in which characters are created in novels. While the authors regret this departure from truth in the literal sense, they feel that this way of presenting reality, while shielding individuals, offers them a reliable and effective way to present some core issues of personality and leadership, and that in the process verity is never compromised.

The Chakras of Leadership presented in this book come to life on www. chakratest.org

The greatest challenge for leadership in this era is to bring love into the corporate sphere

The Enlightened Leader

An introduction to the Chakras of Leadership

Peter ten Hoopen & Fons Trompenaars

JOSSEY-BASS
A Wiley Imprint
www.josseybass.com

Other Wiley Editorial Offices

Library of Congress Cataloging-in-Publication Data

Hoopen, Peter ten.
    The enlightened leader : an introduction to the chakras of leadership / Peter ten Hoopen & Fons
Trompenaars; foreword by Dr Herman Wijffels.
       p.   cm.
    Includes bibliographical references and index.
    ISBN 978-0-470-71396-9 (cloth)
    1. Leadership.   2. Chakras (Theosophy)   I. Trompenaars, Alfons.   II. Title.
    HD57.7.H65 2009
    658.4'092 – dc22   2008052046

British Library Cataloguing in Publication Data

A catalogue record for this book is available from the British Library

ISBN 978-0-470-71396-9

Typeset in SNP Best-set Typesetter Ltd., Hong Kong
Printed and bound in Great Britain by TJ International Ltd, Padstow, Cornwall, U.K.

Contents

Foreword

Recent developments have exposed something which managed to remain hidden for decades: that a fundamental revision of the role of business in society is long overdue. What contribution to society do we expect from corporations? Is their duty limited to satisfying the shareholders – or do we expect something beyond this? Do we expect, for instance, a positive contribution to the world, environmental awareness, a dedication to civic causes? And in strictly pragmatic terms: while we claim that in our present economy, dominated by services and knowledge transfer, people are our most valuable assets, our cherished human capital, are we doing what we need to make this capital yield superior results?

In *The Enlightened Leader*, Peter ten Hoopen and Fons Trompenaars make us aware that as leaders, we are often too busy managing our organisations to notice that the world around us is changing rapidly, and that a new type of leadership is by now required. A leadership which celebrates sustainability as one of its core principles, is marked by a more humane and consequently more inspiring way of dealing with employees, and is based, not on the imposition of will, but on the creation and cultivation of shared passion. A type of leadership that we may variously call 'enlightened', 'authentic', 'transformational', or 'resonant', and which is grounded in authenticity and a sense of connectedness.

How do we attain this authenticity and sense of connectedness? Firstly, by becoming aware of who we really are as human beings, and of our basic connectedness across racial, geographic, religious and gender boundaries. Reaching this awareness is not an easy task, especially for business leaders, because most corporations are still chained to the old mechanistic paradigm, forcefully resist pressures to change, and exert tremendous pressure on both society and corporate leaders to stick to the established *modus operandi*. But a growing number of leaders around the world are

starting to view organisations, not as machines, but as organisms or biotopes. In this conceptual context a new type of leadership emerges, the
contours of which – thanks to an intensifying global public debate – are
now starting to come into focus.

The authors' way of drawing us into the dialogue helps our own process
of awareness, so that we may formulate a clear and resolute answer to the
question: 'What kind of leader am I?' And to the even more important
question: 'What kind of leader do I *want* to be?'

To confidently answer such questions, a fair level of self-knowledge is
required. This book introduces a new system, the Chakras of Leadership,
which helps to attain insight in the fortuitous and rather less fortuitous,
or even detrimental aspects of our own leadership. Wholly apart from the
merits of this specific system, any structured way to look at our own
leadership is enlightening *per se*. Given the corporate world's entrenched
scepticism towards any views not canonised by MBA-courses, it is com-
mendable that the authors have presented the yoga metaphor of centres
of energy as a self-referential system, which requires no belief in chakras.
The only mental state required is belief in the power of one's own vital
energy, and the resulting dedication to careful management of its application in the world.

The title, *The Enlightened Leader*, the authors state emphatically and
repeatedly, is not about pretence, but about aspiration. It is not the exposé
of some people proudly telling us how enlightened they are, and how
enlightened we shall all become if we just follow them, but the modest
report of people who are seeking, and share their findings. That report is
written in a literary voice, caustic where unfortunate cases are presented,
but with a noticeable lightness of being, and a kind of self-deprecating
humour which helps us digest what is in essence deeply serious matter.

I strongly recommend *The Enlightened Leader* to anyone who feels that
there must be more in the world than chasing ever greater profits, whatever the cost to self or society, and who further feels that his or her own
talents, and the power of the organisation, should be applied to make the
world a somewhat better place.

Dr. Herman Wijffels, Executive Director of the World Bank

Authors' Note

Several people, no doubt all having our best interests at heart, have discouraged us from writing this book, or publishing it under this title. 'Be very wary of introducing such terms in the corporate world. "Enlightenment" – what percentage of your target audience do you think is ready for that? You'll end up marginalising yourself! When it comes down to it, no one is interested in anything but profits.' Followed by more and similar advice, all equally well-intentioned. Coming from people who know the corporate world from many years of experience, *and* feel that the world is crying out for messages such as those contained in this book.

This all goes to show how much fear there is in the thinking of otherwise clear-headed people. Unfortunately, fear does not bring enlightenment, but endarkenment. And unfortunately we have seen much of that at the beginning of this century. Anyone desiring to bring more light into his life needs to start conquering fear, because only then can he live and grow in freedom, and attain the stature for which he was intended. To begin with, we have to speak our minds, write the books that well up in us – and read the books that challenge us to rise above our fears.

What wells up in us is an urge to speak to those we know best, corporate leaders, and challenge them to become truly great. The Chief Challenge for corporate leaders in this day and age of globalisation and diversification is to recognise, respect and utilise the power of the heart, because as human beings we are becoming ever closer, both physically and in terms of knowledge and shared (media) experience, and cannot keep our hearts closed to one another without causing conflict, disruption and impoverishment.

This book forms part of a collective work in which thousands of people all over the world are cooperating – all with their own unique contributions and limitations, their own insights, and their own language. It aspires to be no more than a contribution to this collective *magnum opus*; written, it is hoped, in a way that resonates and encourages one to join the effort.

Part I

Enlightenment in Theory

A Lofty Notion

Preface by Peter ten Hoopen

'How can you pass on to your readers things you don't know?'

'They are not things I do not know. Everything written there is in my soul, is part of it, they are lessons that I have learned in the course of my life and that I try to apply for myself. I am a reader of my own books. They give me something that I already knew, but of which I was not conscious.'

Paulo Coelho, *The Zahir*

Enlightenment is a lofty notion – and who are the authors, that they may speak of it? Are they that enlightened themselves? No, unfortunately, there is still a long way to go. The title of this work therefore reflects *not pretence but aspiration*. To further banish any suggestion of self-aggrandisement, let me divulge the trade secret of gurus and management trainers worldwide: we teach what we need to learn.

The subject matter suggested itself to me because I am a seeker. Not in the sense of 'desperately seeking', but in the sense of 'living consciously' – conscious of our connectedness with all living things, of connectedness with our own personal destination. This seeking began around my twenty-fifth with a three year journey to India[1], and was later continued, with varying degrees of application and varying results. My only right to speak derives from this seeking. All seekers have a right to speak, because others learn so much from the accounts of their inner journeys, of their hope and despair, their discoveries and disappointments, the rocks on the path, the sun on the skin.

Stimulated by the strong undercurrent of enthusiasm for the theme of enlightened leadership that I encountered in conversations with friends in the corporate world – like Charles Handy[2] I found no dearth of hungry spirits out there! – I set off on this path by taking a good hard look at myself, by listening to the voices of masters, in person and in writing, and by pairing those impressions with my twenty-five years of experience in consultancy and communication – many of them devoted to helping shape and communicate corporate personality. Since joining up with Fons Trompenaars, serving as Senior Consultant for Trompenaars Hampden-Turner, I have been able to hone my thinking on the whetstone of multiple realities in a great variety of cultural spheres. Many insights were gained from often intense group sessions and individual work with people from fifty different countries, and of course from discussions with Fons, whose vast experience and clear-headed thinking has been a great source of inspiration. Our shared fascination is the relationship between the corporate personality and the personalities of those who give the organisation its face and voice, and are responsible for its stance in the world.

Building on these insights I have developed a structured approach to personality, the Chakras of Leadership, to shed light on personal aspects of leadership, and make it easier to come to grips with them. The companion 'Chakra Test' website (see www.chakratest.org) aims to provide users with new insights into core aspects of their personalities, by looking at the way they apply their life energy. It helps them answer fundamental questions such as: am I a more or less whole being, or do I neglect certain aspects of my personality? What do I really expend my energy on? Is that energy exerted positively or negatively? And which aspects of my personality show most potential for growth? Ideally, the Chakra Test is used in a coaching environment, in the context of leadership development.

A more elaborate version reserved for consultancy clients is being developed to chart the personality of organisations. It compiles the input of all participants, and provides an image of the current corporate personality juxtaposed with the desired personality. This juxtaposition graphically reveals the *aspirations* of the organisation. Because aspirations are the hidden drivers behind every energy application, the Chakra Test for Organisations is an effective tool for those directing change processes in organisations, especially mergers and acquisitions. Incidental use is indicated for 'personality-critical' processes, such as hiring key employees, outsourcing, and reorganisation. Once what I call the 'energy economy' of the organisation as a whole has been charted, the results of subsequent individual Chakra Tests give all or selected participants an opportunity to see how well their own aspirations and energy focus match those of the organisation.

THE SURVIVAL OF THE HAPPIEST

The goal is to create organisations in which people can discover and develop their full potential – not just because *such organisations will be the sole survivors in the new struggle of the fittest*, but also because it will create more happiness in the corporate environment, in my accounting a valuable goal by itself.

Very soon, in fact, happiness may well be the *most valuable* goal, even in a strict fiscal sense. In a world of freely moving talent, the talent will go where it is most happy. Ever more frequently we see highly talented people accept pay below their maximum earning potential to join organisations they love, respect, or simply feel at home with. This changes the rules of the game, certainly in the sectors where human contributions are most vital to the bottom-line.

Which forces us to consider: who really are the fittest these days? The 'lean and mean' shops that manage to pay the lowest hourly wage, no medical? The 'world class combatants' (as one of my clients once demanded to be portrayed) that squeeze the last ounce of juice out of their work force by setting ever higher performance targets? The companies, according to Canadian management-guru Harry Mintzberg, home to over half of all the employed in the USA, where people are scurrying around hectically, living in mortal fear of being fired?[3]

Fons and I – and in fact all of us at Trompenaars Hampden-Turner – believe that a case can be made that the happiest are the fittest, and that in the corporate world, what is really playing now is *the survival of the happiest*. Create happiness, or lose it.

This book grew from great mutual respect, joy in co-operation, and a shared conviction that being pragmatic should not preclude dreaming, and that dreaming should not preclude practical application. Our joint ambition is to enhance your capacity to dream of a better world, and provide tools that help you make this dream become reality.

What is Leadership?

To lead is to find a path forward, to get to where you have not yet been. To lead is to chart the way into unknown territory and make the seemingly impossible possible and actionable.

Aviv Shahar, Founder of Amber Coaching

DEFINITION AND SIZE-UP

Before we can get a clear view of 'the enlightened leader', we should first discuss the fundamental principles, the background that makes him/her stand out so glowingly. Enlightenment is mostly about awareness. Therefore we need to nail this down first: what is leadership, and what is enlightenment?

But far more important than finding the answers to these questions, is the asking itself. As Sue Howard and David Welbourn write in their thorough exploration of *The Spirit at Work Phenomenon*: '... definitions of terms are not as important as actually recognizing the territory and debating meanings together.'[4] The first steps to increased awareness are taken during anamnesis, the exploration of our past: how did our notions about leadership get formed?

And why is it that enlightened leadership – going under this name or others, like authentic leadership, unifying leadership, principle-centred leadership, engaging leadership, et cetera – is such a live topic today? Have we become that endarkened, then? And if so, how did it happen?

So many books have been written on leadership that one might reasonably assume the subject to be exhausted. But the daily news demonstrates that there still is a lot to learn. One of the most quoted phrases in leadership literature is this sentence from James MacGregor Burns' *Leadership*, his wide-ranging study of economic, social and psychological aspects of leadership, canonised as the Genesis of leadership literature: 'Leadership is one of the most observed and least understood phenomena on earth.' [5] He wrote this more than a quarter century ago, but if he were asked today, thousands of books on the subject later, he would probably say the very same thing. Because the social environment constantly changes, and because leading is very difficult.

Why is leading so difficult? Because people don't like to be led and therefore make their leaders' lives hell? No, most people actually are quite keen to be led. The true reason why we keep wrestling with the theme of 'leadership' is, that most people do not like to lead, and therefore make the lives of their subordinates hell.

To preclude misunderstanding: we do not think that people in general are averse to telling others what to do. To the contrary, most people are quite willing or even eager to do so – even when it requires the application of milder, or even ruthless physical force. The Nazis, for instance had no trouble finding willing camp guards, and in Abu Ghraib there didn't appear to be recruitment problems either. No, telling others what to do – people are queuing up for the job. Especially if they get to wear a uniform or a sharp suit. What we mean, is that only very few spontaneously exhibit behaviour that makes others want to follow them. Because that is the essence of leadership: inspiring others to follow.

Many people are allergic to the idea of 'following', of being a 'follower', because it brings to mind the sycophantic, fawning, adulating and brainless following exhibited for instance by some followers of the Hare Krishna movement: 'I haven't got a clue what to do with myself anymore, so I'll just surrender my all to someone else, and then everything will turn out all right.' A kind of spiritual peeing in your pants. A huge relief, and it feels nice and warm, for a while.[6] Let's be very clear about it: this is not the kind of following we are concerned with here. What we are talking about is following in the sense of 'the choice to allow yourself to be directed by someone whose ideas mesh with your own, and who is more advanced than yourself in their development; or someone who makes you achieve insights that you might not have achieved alone, and that suit you so well that they are a constant source of energy'.

Leadership: The capacity to inspire others to follow.

One of the most enlightening texts on this subject is Robert Goffee's and Gareth Jones' classic article in the Harvard Business Review entitled 'Why should anyone be led by you'[7]. A highly confrontational question that many of us should pose ourselves each morning in front of the bathroom mirror: 'Why on earth should anyone be led by you?' Goffee and Jones tabled the question for ten years while consulting for dozens of companies in the United States and in Europe. 'Without fail,' they report, 'the response is a sudden, stunned hush. All you can hear are knees knocking.'

Why this stunned, probably mortified silence? Because the participants found it hard to enunciate why anyone should follow them, of all people. Before trying this yourself, leave alone doing it before the mirror, it may be helpful to take stock of the range of sensible motives to accept someone as your leader – and motives to drop him. Several more will no doubt come to your mind as you go along, but with this short list we cover a fair section of the field:

Reasons for following leader	Reasons to leave leader
• Leader has great strategic acumen, so that following him appears to offer wonderful opportunities to share in his success.	• Leader makes some egregious errors of judgement, opportunities are lost or temporarily diminished.
• Leader promises all who will follow him attractive incentives.	• Incentives turn out to be less attractive than advertised. Or another leader offers yet more attractive incentives.
• Leader has great charisma, that reflects on everyone who works for him or her.	• Charisma is shown to be no guarantee for success (Cf. Jim Collins'*Good to Great*), or reflection is disappointing.
• Leader intimidates and terrorises to such a degree that not-following appears to be a non-option.	• Intimidation lessens or sensitivity to it attenuates as a result of dulling. Or a less threatening alternative presents itself.

Reasons for following leader	Reasons to leave leader
•	• ....
....	....
....	....
....	....
• Leader strives for the attainment of an admirable goal, thereby inspiring to rise to the occasion and make a great contribution.	• None. *(Except in extreme cases, such as dramatic lack of success.)*

Exercise: Tick the reasons why people should follow or leave you, or enter your own into the blank boxes.

Clearly, the last leadership model outperforms all others (except perhaps the one you wrote in yourself) in terms of retention of followers. But some questions remain. What, for instance, constitutes an admirable goal? What does it take to inspire people to make great contributions? And before we rush to applaud the leaders with the greatest host of followers: is follower-retention a sufficient or even a valid criterion for the quality and effectiveness of leadership?

The literature on this subject does not provide an unambiguous answer. To some authors, the single most important benchmark is the sheer number of followers or devotees. To them, Hitler and Gandhi were equally great leaders. Others make a substantial distinction and weigh the quality of the goals set (noble versus ignoble, realistic versus unrealistic), the type of motivation (coercion versus voluntarism or even spontaneity), and the perceived character of the efforts (the human, versus the bestial face).

It will become apparent soon enough where our sympathies lie, so they may as well be exposed right now: the authors of this work belong to the substantive persuasion. In our view, someone who brings death and destruction upon thousands or even millions, can never be called a great leader, at best a great monster. The enshrinement as 'great leader' is to be denied as well to anyone who contributes to despoliation of the environment, direct or indirect assaults on people's health, moral corruption, psychological corrosion, exploitation, usurpation of others' rights, and other negative contributions to the human condition.

A truly great leader has the faculty to unify his followers under the banner of an inspiring vision, based on morally sound principles and socially desirable values – such as integrity, trust, loyalty – and fired by a certain societal or spiritual goal, a shared passion.

To denote this type of leading, James MacGregor Burns coined the term 'transformational leadership', to clearly distinguish it from transactional leadership, the type of leadership which confers power by doing what accrues the greatest number of followers,[8] in politics known as populism. The terminology may be different, but in fact MacGregor Burns is speaking of the same type of leadership that is the subject of this book.

A caveat is called for: the quality of enlightenment is hard to quantify, because we cannot rely on a mere census of the mass of followers, such as suffices for an evaluation of the quality of transactional leadership. Moreover, in the judging of transformational leadership, to stay with Burns' term for a moment, a subjective element will inevitably crop up, because the sympathies of the person who does the evaluating will cast the decisive vote. To some Bush, Sharon, Bin Laden, Putin, Bashayev, Castro, Morales, Berlusconi, or Chavez are great leaders, to others they are devils incarnate. There is no resolving this issue, because the admissibility of subjectively defined desirability as a determinant of value is an essential aspect of this type of leadership.

Those who consider this a weakness, may well reconsider after weighing the potential difference in impact, in specific mass. Transactional leaders, the quintessential deal-makers, may score impressively from time to time, but may equally strike out spectacularly. The enlightened leaders, in their considered, careful, almost subliminal manner, may effect truly transforming changes, and wholly recreate their organisations: with a new sense of purpose, other relationships with stakeholders, another face to the outside world, in other words, another personality. Their effect tends to be far more substantial than that of transactional leaders, which is reflected in their stature.

LEADERSHIP AND MANAGEMENT – RELATED YET FUNDAMENTALLY DIFFERENT

When we got our first glimpses of the corporate world, in our early thirties, to be titled 'manager' meant that you amounted to something in the world, that you had it made – or at the very least that you belonged to the chosen who would make it one day, guaranteed. If you had a business degree such as Fons, to be given such a title or better for your entry level job was a basic assumption. Peter, as an advertising copywriter, laboured in a trade where, until one became agency owner, the title 'manager' was simply not in the offing. A creative person with sufficient ambition and love of meetings might one day be asked to join the so-called 'management team', but everyone in the agency knew that in terms of real power this team amounted to nothing, and that any real decisions were simply taken by the directors. So, there was no alternative than acquiring distinction through the excellence of creative work. What followed were many years of toil and hard graft ...

Nowadays, everyone is a manager or has been a manager, and a new term has taken over the exalted position in the corporate vocabulary: 'leader'. Now, when you are denoted leader, you amount to something in the world, you have it made – or at the very least you belong to the chosen who will make it one day, guaranteed. While in the past everyone with an eye on a career in business or administration made sure that he or she got general management training – Peter included, because one never knew – now all who know which way the wind is blowing take leadership training or study Chinese.

It is easy, and for authors not unappealing, to put this trend down as the new flavour of the month. But the issue is too significant for cynicism or flippancy. Management was and is traditionally practiced from a top-down perspective. With all due respect for the underlings, but still ... You develop your vision, mission, and strategy and impose it. Where practicable without resort to violence, and ideally with some measure of tact. A relatively simple procedure, within the grasp of nearly all primates.

But leadership is not so easily practiced. Because leadership – this is still widely misunderstood – works from the bottom up. You are a leader, not because someone appointed you, but because others see and accept you in that capacity. At many management training institutes these days

Leadership Development is the most popular theme. But in truth, how often have we seen anyone *become* a leader as a result of such programs? In essence you can only *be* a leader and strive to become a better one. The most important condition for embodying leadership is, that others feel that you are not out there to take care of number one, but that you are there for them, or for something even more all-encompassing. In short that you stand for something which transcends your self-interest.

This is so uncomplicated that you need no training course to get it. Yet for many of us it is so hard, that we gladly accept all the help we can get. Fortunately, at Trompenaars Hampden-Turner we can rely on a choice group of colleagues always ready to provide remedial teaching.

Leadership is closely related to management, but wholly different in fundamental aspects. The close relationship is caused by the fact that the one usually does not go without the other. To be effective, a manager needs to be a good leader. Equally, to be effective, a leader needs to be a good manager, or at least a passable one. In real life this combination is rare, because the qualities needed for leadership are so vastly different from the qualities needed for management that it is hard to master both in perfection. The difference is in the mental make-up:

Managers base their goals on what they deem necessary.
Leaders base their goals on what they deem desirable.

Managers are good at directing people, making sure that they co-operate, that the things that need doing get done on time. Where necessary they rely on their status in the organisation – their power to hire and fire, humble or promote, create or crush careers – to achieve the set goals. The best of them deserve gold medals for drive and self-restraint. Leaders see opportunities beyond the horizon, dreams that might one day be realised, ideas too beautiful to relegate to the dustbin just because they seem unrealistic today. The best may not care much for medals, but are amply rewarded as they observe how their vision, fire and tenacity inspire those around them. They rely not on power, but on the respect in which they are held. Their relationship with co-workers is often highly personal and intense, and their demeanour may be chaotic and baffling at times – annoying even, but easy to forgive because of their palpable commitment.

The difference between leadership and management was beautifully elucidated by Abraham Zaleznik in his famous article in the *Harvard Business Review*, 'Managers and Leaders: Are They Different?'[9] Leaders, he said, are inspired, visionary people who are concerned with content, whereas managers are concerned with the process. Psychologically they have an entirely different reaction to order and chaos, and an entirely different concept of their role:

Managers
- hate chaos and insecurity
- tend to plunge into the process to sort things out and bring order
- strive for control and predictability
- find compromises
- try to find a workable solution as quickly as possible – often without having thought out all the ramifications of the situation
- do things right.

Leaders
- are highly tolerant of insecurity
- can live with lack of structure and even chaos for extended periods of time without becoming unduly stressed
- strive to inspire
- find reconciliations
- postpone decision-making till they have a clear picture of all aspects of the situation (like artists, experimental scientists and other creative thinkers)
- do the right things.

But for a leader to become a *great leader*, more is required than these instrumental differences. We trust that you have your own criteria to add, but these seem to be fundamental:

Great leaders
- pair leaders' capacity to create something out of chaos with vision and passion
- inject the moral strength required to let their organisations play a role of importance in the world
- attain greatness less by doing than by being.

Endarkened Leadership

A corporate leader of our acquaintance who takes in vast amounts of management literature and read the manuscript of this book, advised us to omit this entire chapter. 'Oh come on, Taylor and all that mechanistic stuff, there's hardly an organisation out there where that still applies, is there?! Just start with enlightenment straightaway, because that's *new*, that is what readers want to know about.'

The effect of this bit of advice was to reinforce our conviction that a brief look in the rear-view mirror was not just important, but essential for an understanding of what is happening today. There is no greater danger, every psychiatrist will confirm this, than thinking that you are healed when you are not. The stark reality is, that in spite of all the wise books written on the subject in the last decade, only a tiny fraction of all leaders and managers has outgrown the mechanistic model of organisations. And of that tiny fraction, only a minority has outgrown it not just conceptually but also in practice: noticeable in the way that they structure and run their organisations.

People tend to think that, now factory sirens have disappeared, or at least aren't heard that much anymore, the concept of man as a tiny cog in the big machine (immortalised by Charlie Chaplin in *Modern Times*) has disappeared as well. Alas, the truth is far from there. The changes in our society run at such a precipitate pace, that the development of concepts to manage it simply cannot keep up. As a result, many organisations are run – even by young managers fresh from university – with a type of leadership that dates from the 1950s, and which is eminently unsuitable for our current socio-economic reality.

Yes, it all does look so much more humane, with those open plan offices stocked with drip fed plants and colourful display screens, but hundreds of millions of workers have not an inch more room to make a personal contribution than they would have had in the nineteenth century. In fact, thanks to ever more advanced software development, even what little room they have is further restricted by the day. Autonomous decision-making? Forget it, you just tap some parameters into the keyboard and the computer decides.

As Simon Head has pointed out in his *The New Ruthless Economy*,[10] this is one of the most dehumanising and least noted aspects of modern corporate functioning, reducing millions of white collar workers to what is essentially assembly-line type of work, prescribed in minute detail in templates, scripts and service level agreements. The New Robots are not just among us, we are in touch with them everyday. Fortunately, other recent trends are leading in an opposite direction, for instance the trend towards greater focus on creativity, which requires a highly humanised, 'people-friendly' work climate. But the great majority of those on a payroll are still boxed in by the old paradigm of command and control. And don't forget, being told what to do makes people feel miserable. As Nobel Prize winner Elias Canetti said in his 1960 classic *Crowds and Power*,[11] being told what to do is a sting, and a sting which can never be removed.

One of the areas where progress has been made in the last decades, is the moral sphere – both as a result of nascent enlightenment and of the new phenomenon of transparency, which makes the moral high ground seem suddenly so much more attractive, and affordable, too. But still there are legions of leaders who either feel that morality simply has no place in the world of business ('I'll be damned if I'm gonna let my conscience stand in the way of making an honest buck'), or opt for a strict forensic interpretation of the rules: 'As long as my actions do not set me on the path to jail, I am doing fine.'

But are we really doing fine when we limit ourselves to playing by the book? Is unindictability sufficient proof of great leadership? As Danah Zohar and Ian Marshall state in *Spiritual Capital*: 'Corporations exist to make money. They define work simply as making money. In essence, however, people are spiritual beings. Our whole lives are spent looking for purpose and meaning. Ergo, corporate life negates all that is really important to us.'[12]

And for those to whom efficiency is still the guiding principle: how efficient is it really to keep all which is important to employees outside the gate?

HISTORICAL CONTEXT

Let us briefly review the history of leadership. Beginning with the pharaohs and their pyramids. Under what type of leadership were the grand works completed? Is there a wealth of evidence that these massive tombs were built by voluntary effort? That it was a labour of love, inspired by the wishes of the people, the expression of a collective passion of the workers? To the contrary, all indications suggest that they were the fruit of brute force, the crude imposition of will.[13] And wherever in the world we care to look in the ancient world – in the Chinese, Maya and Inca empires, in Assyria and Mesopotamia, in the realms of the moguls and czars – the typical leadership style was always and ever based on this simple principle: the imposition of one man's will on countless others.

Equally typical, always and everywhere, was the support of a sacerdotal class, a clergy whose duty it was to explain to the masses that it was their God-given duty in this life to toil for the benefit of the ruling class, and that great rewards would accrue to them in the afterlife; so that, all considered, you really couldn't drop dead on the job soon enough. And when – after thousands of years that we may as well skip because labour conditions for the common folk turned only a fraction more benevolent – the colonial times began, slaves, christened or otherwise, proved themselves good followers of the preachers, as indeed, die on the job they did, duly and by their thousands, rarely reaching the age of thirty. In the British Empire, the Dutch, French, and Portuguese colonies, whole nations were told what to do. In the Congo, the private domain of Belgian King Leopold I, vast regions (eighty times the size of his kingdom) were ransomed for ivory and rubber, some ten million people in twenty-three years sacrificed on the altar of a single man's personal wealth.

Though there is a tendency to regard the slave trading of the Golden Age and the whole colonial experience as something that happened 'far away and long ago', the effect on the psyche of the traders' and usurpers' home land is not to be underestimated. Slave trading and the deployment of slaves on plantations and in factories, with its concomitant view on work forces and people without power in general, was a large step back into the dark ages, as it reconfirmed 'the use of human beings' as both common and advantageous. Leadership in those days could not be imagined without an element of ruthlessness. Even rulers whom history generally paints as benign would have been highly surprised to learn of a concept of leadership in which their capacity to impose their will might be less than absolute.

And of course, when in the mid-18th century the hallowed Industrial Revolution began, on account of proven effectiveness, the same despotic leadership style was continued, albeit with certain refinement. Corporal punishment for instance, the whipping up of the workers, gradually went out of fashion – even though as late as the early 20th century, many countries, notably the world's model of industry, America, saw striking workers clubbed back to their workbenches by hired gangs of goons and tax-paid police forces. In many less civilised nations – members of the United Nations and all, yes signatories even of the Declaration of Human Rights – this is still happening today. In central India, in 2002, ninety-five members of the Sahariya tribe were rescued from a quarry where they had been slaving in captivity for ten to twelve years, men, women and children.[14] In China similar brutality is frequently heard of. But let's stay with our own, Western line of development, because there is enough work here at home.

After World War II, labour conditions gradually improved, especially the physical conditions, mostly as the result of union organising. Machines were equipped with all manner of security features, in the more civilised nations new rules were introduced to protect workers' jobs, and the life time pain of many workers, the fear of old age in dire poverty, was alleviated by the institution of government pensions, and politicians could promise their followers that soon they would all be driving cars, as indeed they did. But even in those heady days of a New Age of Modernity, the basic concept of leadership hardly changed. It was just refined with human touches.

'I am strong, and you do as I say, or else ...'

For thousands of years, this concept of leadership worked well, to this extent that it yielded what the powers that be wanted. We shall refer to this aspect of efficiency again later, because, although happiness is at the top of our personal agendas, we are also highly respectful of profit, and it is our conviction that behind all profit is the effective application of energy. The question is, if we, heirs to these millennia of exploitation, have the right mind set for effective application of talent in this day and age.

LEAVE YOUR BRAIN OUTSIDE AND BRING YOUR BODY INDOORS

Typifying the 20th century concept of leadership, largely of Anglo-Saxon pedigree, are Frederick Taylor's mechanistic view of organisations, Milton Friedman's exclusive focus on shareholder value, and Albert Carr's advocacy of an amoral stance. This triumvirate of intellectual giants may be held jointly responsible for the consummate dehumanisation of corporate life.*

Taylor, whose 1911 publication of *The Principles of Scientific Management*[15] would turn his name into a synonym for 'scientific management', is the man we have to thank for the concept of man as a cogwheel in a machine; or rather, man as an apparatus that needs to be adjusted scientifically to run as efficiently as possible. Taylor left no doubt about the need for this adjustment. He explained that most workers are not capable by themselves to find out how to work efficiently: 'Now one of the very first requirements for a man who is fit to handle pig iron as a regular occupation is that he shall be so stupid and so phlegmatic that he more nearly resembles in his mental make-up the ox than any other type. The man who is mentally alert and intelligent is for this very reason entirely unsuited to what would, for him, be the grinding monotony of work of this character. [...] He is so stupid that the word "percentage" has no meaning to him, and he must consequently be trained by a man more intelligent than himself into the habit of working in accordance with the laws of this science before he can be successful.'

Taylor's influence was immense, and far-reaching. In no time all major industrial corporations in the US, and soon those in Europe as well, were converted to his beliefs. They employed whole armies of 'scientists' whose job it was to analyse the labour process stopwatch in hand, and to turn out minutely detailed directives for each and every action, similar to the assembly instructions now provided for Ikea wardrobes: 'Slip ring D2 onto bar K while pressing D2 in hole C12 of panel P6'. Except that Taylor

---

* Milton Friedman had the courage, very late in life (at age 91), to repudiate his own prescriptions, stating in an interview: 'The use of quantity of money as a target has not been a success ... I'm not sure I would as of today push it as hard as I once did.' (*Financial Times*, June 6, 2003.) Alas, by then the poison of his erroneous teachings had leached into all aspects of corporate life, all over the world, and was still being sold to a new generation.

also prescribed how many seconds every action should take. His method increased production in many industries, sometimes dramatically, but its effect on the workers was highly detrimental. It aggravated the monotony of what wasn't exactly stimulating work to begin with, produced constant stress to meet the countless mini-deadlines each day, and caused mental dulling through the banishment of even the most immaterial personal contribution to the production process.

Industrial psychologists Alan G. Carter and Colston Sanger in their article *Thinking about Thinking*: 'Taylor gave us mass production before we had robots, by getting people to do the robots' jobs. Perhaps that is an odd way of looking at it, but at Los Alamos [the lab where the atom bomb was designed, *Ed.*], they simulated spreadsheet programs by sitting secretaries at grids of desks with adding machines! He was such a control freak that he used to strap himself into bed every night to counter his morbid fear of falling out. His slogan was, "Leave your brain outside and bring your body indoors". *Our culture, from schools to legislation and concepts of status, is still riddled with Taylorism.*[16]

The italics above are the authors', intended as a call for reflection. Please note that this is not a quote from the middle of the previous century but from the very end of it. In your reflection include our contemporary call centres, with their service level agreements stipulating the maximum number of seconds per caller and the maximum promise of service – irrespective of the seriousness of the issue or the emotional state of the caller.*

When after this you are still in doubt, take a moment to meditate on the workings of our nursing homes. 'Sorry Mr Taylor, an hour ago was time for wee-wee, now you just be a good boy and wait till bedtime.' In modern establishments, the washing of the incontinent, once every x days (where x is a function of profit target over nursing fee), is effected by

---

* All responses of the workers are fully scripted, including instructions on when to smile. Smiling makes the voice sound warmer – suggesting a more humane and more satisfying response than callers are actually getting. This living by template is one of the invidious symptoms of our cybernetic age, that the inventor of cybernetics, Norbert Wiener warned us of half a century ago in *The Human Use of Human Beings*. Psychologically speaking, bringing forced smiles to employees' faces is one of the most degrading and damaging forms of control, little short of psychological warfare.

hoisting the patient into a cubicle fitted with water jets where caked on dirt is sprayed off them in seconds, pretty much as mud is squirted off the undercarriage of your vehicle in a car wash, in about the same amount of time and with minimal human intervention – a showcase of efficiency. 'Oh come on, Taylor and all that mechanistic stuff, there's hardly an organisation out there where that still applies, is there?!'

Frederick Taylor himself predicted the world-wide acceptance of his method. 'That these principles are certain to come into general use practically throughout the civilized world, sooner or later, the writer is profoundly convinced, and the sooner they come the better for all the people.' He may indeed have been a control freak, but one wonders if, had Taylor been alive today ('Wee-wee now, Mr Taylor?'), he would really have been delighted to see that his devout wish has come true.

For those still weighing the trade-off of humanity for efficiency: it is important to understand that the most harmful impact of dehumanisation is not felt by the clients or patients, but by the employees forced to work with less than human, or downright inhuman, and therefore depersonalising priorities. It is particularly hard on care practitioners, many thousands of whom have left the profession in the last decades, on both sides of the Atlantic – not because they stopped caring, but because they could not stand being curtailed in their desire to give more. There is little as damaging to the soul as being forced to withhold care. Naturally, at a remote, the same holds true for the corporate leaders who do the forcing, such as directors of the more greedy HMOs and care facilities. We are told by reliable sources that a special place in hell is reserved for them. It is lived in during this life, often with outward appearance of prosperity, and experienced mostly as a bewildering failure to achieve real happiness.

DOUBLE STANDARDS IN STANDARD CURRICULUM

After Taylor had taken the functional side of human beings into his methodical forceps and dropped it into a mould like so much pig iron, tackling the inner moulding of workers was only the logical next step. We live with the results of this effort every day. The idea was to turn employees (especially those in the higher echelons) into robots, and force them to keep their personal feelings out of the transaction – 'business is business', 'stick to the basics', 'keep yourself out of it ...'*

'Keep yourself out of it', how often don't we hear this? Or, heaven forbid, even *say* this? It is at the same time so common and so damaging.

This classical conception of corporate life, which most of our current managers and corporate leaders have been taught to subscribe to, is not only devoid of feeling, or at least short on sensitivity, it is also consciously and intentionally amoral. As Albert Carr taught the business world in 1968 with his classic article 'Is Business Bluffing Ethical?' published in the *Harvard Business Review*,[17] business is to be conceived as a poker game, in which everything is allowed which is not expressly forbidden by the law, in which personal feelings are to be disregarded, and in which there is no other moral obligation than the enrichment of the shareholders.

Carr stated that business practices such as bluffing (speaking untruths, misrepresenting facts) must be judged by the rules of business and not according to 'the ethical principles preached in churches'. He preached that in the corporate world it is practically inevitable to develop two independent sets of moral values, one for business life and one for private life. And he prophesied that all who take their private values to work, would fail to achieve real success in business.

This piece resonated deeply in the business world, in which, with all the daily fibbing, fiddling, cheating, manipulation and exploitation, many managers were troubled by their conscience. Thanks to Carr, they suddenly were up to it again: that conscience with its constant nagging should simply shut up, because it was talking from another, private morality, which should not even have come along to the office, but sneaked a ride in the back seat.

Anyone who subscribed to this with sufficient depth of belief, was instantly liberated from much psychological pressure, and could act immorally at his or her heart's desire again, with the law as their only limitation – a limitation which, thanks to the armies of lawyers in corporate

---

* The Dutch, past-masters in keeping the heart out of business (during the English-Dutch wars, Dutch merchants would happily sell the English guns for butter), have a unique word for this: 'wegcijferen'. Highly resistant to translation, it means something like 'to discount yourself'. The term is much used in business circles, often with the positive connotation of something rather noble, sacrificing your feelings for the splendid goal of making money.

employ, could be given a wide interpretation, or ignored with impunity. This created a kind of Wild West culture, with the leisure loving sheriff as the only moral force in town. Guys who make the mistake of hurting the powerful are hanged, but other than that it is a free-for-all. Preachers, in supporting roles, are portrayed as either drunk or depraved. The lone individual with integrity is chased into the desert, vultures circling above him, to succumb to hunger and thirst. Alas, with a few magnificent exceptions – namely heroes who take over the town and clean it up – folks who want to keep up moral standards don't survive in frontier country, they don't make it in Fortune, pop. 500.

When we embarked on this project, we had often read *about* Albert Carr's article, so had some inkling of the gist, but when we traced the actual text, we were surprised by the directness of his language. After the sub-heading *Pressure to Deceive* it reads: 'Most executives from time to time are almost compelled, in the interest of their companies or themselves, to practice some form of deception when negotiating with customers, dealers, labour unions, government officials or even other departments of their companies. By conscious misstatements, concealment of pertinent facts, or exaggeration – in short, by bluffing – they seek to persuade others to agree with them. We think it is fair to say that if the individual executive refuses to bluff from time to time – if he feels obligated to tell the truth, the whole truth, and nothing but the truth – he is ignoring opportunities permitted under the rules and is at a heavy disadvantage in his business dealings.'

A heavy disadvantage in business dealings – who shall willingly inflict this on himself? It would be like robbing your own wallet. The most worrying of Carr's piece is that it uses the well documented fact of daily practice, with all the immoral elements he mentions, as an argument to free oneself of any moral or other charges on account of them. Established practice as exoneration for the same. Would it do for eternal salvation? Says the archangel at heaven's gate, staring into the register: 'I am a little puzzled here by some entries on misrepresentation of fact in your business dealings. Would you please explain to me why you feel that your conduct was justified?' 'Well, so many people do it, that if I didn't, I would be placing myself at an unfair disadvantage.'

Or, as the American novelist Sinclair Lewis, one of the earliest censors of corporate irresponsibility, had his protagonist, the real estate broker

Babbitt, say in his famous novel *Babbitt*[18]: 'And then most folks are so darn crooked themselves that they expect a fellow to do a little lying, so if I was fool enough to never whoop the ante I'd get the credit for lying anyway!' In short, being honest in an environment where honesty is not appreciated, is not just useless, you deprive yourself of opportunity, and might cause your own social downfall.

Is this depiction of morality in the business environment, sketched in 1922, still up-to-date? Onc would hope not – but any such hope would be dashed by reading Joep Schrijvers' *The Way of the Rat: A Survival Guide to Office Politics*,[19] published in our days, in which rat-like conduct in a corporate environment is described as both normal and recommended; something you'd better try to get real good at, as otherwise you won't survive. A spoof, as the author maintained in private conversation, but one which many appear to have taken at face value. With this new contribution to the 'adults only' section of office literature, any notion of morality has been left behind, and the door opened to immorality *pur sang*.

No, the rats and Babbitts are among us, and if such books have any use at all, it is that they make us question our own motives. Schrijvers counsels an attitude of suspicion towards all one encounters in the corporate world. We would like to turn his advice around: the only suspicion we need in the business world is suspicion towards our own motives, towards the Babbitts and rats in us, and towards authors who want us to believe that noble, or even simply decent motives are a serious handicap.

WARNING: DON'T ENGAGE IN DUPLICITY IF IT'LL MAKE YOU SICK

It wasn't as if Albert Carr was blind to possible inner conflicts in the people who lived by his precepts, and he was good enough to also serve them with advice for their hours of need: 'But here and there a businessman is unable to reconcile himself to the bluff in which he plays a part. His conscience, perhaps spurred by religious idealism, troubles him. He feels guilty; he may develop an ulcer or a nervous tic. Before any executive can make profitable use of the strategy of the bluff [Carr's euphemism for cheating, used *ad nauseam*], he needs to make sure that in bluffing he will not lose self-respect or become emotionally disturbed. If he is to reconcile personal integrity and high standards of honesty with the practical requirements of business, he must feel that his bluffs are ethically justified. The justification rests on the fact that business, as practiced by individuals as well as by corporations, has the impersonal character of a game – a game that demands both special strategy and an understanding of its special ethics.' For the benefit of the few who might still harbour doubts whether he really means it as plainly as it is stated, Carr adds: 'And no one should think any the worse of the game of business because its standards of right and wrong differ from the prevailing traditions of morality in our society.'

THE CONSCIENCE-FREE CORPORATION

The pernicious character of Albert Carr's philosophy of morality is rendered in high relief when it is paired – as apologists of corporate misbehaviour have always done to great effect – to the vision of Milton Friedman, economic adviser of former US president Ronald Reagan. In 1970 Friedman published his famous/notorious article in the *New York Times* entitled 'The Social Responsibility of Business is to Increase Profits'.[20] Friedman averred that the subject of the social responsibility of corporate chiefs is cut and dried: keep within the law and make as much money as possible for the shareholders. There is no additional responsibility towards society at large, nor to other companies, nor to employees. The game is played for the stake, and morality be damned – business is business. This way of thinking is hauntingly similar to the code of the pirates of old: 'Take what you can. Give nothing back.'

Hardly an organisation out there where this still applies? That would be wonderful. But the reality is, that this Friedmanesque conception of the role of business in society has become the dominant theme of the so-called Chicago School, the powerful coterie of economic thinkers in and around the University of Chicago, *still* the source of inspiration for 90% of all MBA-programs around the world.[21] Friedman, who was awarded the Nobel Prize in 1976 and enjoyed world-wide respect, expounded with professorial patience that we are to view companies, not as something akin to persons (as they are regarded in most of non-Anglo-Saxon Europe), but as strictly legal constructs, bloodless and soulless. Only people can be held morally responsible of their conduct. Because companies are not people but mere legal entities (even though they are founded by and made up of people), they can not be expected to exhibit a social conscience or indeed any form of morality.

These amoral and dehumanised rules of the game are preached in MBA programs all over the world to this very day, and energetically applied by many alumni. They used to work relatively well – if we discount the resultant psychological stress and social disruption – in an economy that was principally geared towards *making things*. They worked well for an economy characterised by tightly controlled processes, stratified organisations with clear hierarchical structures, and assets lending themselves to cost-based or replacement-value based quantification. No one in charge needed to give a hoot about how the workers might feel, because it was immaterial to production. All that mattered, was that they pressed button A at the green light, waited three seconds, and pressed button B. As long as people could be made to do this without disruption, everything was fine and dandy. Whether or not they were happy, was of no concern.

It was of no concern, because, to a high degree, those who organised the production got what they wanted. It worked... At least for the shareholders. And over time also for ever larger numbers of the workers, who made the quantum leap in status from survivors to consumers. But does the same conception of business work equally well in our contemporary society?

IMPOSITION OF WILL – HOW MUCH OF A FUTURE?

Depending on whose figures one chooses to trust, services make up 75% to 85% of our present-day economy, a rapidly growing part of that percentage representing knowledge transfer. In an economy of that nature, how far does one get with the traditional style of directing organisations, the imposition of will?

In the contemporary economic environment, 'production' usually means something *done for* someone else, or something *shared with* someone else. Much of the turnover is realised in interpersonal contacts, in person, by phone, or through a network such as the internet. As a result, the quality of the service rendered, the quality of the 'product' at the *moment suprême* of the transaction, eludes any direct form of command or control.

It is impractical to stand a manager behind the chair of everyone who deals with clients – leave alone to stand a supervisor behind that manager. It is of crucial importance to realise (this applies to the service sector as a whole, but to the knowledge sector in particular) that at the moment of interaction with the client – the moment value is created or not created – the employee is practically immune to direction, and wholly sovereign.

To direct such production, accomplished by employees who operate as sovereign agents, a wholly different type of leadership is called for. Because, unlike in Taylor's days, we can no longer make do with workers' physical/mental contributions only: we also urgently need their emotional, intuitive, intellectual, creative and spiritual gifts and skills. In short, we need them to bring to work their whole being – in all its richness.

The productivity of such sovereign executors of corporate desires – the measure in which they create real, marketable added value – is largely determined by their inner state at the moment that they contribute their energies, and by the percentage of themselves that they are allowed to bring to work. To manage such productivity requires a whole new approach, a new wisdom, and a new type of leadership.

What is Followership?

Much has been written about leadership, but little about followership. Some of the more interesting recent publications are Robert E. Kelley's article in the *Harvard Business Review* 'In Praise of Followers',[22] and Ira Chaleff's *The Courageous Follower: Standing Up to and for Our Leaders*.[23] But, helpful as these contributions are, if only by their original, almost contrarian choice of subject, one would wish that the authors had gone a step further than the functional aspects, and revealed to us the true power of the follower. Or more specifically, the true power as we see it, from the perspective of pragmatists with a firm belief in the value of 'values-based' management.

Let us explain the origins of this belief. As soon as you start charting the values in an organisation, looking at the *values distribution* across the board and in various cuts, you soon discover something truly fundamental: the amalgam of the value sets of the few people in the top is reduced almost to insignificance by the amalgam of the value sets of the hundreds or thousands or hundreds of thousands of employees. Accepting this observation and drawing your conclusions from it, leads to wisdom.

Why? Because the many fervent attempts by consultants in the previous century have demonstrated that it is next to impossible – short of wholesale firing and replacement – to change the values of large numbers of employees in any significant way. It is far easier to adjust the values of the few people at the top. Awareness of this reality is highly enlightening, and constitutes the fundamental insight required for practical enlightened leadership.

THE LEADING ROLE OF THE FOLLOWER

More than most leaders realise, the followers call the tune. Dee Hock, the visionary founder of Visa International and more recently of the Chaordic

Alliance, states it beautifully in 'The Art of Chaordic Leadership': 'In a very real sense, followers lead by choosing where to be led. Where an organizational community will be led is inseparable from the shared values and beliefs of its members.'[24]

Elsewhere in the same piece, Hock states: 'Leader presumes follower. Follower presumes choice. One who is coerced to the purposes, objectives, or preferences of another is not a follower in any true sense of the word, but an object of manipulation. Nor is the relationship materially altered if both parties voluntarily accept the dominance of one by the other. A true leader cannot be bound to lead. A true follower cannot be bound to follow. The moment they are bound they are no longer leader or follower. If the behaviour of either is compelled, whether by force, economic necessity, or contractual arrangement, the relationship is altered to one of superior/subordinate, manager/employee, master/servant, or owner/slave. All such relationships are materially different from leader/follower.'

Hock goes on to explain that induced behaviour is the hallmark of true leader/follower relationships, whereas coerced behaviour marks nearly all other corporate relationships. Where behaviour is coerced, there is tyranny, however mild in its manifestation. Wherever behaviour is induced, there is leadership, however firm in its manifestation. He warns that the term 'leadership' as such does not imply constructive, ethical, open conduct. It is wholly doable to induce destructive, malign, deceitful conduct, and, moreover, do so in a depraved manner. That is why each organisation should be built upon a clearly outlined constructive goal and strong ethical principles, valued and shared by all its members.

The best way to start is to define the organisation's purpose, its *raison d'être*, in full clarity, state it unambiguously, attract people who are inspired by it, followers indeed, and wave goodbye to people who feel, think or act at cross purposes.

Keep in mind that followers tend to flock, which may lead to an increased reverence for the shepherd. It is the wise shepherd who is not led into the thorn bushes of vanity.

Followership: the capacity to induce leadership behaviour in others.

THE HIGH ART OF INSPIRING OTHERS TO LEAD

You inspire others to exhibit leadership traits by making them feel your expectations in this area. Most people are ashamed of their weaknesses and are pleasantly touched by respect for their capacities, expressions and conduct. The penultimate form this can take is an appeal to their noble nature. It is on the edge of manipulation, but for the good cause such subliminal exploitation of vanity is absolutely in order.

In leadership courses Peter often cites a case involving himself as the manipulatee. Years ago he was working in Paris with Jean Feldman, one of the founders of the French advertising agency FCA!, which at the time was acquiring the Amsterdam agency he had co-founded. The FCA! group was involved in an international competition for a large oil company account, and they were trying to come up with a winning concept. At one moment Peter got what he thought was a great idea – one that he knew the oil boys would fall in love with instantly. It was so Big Oil.

But Feldman was not pleased: 'Peter, do you really think this idea will make them sell a single litre more?'

'No Jean, of course not! But this idea will win us the competition!'

Feldman, one of the dons of French advertising, looked him deep in the eyes and said: 'Peter, you are a greater man than that.'

Ouch! That straightened the spine! Rarely was a man so gently, yet so forcefully corrected. And how was it done? According to the patient: 'Simply by an appeal to my inner nobility, such as it is. Or, put more prosaically, by an appeal to my self-respect.' This principle can work wonders in the induction of leadership behaviour in colleagues and superiors.

Obviously, any such appeal to nobility is effective only with people in whom this quality is a somewhat developed aspect of the personality. We once had it fail dismally. A values assessment at the XYZ Corporation, a German high tech company with a staff consisting largely of PhDs, showed that the organisation was in dire need of more leadership. In fact it was fairly screaming out for leadership. This was in itself not surprising, because Tom S., the charismatic CEO, was on the road much of the time, attending conferences and functions all over the country, and between these social obligations and his managerial duties had little time left to show his face in his own organisation. When he did, he was not very directive, believing and preaching that all that people need to develop their talents, is to be given the freedom to do so. During the pre-presentation we showed him the assessment results, with their loud call for leadership.

'Yes,' Tom said, 'I recognise this.' He looked at us defiantly. 'But I am not going to do it.'

'Listen Tom, it's rather painful to have to say this, but we really feel that the organisation has been emotionally neglected.'

'Absolutely, no doubt. But you know what's the worst of it? The worst is that hearing you say this is not really painful for me – because I know this for a fact, and have accepted it. It's like when you come over to my place and say "Gee, what a mess!". That doesn't hurt me a bit, because I know it's a mess and I have accepted my lack of tidiness.'

Fortunately, this facile acceptance of one's own shortcomings is quite rare. The only leaders who manage to get away with it, are those with oodles of disarming personal charm. Most men and women of character, charming or otherwise, will rise to the occasion when called upon to lead.

What is Enlightenment?

Do not believe anything because it is said by an authority, or because it is supposed to come from angels or from Gods, or from an inspired source. Believe it only if you have explored it in your own heart and mind and body and found it to be true.

Gautama Buddha

Using the term 'enlightenment' is risky, especially in a business context, because it can refer to widely divergent concepts. In the original sense it stands for the illumination of our earthly darkness (think caves) by means of torches and other forms of domesticated fire, the gift of Prometheus, latterly of Philips. Then there is the 17th–18th century Age of Enlightenment presided over by philosophers like Voltaire, Rousseau and Hume; a transforming period in European history, during which, after millennia of submission to religious dogma, reason began to prevail over belief. (A period which now appears to be ending for Americans, 54 percent of whom believe that the Bible represents the literal truth,[25] and who appear to be ushering in an era of regression that Kevin Philips, author of *American Theocracy*,[26] calls the 'American Disenlightenment'.) There is also the enlightenment preached by Buddha and other wise men from the East, nowadays sought by increasing numbers of westerners, and which largely boils down to detachment. The word is also used in a more general sense as a synonym for wisdom, culture, education. So, it is essential to make clear from the outset what type of enlightenment we are talking about.

Enlightenment in the sense used here certainly does have an aspect of detachment – namely detachment from much of that which brings darkness and misery – but it largely consists of raising awareness. There is nothing scary or woolly about this, because the only effect is, that one becomes more aware of what is. Nothing will happen during the process that was not already happening before you became aware of it. In other words, you have nothing to lose, but much to gain. There are no visions involved, at most a few visionary moments. You don't have to start wearing pink robes or burn lots of incense. To many corporate readers this may come as some relief.

The type of enlightenment we are concerned with here is marked by a level-headed, pragmatic view of what is going on in the (business) world and the advantages will be argued in a rational manner, without the need to believe anything at all. The greatest advantage, it will be reasoned, is that enlightenment makes people more happy. Enlightened leadership makes leaders more happy and through them the organisations they lead. 'Happy' organisations work wonders for all stakeholders and generate more money in the long run than unhappy organisations driven by greed and fear.

But the greatest gain this book aims to bring about is your own happiness: the product of a new view of your own leadership and the discovery of an energising sense of purpose, a goal worth dedicating yourself to body and soul.

PRACTICAL AND IDEAL ENLIGHTENMENT

Because the term 'enlightenment' has such a rich range of connotations, we shall speak of it in a manner that relies more on inspiration and evocation than on presentation and analysis. To make things even more challenging (but actually more yummy for the analytically minded), there is enlightenment on several levels. This is said, not with the intent to start a competition about who is the most enlightened, but because there is a significant distinction between awakening awareness of a few aspects of the self, and full consciousness of all aspects, from the most basic to the transcendental, encompassing both one's own psyche and universal consciousness.

The most fundamental distinction is the one between practical and ideal enlightenment:

- *Practical*
  Enlightenment means clarification, becoming aware, seeing things in a clear light. Things become clear that were not clear before. From a

business point of view this has great advantages. For instance: a leader who just wants to make better use of the human potential in his organisation and comes to see that this is feasible only by making people more happy, may already be called quite enlightened, and he will have an enlightening effect on those he leads. To reach this stage of enlightenment he needs to be no more than a smart businessman who reads the signs of the times.

* *Ideal*

   Advantageous and socially beneficial as practical enlightenment may be, it is of another class – more limited in terms of ambition – than the enlightenment we recognise in a corporate leader dedicated to make the world a better place, starting with his or her own organisation. Ideal enlightenment requires an inspiring vision, integrated in a coherent conceptual framework, and devotion to a self-transcending cause. It also brings great practical advantages, but first and foremost for others. Any personal benefit accrues incidentally, as a result of increased esteem or even admiration.

To differentiate between these two levels of enlightenment, we need only check who stands to benefit primarily. In the former it is mainly the leader (as a consequence of improved running of the organisation), others benefiting consequently. In the latter it is primarily others who benefit, the perpetrator consequently. Leaders in a transformational phase may operate now on one level, then on the other.

   This dichotomy by itself is quite enlightening already, but for a thorough understanding of all aspects of enlightenment we will have to start making some finer distinctions. In anticipation of the seven Chakras of Leadership to be introduced hereafter, the following progression sheet constitutes a useful first test.

SEVEN LEVELS OF ENLIGHTENMENT

Level 1: Awakening awareness

Moments of reflection, followed by a clearer perception of reality. (This may occur on an utterly pragmatic level. You may become aware, for instance, that the 'tried and true' way of directing employees is no longer effective, that new times require new ways. For many leaders and managers, this is a giant step forwards. Most simply live their agendas, and, beyond the immediately apparent, hardly notice what goes on in their organisations, leave alone in the world at large.) The awakening awareness brings about a new type of rootedness – not in pay dirt, but in your own body, the greatest source of inner strength.

Level 2: Awakening social consciousness

Development of a clearer view of the role played in other people's lives. (This used to be a mark of middle age, the onset of maturity, but is increasingly seen in relatively young people. Apparently humans are now maturing faster, possibly as a result of richer information about the world we live in.[27]) Enhanced sense of connectedness on interpersonal level. Productive urge: the longing to seriously do something with your life energy, to create something of substance.

Level 3: Awakening self-respect

Increased sense of self-worth, fortification of the will as an instrument for the expression of the inner self. Development of the will as an instrument for shaping the world. Nascence of ambition to 'make a difference'. Authenticity as guiding principle for all activities. Humility.

Level 4: Awakening 'heart power'

Allowing yourself to become aware of your heart's promptings not just in your private life, but also *while at work*. By extension: admitting feeling to the corporate realm. The next step is the installation of feeling as the touchstone for all professional conduct – not instead of the will, but above it, as a kind of supreme judge. Awakening 'heart power' is at the core of all forms of personal transformation.

Level 5: Awakening connectedness

Birth of a new sense of connectedness: with others, and with your inner self. Taking ownership of the talents you were given, specifically in the sense of (great power implies great responsibility) shouldering the responsibility for your own power. What effect do my actions have on others? Walking your talk: conduct in accordance with new insights.

Increased powers of communication: the conscious use of communication to involve others.

Level 6: Discovery of the secret

Discovery of the true nature of leadership: focus on a greater good than personal well-being. Comes with more acute awareness of your own inner strength, your talents and your capacity to change the world. (This discovery can be a powerful experience, which, alas, in some subjects leads to a sense of omnipotence, or even megalomania, so that further growth is blocked, a common trap for gurus of all persuasions.)

Level 7: Assuming the stance of a leader

Inception of a clear vision, a coherent conceptual framework and devotion to a self-transcending cause – either declared, e.g. by publicly working for a cause, or 'secretly', as a transformative force within organisations with essentially selfish goals. Initiation of activities, either on request or of your own accord, that help others with the development of their own leadership.

EXERCISE: Check which levels correspond with your own inner state. Before you start out, try to lock your ego into the broom closet, and observe yourself without positive or negative bias. A good method is to tell yourself that a) I am nowhere near as highly developed as I like to imagine, and that b) I have sunk nowhere near as deep as I fear in my darkest moments.

What is Enlightened Leadership?

The ultimate test of practical leadership is the realization of intended, real change that meets people's enduring needs.

James MacGregor Burns

Enlightened leadership starts with awareness, with raising consciousness*. And raising consciousness starts — leaving aside visionary experiences and the insights of lucid moments — with questioning. The questioning, searching attitude is its hallmark, until habituation turns it into simple openness; though openness on a higher level. As the novelist Jack London counselled: 'Be one of those whom nothing escapes.'[28]

Also, we would never use the term 'enlightened' for anything other than leadership with a human face, and frankly, if we whittle it down to the bone, we are speaking of loving leadership.

Because this expression may put off some readers by seeming too mushy, and others because they have heard saccharine sweetened talk too often, we will not mention it again. But, as you read on, do keep in mind that this whole book is reducible to a simple call to switch to this unmentionable type of leadership. So, as soon as you have been converted, you can safely skip the rest. Go do something nice with your loved ones.

In *Enlightened Leadership*,[29] Ed Oakley and Doug Krug define enlightened leadership as 'the willingness and ability to draw the vision from

---

* Unfortunately the term 'raising consciousness' has been flogged to death by New Age writers. And it is arguable anyway if consciousness can be raised or lowered. Any such quantitive thinking raises nagging issues around hierarchy (as evidenced by the sharp discussion on Pop Occulture Blog, URL: http://www.timboucher.com/journal/) by calling up the 'I am more enlightened than you' phenomenon. We use the term in a rather technical sense, to indicate a process of enhanced pattern recognition: the discovery of more links between nodes of information about the self and the world.

their people and inspire and empower those people to do what it takes to bring the vision into reality.'

This is one of the best definitions we have come across so far, specifically on account of the phrase 'to draw the vision from their people', which so precisely and poetically describes the crucial aspect of servitude to others' aspirations, but it is not memorable. In our attempt to include some of the forgoing, we hit upon: 'Enlightened leadership is leadership that returns to followers the part of themselves that they lost as a result of endarkenment.' (With this golden investment tip: whosoever manages to return to others a part of themselves that they lost, enriches himself beyond measure.) But of course we're not primarily concerned with restoring something that went askew, however urgent that may be. More important is the positive aspect, to wit, that enlightened leadership should lead to desirable ends.

Oakley and Krug: 'Indeed, Enlightened Leaders nurture and encourage their people to be open, creative, and innovative and find what it takes to achieve their shared objectives. They get the members of the organization to accept ownership for that vision as their own, thus developing the commitment to carry it through to completion.' How true. But again, how to memorise it long enough to tell your friends? To us, and the authors above quoted will surely concur, it all boils down to developing the best that people have in them – starting with yourself. So if you agree we would like to phrase it like this:

Enlightened leadership develops the best that people have in them – starting with yourself.

WHAT ENLIGHTENED LEADERSHIP IS NOT

To get a topic properly in focus, it can be useful to examine what it certainly is not. This list may serve as a preliminary inventory for our chosen subject. Enlightened leadership is not:

- *A more elevated type of management*
  Enlightened leadership is not a more lofty way of directing people, but a way to help them realise real growth, and do better business. It may not be elevated – but it is uplifting.

- *Transcendence of the material*
  There is nothing inherently base in the material, and transcending it is not worth striving for. Everyone should enjoy the material to his or her heart's content, and the more people can do this, the happier we all shall be. I highly recommend my personal motto, with thanks to Satya Narayan Goenka, the great teacher of Vipassana meditation: 'As we humans consist of spirit and body, the spiritual and the material are two sides of the same coin. It is the combination of spirit and matter that makes us whole living beings, and it is that wholeness which brings us true wealth.'

- A *management fad*
  [Item included for the benefit of hard-nosed businessmen who don't mind some enlightenment, as long as it doesn't cost any money.] The only sensible approach to management is to do what makes the most money. The rest is fashion, window-dressing – right? If you look at it that way, then try to see enlightened leadership as the current cutting edge in business thinking. Enlightened leadership implies becoming aware of transformational forces in the world, with consequent adaptation of operational behaviour. That is not fashion, but classic survival skill, which is of all times and all cultures. And in this day and age, the true survivors note that opting for a humanist type of leadership starts to give real competitive advantage.

- A *badge of honour*
  The choice for enlightened leadership is not noble *per se*, because the profit to be had from this choice is too obvious. However, a noble soul certainly will be able to make more of it than a more selfish one. Still, it would be a shame if, in a few years, enlightenment or something resembling it would deteriorate into a kind of self-issued certificate of inner quality. At some organisations and conferences this sort of scene is starting to develop: 'Hey, check out how enlightened I am ...' 'Oh, no! I am much more enlightened than you!' 'Of course, and more modest, too!'[30]

LEADERSHIP FROM WITHIN

A truly essential mark of the type of leadership that one might call enlightened, is that it comes from within. An enlightened leader is driven by his own convictions, which give him the strength to overcome obstacles – not the brutal strength of willpower, but the soft and warm, continuously flowing strength derived from the feeling that you are doing something worth doing. A force like the water in a mountain river, which surges around rocks, takes dead drops fearlessly, rips trees off the banks where necessary, or simply changes course, unstoppable in its journey.

This inner force manifests itself not in rage; it is never threatening, humiliating or demanding. It is not compelling but patient: focused, not on result but on contribution. All exertion is made in a joyful mood, spiked by thrill and expectation; the mood of a child which in play develops its abilities by exploration of their outer limits.

HOW VALUABLE IS THE CORPORATE PERSONALITY?

Many financial analysts feel that there is little worth knowing about a company that cannot be put into a spreadsheet. We do not expect the breed to die out any time soon. But we do predict that in ten years from now, it will be routine to include unquantifiable factors in the valuation of companies, a notion that PriceWaterhouseCoopers already endorsed a few years ago by supporting the publication of *The Value Reporting Revolution, Moving Beyond the Earnings Game*,[31] a work that is almost subversive in its stridency, practically a revolutionary manifest, written by PwC accountants. ValueReporting™ takes not just the balance sheet into account, but cultural and human capital as well. The authors stress the great value of important immaterial assets, so far left off the books – such as creativity, sense of purpose and collective passion – and the urgency of a revaluation of cultural and human capital. High time to activate these hidden reserves in the books ...

In the last two decades we have seen numerous companies grow from nothing to mega size, not just on the strength of their offerings, but on the strength of their corporate personality. What corporate personality is, could be the subject of lengthy scholarly debate, but we all understand what it means when we talk about people. Now that we tend to see organisations not as mechanical constructs, but as organisms, let's go the whole hog and look at them as people – and the whole issue of what constitutes corporate personality is at once cleared up. What we see is a set of character traits manifested through conduct. Appeal and success of the manifestation are largely determined by the quality of the core values and the degree of authenticity, i.e. the degree to which values are actually lived, which in turn determines the attainable energy level of the organisation, the creativity, intensity, vitality, and charm.

And as for a reporting revolution, let's begin by not undervaluing charm. Look at companies like Virgin, Vodafone and Starbucks: no better seats, no cheaper calls, no better coffee, but oodles of charm. Starbucks achieved its super-mug size in no time, not only by serving good coffee, but also by its involvement, supposed or real, in the betterment of the lot of coffee growers in photogenic tropics. It is not likely to make you drink one extra cup of Double Mint Mocha Skim Latte or Grande Non-fat No-Whip Mocha, but it leaves a nice aftertaste to hear that Starbucks helps farmers in South-America to conserve water and use fewer chemicals.

Starbucks claims socially conscious conduct throughout the supply, production and marketing chain. Purchase guidelines reward farmers who comply with strict ecological and socio-economic demands with preferred-supplier contracts. The 'Bring Your Own Mug' program stimulates customers to bring their own mugs. Come in with your own mug today for a $0.10 discount. In 2003 customers participated 13.5 million times, saving 266 tons of garbage. (Remains the enigma why Starbucks does not switch to regular, washable crockery for all coffee consumed on the premises, but keeps serving those shabby paper cups.) Even the coffee dregs are disposed of in a socially profitable manner: given away to customers, parks, schools and nurseries as a nitrate-rich compost. Such corporate conduct exemplifies the type of leadership in action that we might call enlightened. Not just enriching in terms of moral content, but economically effective as well.

Unfortunately, there are lingering doubts about this specific case of corporate nobility, caused by the many protesters and bloggers who question, often in shrill language, if Starbucks' moral brew is truly all that tasty. In that same year 2003, the company's shareholders meeting in Seattle was assailed with over 2000 fax messages, e-mails and phone calls urging Starbucks CEO Orin Smith to start complying with the company's espoused ethical values, that he broadcast to the world so proudly. There is a whole subculture of Starbucks haters, who publish on the web serious allegations regarding Starbuck's sourcing, social behaviour, employment and remuneration practices, quality control, and general integrity. One even built a dedicated website, www.ihatestarbucks.com – clumsily built and poor in content, but with a high page ranking. A recent Google search on 'starbucks slave labour' (to pick the most hair-raising allegation of misconduct by the coffee brewers) produced 51,100, on 'starbucks slave labor' another 40,300 hits. Of course this proves absolutely nothing – nothing beyond the fact that, despite Starbucks' sustained communication efforts, many people remain unconvinced of Starbucks' nobility. Corpwatch, at www.corpwatch.com, motto 'Holding Corporations Accountable', has 840 references to the company. Again, no proof, beyond the fact that Starbucks has many critics, with many different issues.

As far as we can tell, the jury is still out. But this is not about putting Starbucks up on a pedestal or ripping it down. This just goes to show how important corporate personality is becoming, and how crucial it is to develop a type of leadership that helps to make the organisation a lovable personality on the world stage.

We cannot stress enough the economic value of that unique quality of being lovable. In people we immediately recognise it as an asset that will ease the person's path through life, giving 'unfair' advantage always. More and more people start to recognise this same quality in organisations – and get alerted by its absence.

Let's see then what it takes to become lovable and enjoy the same advantage.

How to Reach Enlightenment

> **Enlightenment** is not about becoming, but about being.
> Enlightenment is not about action, but about awareness.

Let us start off by saying that if we knew how to get enlightened, we would go for it today. But alas, like you we are just seekers. So don't expect us to hand you a magic key that suddenly gives you access to a whole new world – a world in which you are both perfect and happy, a blessing to mankind. So leave that saint's gown on its hanger for the moment ... Still, reading this book does not have to be a waste of time, because even if the authors have no magic key, there may be magic cues, some perhaps passed on unintentionally, as occurs in novels all the time.

The magic is not in the sending, but in the receiving. The magic is in being open, in allowing information to sink in. This is the essence of any learning from others: the incorporation of others' experience, based on the wisdom, given to all higher animals, that anyone who works with certain material for any length of time acquires a few insights that can be helpful to others. Experienced stable hands, for instance, teach the inexperienced that it is unsafe to stand behind a horse, and many have profited from this transferred knowledge, obviating the need to learn the hard way. It is the student's duty to integrate the new information with existing information to achieve new insights, ideally surpassing those of the teacher, expanding on them, or making them more actionable.

Ideally, of course – as happened to the apostle Paul – you are simply struck down with a vision, in the middle of the street on your way to work, and find yourself transformed instantly. But with most people, enlightenment will come into their lives the way friendship does – from a first encounter that was agreeable to a next encounter, from there to growing familiarity, increasing confidentiality and intimacy, to amity and finally to a merging of souls that needs no language to explain itself.

In the language of enlightenment the induction process runs from transforming insights (insights that give life a new direction, for example the insight that you are obstructing your own self-realisation or impeding further growth) to changes in your behaviour (changes that enhance your personal effectiveness, especially in terms of happiness), and finally, *deo volente*, to a state in which you are entirely yourself, free from ego and other ballast, and your inner qualities get optimal possibilities to manifest themselves. Then it's time for those robes.

HONESTY AS A FIRST STEP

One of the more fundamental steps to practical enlightenment is taken when you confront yourself honestly. No more evasion or fabrication to make yourself look better, no more spin. You are who you are, and there is no theatrical diversion. You love what you adore, and abhor what you despise.

Part of this honesty involves openness towards others. Not that you may never keep anything from anyone anymore – because some people are better off not knowing certain things – but openness in the emotional sense: don't act as if you feel good about something when you don't. And don't be ambiguous about that which you really value. Don't be too meek either, be explicit about what it takes to make you happy. Take your staff in hand and take a stand. The world is not changed by wusses.

We will return to this theme later because there is much misunderstanding about the true nature of spirituality. The truth, well known to circles of initiates throughout the ages, is this: *the softer you get, the tougher you need to get.*

To anyone seriously undertaking the path of full honesty it soon becomes apparent that being honest towards others is not as hard as being honest to yourself. Disappointing others is not quite as painful as disappointing yourself. Losing the respect of others hurts, but not as much as losing your self-respect. Yes, there can be plenty of hurt to go around ... But fortunately, there is a golden rule which applies both to your relationship to others and your relationship to yourself: *anyone who really loves you can handle the reality.* Love yourself, even if you should discover that you really aren't as great as you thought. If you do, soon enough you will discover that you really aren't anywhere near as hopeless as you made yourself out to be.

No one who switches to being honest likes all of the process initially. There are many defence mechanisms in place and all want to be played, bringing up spurious arguments, pleading for continuation of the *status quo*, throwing up tantrums. But don't let these upset you. Go easy on your shortcomings, we need all your talents on board, and all your energy; don't waste it moping about how much greater you could have been. Go live with yourself and show us what you've got.

THE WILL AS AID AND OBSTACLE

Equally fundamental, something you need to grasp and exhibit in practice, is that the will may be the most important means to achieve self-realisation, yet it is also a potential obstacle of huge proportions. Grasping this is not easy, because in our culture, willpower stands in high esteem. We strive for wealth, we strive for perfection. We applaud signs of willpower in our children, in our sports heroes and corporate leaders. Rightly so, as without willpower, little of any substance is ever achieved. Even apart from the larger question whether it would not be desirable to bring other aspects of the self to the fore, the immediate question is, which purpose does the will serve?

Many people's will is not sovereign, but enslaved – either part-time or 24/7 – by the ego. I call this the Inner Slavery. Those entrapped in this deplorable state direct their will forcefully, but much of what they are striving for does not do them or anyone else any good, and they would be better off willing something else. In such slaves of their own ego we see a will that has been kidnapped and perverted*, often in the service of short term wants created by the ego itself, e.g. for the advancement of status.

---

* In this abduction by the ego, often there is what we might call a solo-version of the Stockholm syndrome at work: the pattern of gradual acceptance, familiarisation and sometimes even creation of a love bond with the enslaver that is so common in kidnappings, especially with long periods of captivity, such as the well-documented Natasha Kampusch case. 'He was part of my life,' she wrote in her first note after she freed herself. And so it will feel for someone freeing him or her self from domination by the ego, which makes it so hard to part ways. Ours still cling to us like whining children.

For an illustration look at those chiefs of Enron,[32] WorldCom,[33] Tyco,[34] Sunbeam,[35] Qwest,[36] Samsung,[37] Adelphia,[38] the re-packagers of sub-prime mortgages who managed to get their 'toxic waste'[39] wrapped in AAA ratings, and all those others with an iron will, who at one time or another appear to have thought: 'I don't care what it takes, but I will and shall rake in those millions.' Or like the agitated diner in a fancy restaurant, we all know him from our own or a neighbouring table, already somewhat overweight for better theatrical effect, who suddenly gets up, flushed with impatience: 'Dammit, even if I have to get it from the kitchen myself, *I do want cream in my bisque!*'

People with a modest ego are recognised by their easy acceptance of circumstances, even when these turn out less copious than they had expected. A degree of enlightenment makes people *easy*. This is caused by their detachment from things that others find important. No curry on the coriander? Don't kill the chef. No ten million this year, but six? Keep pouring that champ. No award, no place on the stage, no cover story, no applause, no knighthood or elevation to any other high stature? Then let's share the joy of those favoured by fortune.

People who resign themselves to the course of events, save their will power for moments when it is truly required – to initiate, promote or implement important changes. 'I want to reduce the amount of poison we bring into the environment by fifty percent in five years.' 'I want to help women in my organisation enjoy both their work *and* their children.' 'Even if it costs me my promotion, I do want to see more of my kids than just that glimpse around bed-time.' Anyone who deploys willpower for such ends, frees him or herself from self-imposed slavery and opens the doors to self-realisation.

It is not so, alas, that enlightenment may be achieved simply by willing it. But what you can direct your will at – and this really works – is to step out of your own darkness, your own dungeon, to free yourself from the slave deck on the galley that you row across the oceans. Once you have freed yourself, all you need to do to is to open your mind to the light, and it will come of itself. Now, if it doesn't come as soon as expected, don't get worked-up and run into the kitchen. Light comes in waves. And as every surfer knows, if you miss one, lay in there, for there'll always be a next one.[40]

Enlightened Leaders Speak Out

Because 'enlightenment' is so hard to define, and at the same time so rich in content, it is worth hearing what enlightened leaders themselves have to say about it. It must be noted, that as a rule these are not people who tag themselves as 'enlightened' – but most use terms that are closely related to our theme, promoting concepts like 'authentic leadership', 'true leadership', 'leadership from the heart.' What they share is a conviction that in the long run, and often in the short run as well, an approach informed by humanitarian sentiments, by love, *excusez le mot*, gives a better return than the traditional and impersonal 'business-is-business' approach.

BILL GEORGE, EX-CEO MEDTRONIC: COMMITMENT TO A PURPOSE OR MISSION

'We are all called to be leaders, each of us in our own way. We are the servants of the people we lead, and stewards of the assets of the organizations we are chosen to lead, most important of which are the human assets.'[41]

'Authentic leaders are those who are committed to a purpose or a mission; people who live by their values every day and who know the true north of their moral compass. They lead with the discipline and commitment to get great results for all their stakeholders: their customers, their employees, and their shareholders, as well as the communities where they serve. It sounds old-fashioned, and yet it's almost revolutionary.'[42]

'We've lost sight of the basics of doing business. The greatest misnomer in the business world is that companies are set up only to serve their shareholders, especially those shareholders who invest in the stock just for the short-term. I would argue that companies are set up to serve their customers. That's the only way you can create lasting value. And the path to serving your customers best is to get employees passionate and motivated about creating better products, and about providing better service. Ultimately, that's the competitive edge, which translates into a healthy bottom line. Authentic leaders focus on making a difference in the lives of the people they serve: their customers and their employees.'[43]

DEE HOCK, FOUNDER OF VISA INTERNATIONAL: INDUCED BEHAVIOUR

'A compelling question is how to ensure that those who lead are constructive, ethical, open, and honest. The answer is to follow those who will behave in that manner. It comes down to both the individual and collective sense of where and how people choose to be led. In a very real sense, followers lead by choosing where to be led. Where a community will be led is inseparable from the conscious, shared values and beliefs of the individuals of which it is composed.

True leaders are those who epitomize the general sense of the community – who symbolize, legitimize, and strengthen behaviour in accordance with the sense of the community – who enable its conscious, shared values and beliefs to emerge, expand, and be transmitted from generation to generation – who enable that which is trying to happen to come into being. The true leader's behaviour is induced by the behaviour of every individual who chooses where they will be led.

The important thing to remember is that true leadership and induced behaviour can be constructive or destructive, but have an inherent tendency to good, while tyranny and compelled behaviour have an inherent tendency to evil.'[44]

ROBERT E. STAUB: LOVE GENERATES MORE PROFITS

'You generate wholehearted leading by having the courage to pose key questions: What is the purpose of the work you do, of your enterprise? What is the aim of your life? How do you want to engage others and deal with different needs and agendas? What value do you place on surrounding relationships? Why should your customers want to be in an ongoing relationship with you and your organization? What are the core values that drive all interactions? What will continue to distinguish you from the competitors available?

As you formulate answers, you discover a deeper sense of meaning emerging, liberating energy, commitment, and creativity. Customers and suppliers begin to be engaged by the magnetic power of the interactions generated, creating significant bottom-line results. As James Autry, retired CEO of Field and Stream, expressed it, "Love generated greater profits."'[45]

ANDREW COHEN, SPIRITUAL LEADER: BECOMING ONE WITH YOUR DESTINY

'The thought of being a leader may seem like an appealing idea to the ego, but the reality of what being an *authentic* leader implies scares the ego to death. It means ego *death*. Why? Because it means that we actually care so much about a higher purpose, a higher principle, a higher goal, that we're willing to make the most important sacrifices for the sake of what we are aspiring to accomplish. It means we care so passionately about others also reaching that goal that we unhesitatingly sacrifice our own peace of mind, comfort, and security in order for them to succeed. It really means that we have no choice left anymore because we have realized without any doubt that from now on, *it's up to us.* We have realized that One Without a Second. We have realized that there is no other and there never could have been. What is so interesting about authentic leadership is this very insight: that once we have arrived, there is no longer any point of return. We have become one with destiny itself.'[46]

Note by the authors: This quote by Andrew Cohen is included here for two reasons. The first is, that it tackles a serious issue that many of us are confronted with as soon as we advance on a path that involves taking ownership of our leadership talents. The ego screams out, fearing its hold on the individual, and can make further advancement difficult. Being aware of the true nature of this constant obstruction helps keep up the spirit in moments of inner strife. Accept the sabotage as a common trick of a dying ego, and thereby weaken its force.

The quote is also included because of the moving image of someone dedicating her or himself to something higher, heart and soul. Which raised another serious issue. We have no ambition to diminish a word of what Andrew Cohen says, but let's stay grounded here: how many holy men and holy women does the world count? And how many of them are found in the corporate world? The problem with sayings like these about complete surrender to a higher cause – led by the hand of someone who extends his hand for this purpose – is that the followership can easily drift into a sectarian direction, with plenty of potential to be elaborated into a proto-fascist system.

When the one who extends his or her hand is a truly noble leader, this celebration, and almost veneration of the leader in the fullness of his dedication, is touching and deeply inspiring. But the same expressions have in the past been uttered by fascist demagogues, by cult figures like Jim Jones of the People's Temple, who drove 914 people to collective suicide in Guyana, and by the clever leaders of business operations pretending to be 'churches' – and under their direction a script like this works out awfully wrong. 'There is no longer any point of return,' the jihadi said as he strapped on his bomb pack. 'Now I am becoming one with my destiny,' he said as he ripped the cord.

Again, we assume that the leader you find on your path has only the noblest intentions, but hold your step when you hear that there is no more going back, because at that moment maybe there still is. How do you know when to follow, and when to back out – either to continue on a path of your own, or to be led by another? Listen to your heart, because it is the only voice that always rings true. Never follow anyone, follow only your heart.

AVIV SHAHAR, FOUNDER OF AMBER COACHING: A NEW TYPE OF AWARENESS

'Do you experience a new kind of awareness about yourself and the world around you? Are these moments of reflective awareness mixed with internal pressures and anxieties that you cannot fully explain?

If yes, you may be part of the quiet transformation that is underway. Simply put, yesterday's ways and holding patterns can no longer support the shifting dynamics at play. On the positive side, this shift awakens in many a new kind of creativity, a need to redress balance or a wish to alter things and make a difference. On the struggle side there is a pressure to assimilate, adapt and respond to a changing world with increasing ambiguity. As the 21st century unfolds, we find that the models of the past still offer lessons but cannot provide the answers and solutions we now need. Leaders from all sectors of society are discovering that the demands of true leadership are much greater than a skilfully learned behavioural model. The essence of this transformation concerns a need in oneself to envision an integrated whole-person-development. [...]

Today's managers are challenged inside circumstances of unprecedented change, speed and intensity. Imagine the following scenario: driving out to the country you take along a roadmap. Well, imagine the roads changing as you drive. The map no longer matches what you see. You hope the compass is going to give you direction but it starts spinning because you enter a higher magnetic field. Sounds like science fiction? Perhaps, but isn't your experience as a manager these days a bit like that?

You come to a point where you can no longer trust the map or the compass. What you need is to know where you stand, to know where you are. You are compelled to discover an integrated big-picture view and find yourself inside it. You emerge with questions such as: what really matters? What is really important for me as a leader? What is long-lasting and how can I do the best for my people?'[47]

JIM DREAVER, MANAGEMENT GURU: BEING PRESENT WITHOUT AGENDA

'If you are a student of the art of leadership, the subject of enlightenment will probably be of interest to you. It may be that you are a leader in your industry, your community, your field or area of expertise. You find yourself inspired by stories of great leadership. You are moved by the example of individuals who embody such qualities as vision, courage, compassion, creative thinking, bold decision-making, and selfless service to humanity.

You want to be the best leader you can possibly be. It makes you feel good to be a positive force in helping influence, shape, or direct the creative energy of others. You want to be of service. You like being part of a group, team, or organization that has good chemistry, one where every member or player feels a sense of kinship with each other, and is united around a common goal. You know from experience what it takes to create such unity, and you are willing to take responsibility to help in making it happen.

You understand the power of multiplication, and what can be accomplished when a group of conscious, focused people come together in the pursuit of a shared vision. You want to use that power to not only produce great results, but to make your organization, your community – and ultimately, our world – a better place.

If this is the kind of leader you are, or want to be, then *whether you think of it in these terms or not, you are on a journey to enlightenment.* [our italics] The greatest leaders in history, after all, have been the enlightened ones. This has always been the case. The ancient Chinese philosopher, Lao Tzu, spoke about this thousands of years ago, in the Tao Te Ch'ing, his classic guide to enlightened living:

> *"If you want to learn how to govern... Show people the way back to their own true nature."*

If, as a leader, you want to be able to bring out the highest and best in others, you must have achieved a certain level of mastery within yourself, a true meeting of wisdom and love. You don't have to be a saint, you don't have to be completely without ego. But your mind must be clear, your heart open, and you must know how to be present without any personal agenda, which is one of the signs of enlightenment.

Anyone can be present with an agenda – a self-centred motive – but it takes a very conscious and inwardly free, or awakened person, to be present without one. Only then can you be truly open and available to the untapped creative potential that exists in each moment. Only from that place of clear, loving presence can you build, create, and nurture an enlightened team or organization.

Nagarjuna, a philosopher-sage who lived in India about five hundred years after the Buddha, understood how critical enlightenment was in the art of leadership. He went so far as to say this:

> *"If a ruler cannot implement a politics of enlightenment, then he or she must abandon the throne to pursue enlightenment first."*

Now, to me, this does not mean that if you are struggling, say, with fostering an enlightened and harmonious work environment, you need to necessarily resign your position or office and go off on a long spiritual retreat in a mountaintop monastery somewhere. But it does mean that you must take some time out from your busy schedule to do some inner work.

Make enlightenment, your own inner peace and clarity, more of a priority in your life. Draw upon the resources that will feed your soul, nourish your heart, and enlighten your mind. Read the books, take the trainings, and get the coaching that will support you in this process and that will allow you to return to your leadership responsibilities with renewed clarity, vision, and passion.

Above all, take your own counsel. Spend time alone in meditation and contemplation. Listen to the voice of truth that comes from deep within you. Develop a trusting relationship with your own intuition and inner guidance. The more you do this, the more you will be able to empower others to do it. You will model conscious, enlightened behaviour for them. You will inspire them to dive more deeply within themselves. This is how you become a great leader.'[48]

Part II

The Chakras

The Seven Chakras of Leadership

WHY CHAKRAS?

When we want to get a complete picture of something, in all its aspects, it often helps to differentiate and name these aspects. For organisations we do that with instruments like Balanced Scorecard®, SIPCO Analysis, Business Process Mapping, and the whole battery of surveys including Integrated Scorecard that we use at Trompenaars Hampden-Turner. For individuals we may use Eysenck Personality Test, Myers-Briggs, Keirsey Temperament Sorter®, enneagram, astrology, and other tools to chart personality traits, some of them of recent development, others ancient. In the realm of leadership, the way we see it, what we most urgently need to differentiate is levels of consciousness – which, for the purpose of this book, we equate with *the areas where you focus your life energy*.

What is it that you really do with your life energy? In which areas are you most active, and where more reticent or even dormant? And is that energy spent in a positive way that charges you with new energy continuously, or is it spent in a way that drains you and hinders progress? Where are blockages, where new opportunities for growth? To identify this helps you to see how you are doing in terms of your 'energy economy', and how you may improve your effectiveness.

This book presents a new analytical instrument to chart these energetic aspects of personality, inspired by the seven energy centres of classic yoga philosophy: the Chakras of Leadership. Its aim is to facilitate recognition of aspects of leadership, one's own and others', reflection on the same, and re-focusing. A web-based survey, more on this later, has been created as an aid to analyse the energy distribution of self and others. Eager to jump right in? Go to www.chakratest.org.

Why have we used the image of the chakras, instead of stars, pillars, pie sections or consecutive layers, as Richard Barrett, prophet of values-based management, does in his Seven Levels of Corporate Con-sciousness?[49] The reason is, that as a young man Peter spent several years in the East, where he became acquainted with yoga and the chakra system, part of an immersion in Indian culture which he enjoyed immensely, and which touched him deeply by its blend of gentleness and academic rigour. This enriching acquaintance was deepened over the years by meditation, personal instruction, reading, music study or Nada Yoga, and further journeys to India. At mature age, when he began thinking about 'enlight-ened leadership', he recognised that the seven chakras would make a very apt symbol set to discriminate levels of personal and corporate conscious-ness, or levels of energy distribution.

In 2001 when Peter was training with Richard Barrett, fascinated by his system, essentially a raising of Maslow's pyramid with another two levels, he instantly saw the correlation of Maslow's hierarchy with the chakra system, a correlation which had not occurred to him before Barrett's upward extension. Maslow originally stopped at the level of self-realisation. Later in life he added a sixth and a seventh level above it: the Desires to Know and to Understand, and the Aesthetic Needs.[50] Given his interest in Vedic literature and other aspects of Indian culture, Peter had no doubt that Maslow's pyramid was a conscious attempt at transposition of the chakra system to western psychology. Given Maslow's original reluctance to go beyond self-realisation, it appears that his con-fidence in correlating the higher levels increased as his own insights deepened. Later in life he became increasingly explicit about the essen-tially transcendental nature of these higher needs, relating them to reli-gion and universal consciousness.[51]

Given Richard Barrett's erudition, Peter had no doubt that he, too, had a certain familiarity with Indian philosophy, so in their first meeting face to face (on 9/11, far away from the events, of which both were as yet unaware) he asked Richard why he had not chosen the chakra system, instead of his effective, but rather dry, numerical system. Richard answered that he had indeed considered it, but felt that his more business-like system of presentation was better suited to the corporate world. From the European perspective: let's not forget that much of the American corpo-rate world is more conservative than ours, and more provincial to boot. Not that we have many CEOs standing on their heads every day, but there is more openness for ideas from other cultures, and it is becoming hard to conceive of a European leadership training programme without at least a few blocks of yoga, tai-chi or chanting.

Being Europeans, we feel that we can safely introduce the chakras as an apt and visually attractive way to symbolically represent aspects of leadership. For the moment, see them as empty containers of meaning. Over the next chapters we shall fill them with associations – guided by what Peter learned about the subject in India and elsewhere, in gratitude to what masters such as Yesudian,[52] Iyengar,[53] Yogananda,[54] Satchidananda[55] have said and written – and what Guru Girnari[56] taught him in silence. We also draw on the work of Abraham Maslow,[57] read to shreds, but still bringing fresh insights, Richard Barrett[58] mentioned above, Stephen Covey,[59] Jim *Good to Great*[60] Collins, – whose Level 5 Leader corresponds marvellously with the fifth chakra – and various other authors who have described systems to differentiate between different levels of consciousness.[61]

Assuming that by now the credentials of the Chakras of Leadership may be considered established, let us admit that we have allowed ourselves free association with the classic framework. Like an Indian raga is played: there is a strong and rigid academic element, defining the structure, associated rhythms and moods, but there is at the same time a great amount of freedom to improvise. We hope that these improvisations will touch something inside you and help you to look at yourself and your behaviour with a clearer view, and become more conscious of your role as a leader. That increased consciousness of yours is the enlightenment the world is yearning for.

CHAKRAS AS CONTAINERS OF MEANING

Chakra is a Sanskrit term from the ancient Indian yoga philosophy, meaning literally 'wheel', used to refer to human energy centres at various locations in the body. These centres, traditionally represented as lotus flowers with varying numbers of petals, are immaterial – they are not found in even the most incisive autopsy, they do not show up on X-rays, MRI or CAT-Scans. According to many, this would mean that they do not exist. Or, put more kindly, that they are imaginary. Indians, who have worked with the chakra system for thousands of years, would retort that our problem is that we accept as 'real' only the material world. And that thereby we are depriving ourselves of much vital energy and wisdom. The Bengali poet/philosopher Samuel B. Lall once said to Peter, with his characteristic disdain for materialist thinking: 'Those poor people recognize as relevant only that which they can dissect, pulverize, bombard with rays, test with chemicals or destroy otherwise.'

An interesting discussion, but (and it is only to stress this that we brought it up) irrelevant in the context of this book, because we use the chakras merely as symbols for certain levels of consciousness: containers of meaning that are standing here empty as we speak and will be filled in the next pages. In principle these containers could be called anything, as other writers have created symbol sets based on colours, planets, archetypes, metals, precious stones, mountains, numbers, or classical deities to differentiate aspects of personality, attaching values to their chosen symbols. Our preference for chakras may be regarded as a personal quirk, which we hope you will accept, because to us the terminology opens the door to a rich realm of associations, a fair dose of which we hope to share with you. So, materialist or otherwise, this is something we should be able to agree on: *within the context of this book chakras exist.*

The advantage of employing a symbol set at all, instead of just naming the different levels of consciousness, is that symbols may be charged with a large, and ever expandable, quantity of related information, so that this whole body of wisdom can be shared simply by reference to the symbol, in this case a particular chakra. In terms of computer programming: we don't pass the value, just the pointer. This tremendously speeds up the processing of information.

The use of symbols, which predates language, is one of the most primordial and most powerful human qualities; an ability that chimpanzees and other higher primates can attain with training, but do not appear to use in their own culture. It may be argued that the path of humans and apes separated when we developed our mental capacity for referencing and dereferencing blocks of mental content, which led to the rapid development of language and our ability to map and explore our environment. The use of symbols, we believe, is where the road forks. And where God came into being.

In astrology, one of the oldest symbol sets in existence, the zodiacal signs stand for a whole gamut of aspects. The cross in all its simplicity has enough content to move millions. And, to stay closer to earth, the names of major cities evoke a whole gamut of positive and negative connotations: 'New York' and 'Shanghai' stand for hecticity, ambition, challenges and kicks, but also for power and exploitation, the corporate jungle; 'Paris' stands for joie de vivre, *élégance*, cultural riches, the good life, but also for decadence and arrogance; 'Amsterdam' stands for freedom, creativity, but also for dereliction. In exactly the same way the chakras to be introduced here will be charged with a series of related associations, allowing concise reference to a complex of urges, values, notions, talents, aspirations and attitudes that jointly determine one particular aspect of leadership.

The reason why we speak of this issue so explicitly, is that we are avoiding two trapdoors at once. We do not wish to impose on readers a belief in the existence of chakras, because no such belief is needed to develop one's leadership. The second is, that, although we admit being deeply indebted to it, we do not wish here to be bound to the classic canon of yoga philosophy, so insights from outside this system can be brought in without possible charges of adulteration of an old and venerable tradition. The chakra system that Peter developed, therefore, the Chakras of Leadership, is not ancient, but brand new. It is also entirely self-referencing: it does not rely on any outside values to exist.

HOW DOES THIS WORK IN PRACTICE?

To illustrate where we are going in practical terms: when we say that someone's existence is dominated by her Root Chakra, it calls to mind someone with a strong presence, who manifests herself with gusto, has extensive material needs and probably the possessions to match. She loves nature, has strong bonds with her tribe or family, and a practical mind. An inexhaustible doer ... Should, as is the case with both present authors, the Throat Chakra be dominant, then we see someone who likes to talk about the things he finds important, in the hope that his words will resonate with others, because it is very important for him to live in an environment of shared values.

The next step is to look at the balance between the different chakras: are all roughly equally active, or do one or two appear to preside over the personality? Are there sleepers, holding up true self-realisation, leave alone enlightenment? Then look again at those chakras that are powerfully active, the most strongly manifested aspects of the personality: is their development desirable or undesirable, destructive or constructive, injurious or healing?

With increasing familiarity you may discover aspects of yourself that you were not, or only dimly, aware of – and that, most likely, are a delight to discover. Most people, deep down, are greater than they think.

THE CHAKRAS AND THE HUMAN PHASES OF DEVELOPMENT

This section would expand beyond its targeted size (brief, the sooner to get to the beef), if we also covered the subject of chakras and their relationship to human phases of development. But touching on it for a second may be enlightening with regard to our changing view of leadership.

Human consciousness develops from a state of universal existence (prenatal existence in the womb), through merged existence in infancy, to individuality – and later, when development is not stunted, back to universality; back to a dissolution of self in the universal whole, but now in full awareness. Question: is this a western or an oriental view? The answer is, both. These stages of development are widely recognised in the west, extensively covered by Sigmund Freud, Norman Brown, and many others. But in the east we see exactly the same, essentially mystical motif. The classic image in Advaita Vedanta philosophy is of a drop of water in the surf which breaks free of the sea, flying through the air, and for a brief moment may cherish a sense of individuality, before falling back into the ocean.

A surprising new addition to literature on this subject was provided by Jeremy Rifkin in his book *The European Dream*.[62] In a brilliant display he speaks of the phases of life of human beings, and the striking parallels with the phases of life of cultures; all this to prove that European society, which now tends towards a holistic approach, is moving towards a higher level of development than American society, which is still in the phase of individuation and possessiveness.

The most important relationship between the life phases and the theme of enlightened leadership is, that according to the classic Indian teachings, the higher chakras tend to develop somewhat later in life. So don't feel too bad if not much is happening up there, you must still be too young. On the other hand, as we said earlier, many young people these days show precocious levels of maturity. Perhaps man, as a species, is going through a phase of accelerated development. The normal, and desirable route of personal development goes like this: acquiring the self-confidence of a survivor, relational effectiveness, and willpower; then, after a turnaround in the heart region, achieving purity, insight and universal consciousness.

CHAKRA TEST HELPS TO SEE YOUR OWN CHAKRAS

Any reader who wishes to know more about chakras has a wealth of literature at his or her disposal, some of it referred to elsewhere in these pages. (One title we would strongly recommend is Anodea Judith's *Eastern Body, Western Mind*,[63] though rationalists may want to skip the bits about healing and just absorb the psychology.) Our aim is exclusively to link the chakras with the theme of leadership – and to explore what leaders today might learn from the ancient teachings about energy centres that determine what our life force effects in the world – and thereby, who we really are.

To assist you in this exploration Peter developed the Chakra Test mentioned above. This web-based survey, which takes about 20 minutes to complete, leads you through seventy statements in the first person singular, asking you to indicate to which degree it accurately describes you. 'I constantly worry about money', 'I rely more on my intuition than on rational considerations', 'I am already quite a bit more enlightened than most people', and so forth.

The results are presented as circles composed of coloured and grey concentric rings, respectively representing positive and negative development of the particular chakra. To see this on the screen makes Peter's ego swell up a little, because no other chakra test on the internet (so far at least) represents the chakras so smartly, created in real-time by algorithms that analyse the input data and create a unique set of images for each user. The site was programmed in PHP, new to him when he started out, but fortunately similar to C, a language that he has been addicted to for years.

The web survey project has the creativity of the Sacral Chakra to thank for its existence, the Third Eye Chakra for its analytical powers, and for its completion the willpower of the Solar Plexus Chakra. The poor Root

Chakra, normally quite active during professional activities, got little attention, because, the site being free (for the moment at least, survival instincts may yet surge), we are not likely to make any money out of it. Should it ever become commercial, you as a reader of this book, will always have free access.

Please note that the Chakra Test does not pretend to be a diagnostic instrument, or a kind of virtual CAT-scan. We hope, and this is the only ambition we have for this test, that it will stimulate thinking about levels of consciousness, about the real-time effect of who we are and what we do, and facilitate self-observation. We particularly hope to promote awareness of the fact that any aspect of personality, which in itself is largely a given, the fruit of nature and nurture, may develop in a positive or in a negative way. And we ourselves determine which it shall be.

Your personal Chakra Test is ready for you and waiting at www.chakratest.org.

1. ROOT CHAKRA: SURVIVAL

Sanskrit name: Muladhara Chakra
Aspects: survival, independence
Location: the perineum, between genitals and anus
Colour: red
Element: earth
Sense: smell
Right: right to exist
Demon: fear
Figure: four-petaled lotus, pointing to the four corners of the earth
Maslow: levels 1 and 2 combined, need for survival, need for safety

Personal Aspects

Favourable development: This is the chakra of survival, comprising care for physical integrity, food, clothing, shelter and procreation. Dominant themes are independence, stability, groundedness. Other aspects are level-headedness, energy, assertiveness, ambition, material gain.

Negative development: Addiction to material wealth or sensual enjoyment, fear, lust for power, exploitation.

Corporate Aspects

Favourable development: This is the chakra of organisational continuity – and on a personal level, the chakra of continuity of your professional existence. Given positive development of this aspect, core themes are financial health, profit, shareholders' value. Also covered by this chakra are safety and health of employees. Leaders with a powerfully developed Root Chakra never lose sight of the bottom-line. This is their strength, and may at the same time be their weakness.

Unfavourable development: Totalitarian management style, exploitation, profit-at-any-price, share price manipulation, inhuman behaviour, criminality. Former WorldCom CEO Bernard Ebbers, sentenced to 25 years of imprisonment, has done the world a great service by becoming a poster child for negative development of the Root Chakra.

Chief Challenge: To transcend the worldly without uprooting yourself.

THE CHAKRA OF SURVIVAL

The Root Chakra is all about survival, the strongest of all human needs, the most deeply rooted of all primal urges. Its seat is the perineum, the saddle between anus and genitals. It is the root of all development. The Root Chakra provides the impetus for our first phase of growth as human beings, from the prenatal stage up to the onset of individuation, the recognition of the self as an individual entity. It is the centre of our connectedness with the mother and through her with the earth. Its manifestation is seen in the success, or lack of it, of our struggle for life. Simply put: the Root Chakra is the spiritual hub of everything material.

Envisage yourself for a moment as a cave-dweller ... Next try to imagine what might most occupy your head. This, and everything derived from it, is the realm of the Root Chakra. The central theme is security. For early man this meant first and foremost bodily integrity (the survival instinct) – almost all energy went into this. Development of higher chakras? Expending any energy at all on something other than food, shelter and sex? Forget it, not for ten thousand more years. Pick up your club and go get dinner. For modern humans it means all this – there is an early man or an early woman in all of us – but at a low level of awareness. In our daily consciousness we are mostly busy arranging less immediate forms of security, manifested in a predilection for cars that do well in crash-tests, provisioning for old age, and calling in sick on the day that the whole department goes bungee jumping.

Survival is a matter of life and death – and the latter we wish to avoid at all costs. In primeval ages survival meant victory in the fight with wild animals and other humans. Later it meant growing and harvesting, battling with the elements, rodents and other vermin. It also meant developing a new, less assertive and more humble posture, namely squatting, and a new kind of cunning, directed at smaller animals. Nowadays, for the majority of people in our culture it means mostly financial survival: the struggle to get money for rent or mortgage, taxes, the energy bill. This battle forces us to focus on the material – the worldly, the earthly, and indeed the earthy.

The Root Chakra connects us with the earth, in which we are rooted so deeply, and which is the source of our vital energy. This energy, absorbed through, yes indeed, the roots, helps us in the 'struggle for survival' – a term that for most westerners has lost the sharp edge it had in earlier centuries, actually until well into the 20th century – which most of us are engaged with one way or another; albeit, thank heaven, in a veiled and softened form. Such a veiled form may be the filling out of your tax returns, especially when it involves some fiddling, or looking for a parking space when you are late for your appointment already and get on the phone to your secretary to let her call in an excuse, an archetypal Muladhara-moment.

Other, more positive moments in which the Root Chakra makes itself felt strongly, are the occupation of a new house (superlative form: building of your own home), making a major career step, founding of your own company, and any time you work at keeping your body in good condition.

THE CHAKRA OF OUR RELATIONSHIP TO
THE MATERIAL WORLD

The Muladhara, as already indicated above, is the chakra in which our relationship with the material world is manifested. Whether this relationship manifests itself in contentment with material well-being (as many in the western world enjoy in historic measure) or greedy materialism, a hunger that keeps feeding on itself, is a function of the development of this aspect. The way we use the worldly energy determines whether we get hooked on worldly pleasures and possessions (so that they start to possess us) or can use them for our spiritual development. World-renowned guru Bhagwan Shree Rajneesh, a.k.a. Osho, was so keen to show that he was above the material, that at the end he owned hundreds of Rolexes and ninety Rolls-Royces.[64]

A properly functioning Root Chakra makes a well-grounded individual, a capacity to live in the here and now, and a lively personality, bursting with energy. It provides a healthy relationship with the material world, a proper balance of giving and receiving. The ideal image is that of a man or woman who stands with both feet firmly planted on the ground, of radiant health and full of confidence, arms loaded with the earth's bounty.

THE ONE YOU NEGLECT AT YOUR PERIL

Many somewhat cultured individuals tend to look down upon the realm of the Root Chakra. We notice it ourselves working on this chapter: this is not the most attractive chakra to write about. Not really glorious, not sexy, and in Freudian terms pretty darn close to anal. No, then we would rather discourse on the Third Eye Chakra or Crown Chakra, proper subjects for gentlemen of standing ... Horribly elitist, and at the same time so common. Unadulterated snobbery, rooted in age-old class sentiments and an attendant sense of superiority. We feel we are too fine to have to dig into our primal urges to find our truths ... Wholly wrong of course, but to deny it is worse. Still, we need to outgrow this, because if we forget our roots we can never grow tall.

Historically, it has always been the case that rich people who developed themselves, began looking down their noses at the material resources that helped them to transcend the material, and started preaching a reformist gospel to the classes below them: 'Do not think for one moment that you can buy happiness. And frankly, the way you folks live ... It really is rather base, you know, to always be after the material! Look at me, I prune my own roses, but other than that I do not concern myself with the world, leave alone worry about my daily quiche.' That is why very rich people always have trusts, managed by people who know everything about money – or do a good job pretending – so that the owners need not mind it ever again, and can safely start cultivating an image of themselves as having risen above it.

For the class of common people (people without trusts) to which 99.9 percent of the world population may be counted, such disdain for the material is not just inadvisable, but also unhealthy. Financial security – defined as a position in which medium term needs are met by income from capital gains, private enterprise or secure position of employment – is a minimum requirement for the development of the higher chakras, in particular the three highest. Universal connectedness is beautiful, but when we are starving we may find ourselves grabbing from others what we feel we need. If worst comes to worst, we will eat one another.

Cannibalism (not the contemporary internet hobby, but the traditional form) is the most revolting, but also the purest expression of the power of the Root Chakra. In the trenches around Stalingrad the SS were chomping the arms and legs of fallen comrades, attacking them fresh, before they'd get frozen; there are numerous well documented cases of pole explorers and seamen on rafts who ended up drinking each other's blood and eating each other's flesh; the survivors of a Uruguayan Air Force plane crash in the Andes in 1972 filleted the best preserved dead with pocket knives, laid the strips of meat to dry on the wings and kept themselves alive chewing up their fellow passengers for 72 days. Don't look down on this kind of energy, don't denigrate the associated chakra, because maybe one day you'll need its force badly.

It may be useful to remark that financial security, and the attendant inner peace, is easier to achieve with an unpresumptuous set of demands. As our late friend, the psychologist Herman Cohen, used to say when he heard someone complain about not achieving one grand objective or another: 'The people most likely to achieve happiness are those with modest demands.'

THE ROOT CAUSE OF MANY PROBLEMS

A Root Chakra that is wide open and allows an uninterrupted flow of energy is an absolute prerequisite for development. It is impossible to have properly functioning higher chakras, while there is something wrong at the base, because a problem at the root of our functioning will demand so much attention that little energy will be left for higher causes.

A Root Chakra with a choked energy flow manifests itself in various ways, including fear (often fear for life itself – an inverted form of the primal fear of death), suspicion and a defensive attitude. The worst risk of a stalling Root Chakra is a possible lapse into violent behaviour, caused by an intense, built-up sense of insecurity. Like a hunted animal, a man or woman who feels his or her very existence endangered, can suddenly lash out fearsomely – commandeering the iron will of the Solar Plexus Chakra, and go all out when needed.

The second great risk is a spasmodic seizing up of the attention, directed at all things material and sensual. The results come in two variations:

1. The material and the sensual fail to flow in. One is left poor and miserable. Always broke and in hock, not a penny to scratch an itch. A credit rating from hell.
2. Material success is achieved, but comes with symptoms of excess, attachment, or ostentation. Lakeside villa with boathouse for ten jet-skis, Lamborghini with gold-plated wheels, male guests with bejewelled watches. The maintenance of white elephants. It looks great, but commonly causes many problems.

In other words, a greedy attitude either blocks an uninterrupted inflow of the objects of desire, or blocks their true enjoyment.

MARKS OF A PROPERLY FUNCTIONING ROOT CHAKRA
- a well grounded personality
- physical health

- zest and dynamism
- everything one attempts succeeds, with at most a few exceptions
- solid standing in society – which may not necessarily lead to wealth, but is likely to produce sufficiency, the good life, general well-being
- common sense, level-headedness (perhaps manifested in scepticism towards chakras and all that stuff)
- tons of courage; confidence that even if there is trouble today, it will all turn out alright in the end
- contentment.

SYMPTOMS OF A BLOCKED ROOT CHAKRA
- feelings of insecurity, negative assessment of one's own chances of survival, *Lebensangst*
- obsession with security, seeking cover from all kinds of threats, real and imagined
- materialism in all shapes and sizes
- a feeling of being 'unwanted' here on earth
- no inner peace, nervousness, drifting about, an unsteady gait
- mania for utility: everything you expend energy on has to *yield* something
- relationships based on dependency, clinging and clasping, directed at the fulfilment of an inner need
- ostentation (showing off material attributes is an overcompensation of the fear not to survive)
- health problems
- no grounding in passions, deep-seated convictions, strong set of values
- weak self-discipline, self-indulgence
- suicidal tendencies (a longing for death in a physically healthy human being points to a deeply disturbed relationship with the Root Chakra)
- wearing a Ferrari sweater with the imprint 'Life goes too fast to be driving Porsche'.

SHORT TERM ORIENTATION KILLING LONG TERM POTENTIAL

Globalization through mergers, acquisitions and strategic alliances is big business – estimated to be worth in excess of $4 trillion per year.[65]

According to the Washington Post, benefits of globalisation, in terms of increased income, for the USA amount to $1 trillion annually.[66] In 2007 the total volume for mergers in the US topped $1 trillion within the first half year alone.[67] Mergers, acquisitions and strategic alliances are increasingly pursued, not just to implement globalisation strategies, but rather as a consequence of political, monetary and regulatory convergence. The phones at consultants' are ringing off the hook.

Creating wealth in an integration process is not easy since it requires joining values that are not easily joined: two out of three deals don't achieve anywhere near the anticipated benefits. This alarming statistic was first brought to the world's attention by the *Economist* in 1999.[68] Larry Selden and Geoffrey Colvin, writing in the *Harvard Business Review* in 2003, came to a failure rate as high as 70–80%.[69] Similarly, a 2001 McKinsey study by Mathias Beier, Anna Bogardus and Timothy Oldham, referenced by the Institute of Mergers, Acquisitions and Alliances, finds that 80% of M&A deals completed during the 1990s failed to justify the equity that funded them.[70]

Since then many others have looked at the success rate of mergers and acquisitions, and found on average the same ratio: about one-third are successful, two-thirds fail. Alas, researchers do not go by a common standard for what constitutes success and what failure, so any numbers on the subject are inherently dodgy. Recently, New York University's Stern School of Business,[71] looking at the varying assessments, arrived at a ballpark figure that appears to be widely shared: a failure rate for mergers and acquisitions of 50–70%.

Why is the failure rate so high?

The short answer is: because of greed. The mad hunger to make as much money as quickly as possible, to hell with the consequences. Or, more precisely, to hell with the people – because that is what it usually implies, as we have seen again in the banking crises. The big guys sail off with their multimillion dollar golden parachutes, the employees stand at the door empty handed – if we forget their carton boxes with private belongings. A Root Chakra that is both hyperactive and unfavourably developed can lead to gross disregard for other people's needs. The somewhat more elaborate answer is that organisations are traditionally acquired on the basis of their inherent value, rather than with the intention of achieving full integration. Increasingly however, we see motives originating from a range of other expected benefits, including synergistic values (e.g. cross-selling, supply chain consolidation, economies of scale) and more direct strategic values (e.g. become market leader, expand customer base).

This fills us with hope that the M&A world will eventually enjoy better weather. Unfortunately, the short term forecast is still rather dim: the emphasis in pre-deal and post-deal management is too often focused on immediate exploitation of new opportunities. To make matters worse, this is commonly done with a mechanistic mindset, steeped in the acids of financial due-diligence, which probably dropped a full pH point in the 2008 credit crunch.

CEOs commonly assume that delivering M&A benefits requires primarily the alignment of strategic, organisational, technical, operational, and financial systems, market approaches and sundry other structural elements. This is where things go wrong. In fact what is required first and foremost, is to align the culture – in other words, the people. It strikes us as curious that this is still not universally understood, whereas to us it seems obvious that in a world economy dominated by service and knowledge transfer, the human factor is the key to success.

Our practical experience of the last two decades reveals that the most common underlying reason for any failure to deliver M&A benefits is found in the absence of a holistic, and ideally also emotionally binding methodological framework. A framework that comprises not just the above-mentioned structural elements but the human element as well, and that has the capacity to engender collective passion. Because of this absence senior managers do not know what to integrate, what to prioritise, and what types of decisions are needed to deliver the anticipated benefits. All they know is that money – ideally big money – is somehow to be made. And that *they* as chief executives are to deliver this money at short notice, or will be seen to have failed. All this leads to regressive use of command and control, power displays, and panicky, fearful approaches: managers armed with freshly honed bush knives slashing wildly through the cultural jungle. To prevent these often ruthless and fruitless treks into the heart of corporate darkness, we need to go beyond the Root Chakra and strive for well defined goals over and above the short term materialistic gains that mergers and acquisitions are supposed to bring.

The absence of a holistic methodological framework also results in an information vacuum: those responsible remain in the dark about the success or failure of their decisions. Even where strategists and senior managers recognise the importance of culture, frustration often sets in because they have no means of assessing or quantifying causes and effects, and therefore no way to design effective action. Part of what we are trying to do here, is provide such a holistic framework: a way of looking at the issues across the full spectrum of energy levels.

SOME FUNDAMENTAL STUFF

Issues at this level are truly fundamental for M&A – if there is no agreement on the importance of bottom line results, any effort to merge or integrate acquired companies will be messy, with fierce recriminations dominating management discussions. We recently saw a case that perfectly illustrates what may go wrong if intentions on this level are assumed rather than discussed in depth as part of the cultural due diligence process – and how to resolve the issue.

TCON* is a rapidly globalising company in the technology sector, very successful on its home market, and an aggressive pursuer of new markets. After a successful IPO it is still run largely by the founders/ owners. Known throughout the mother organisation for its relentless focus on short term results and disregard for relational and developmental needs of its people (many employees are on board only because the rapid expansion challenges and stretches them, something we have observed in many fast growth companies), TCON acquired a whole string of operations in a score of countries, most thousands of miles away – only to discover after a year of struggle, that the majority of the managers of the acquired companies had entirely different basic assumptions as to what constitutes good leadership and good management. They regarded bottom line results as the natural results of commitment to employees and customers, not as a purpose per se. *To serve their markets* had been their purpose, and because they cared for their employees, these had served the customers with passion, thus setting in motion the virtuous circle of value generation that we preach every day. In so doing, they had done very well – and this was what had made them attractive takeover targets.

* Like all other names of organisations mentioned in these sections, true name and corporate activity were modified to protect the identity of clients.

Group management became puzzled. On the one hand they wanted to maintain their habitual focus on Results Now, on the other hand they became aware of the low degree of support for the management style that they tried to impose, and the need to do something about this urgently – if only for the sake of employee retention. How to reconcile the dilemma? Several of the outlying operating companies were already bleeding talent, and finding it harder to recruit top candidates. What to do? Replace the management in all the 'affected' companies? Lose more people? But then, who would be left to make all that dearly wanted money for the founders/owners?

A thorough cultural inventory through interviews and THT 'Culture Labs' in about half of the country operations, *and* in the home country, showed that employees across the whole multi-continent footprint were unanimous in their desire for a more people-oriented approach, and would be energised by leadership that manifested true interest in their values, ambitions, and needs.

After careful but forceful prodding, top management decided that maybe they should try to *learn* from the companies they acquired – something so rare in M&A that we should award them the Golden Globe for Cultural Sensitivity. TCON, being a group of doers, sat down and redefined the company's purpose, vision and mission.

To specify what we mean by these often confused, interchanged, or otherwise nonchalantly used terms:

Purpose
Question: *What do we want to achieve in this world?*
Deliverable: *This is what we go for.*

Vision
Question: *How does our purpose relate to current realities?*
Deliverable: *This is what we see.*

Mission
Question: *How do we achieve our purpose in this current reality?*
Deliverable: *This is what we do.*

We aided TCON using a web tool that Peter created based on the work of Nikos Mourkogiannis, author of the inspirational work *Purpose*,[72] unique in the way he sheds light on one of the most fundamental issues any organisation can be faced with: 'Why are we here? What do we do with our collective energy?' Mourkogiannis posits four archetypes: Discovery, Excellence, Altruism and Heroism. We added Materialism, in other words Money. Loot is a powerful archetype, Lord of this Chakra, as old as the world. It is essential to add 'Big M' to the paradigm because for many companies this is their *only* purpose, and the only one they can possibly imagine. We should also add Employment. More than half a century ago William Hewlett and David Packard chose to make quality employment and care for the individual a core element of their corporate purpose. People were at the heart of their culture, the 'HP Way'. They lived it, found it profitable, earned great admiration and created a legacy.

At the time, such recognition of employee satisfaction as the source of all wealth creation ('HP's performance starts with motivated employees; their loyalty is key') was relatively rare. Now it is rapidly gaining prominence; with some truly tough, mostly American hold-outs and a few new entrants, mainly Chinese, fighting the rearguard of exploitation and inhuman use of human beings.

After consensus about TCON's purpose was established by group management and a team of top managers from half a dozen of the larger opcos, vision and mission were redefined in a few weeks – weeks of frequent brief contacts. PowerPoints were flying across the network for amendment, emendation or other revision. A few weeks later, when TCON's CEO announced the new course at the company's annual leadership forum, he was greeted with a spontaneous outburst of applause.

It is too early to tell what this whole operation will do to TCON's bottom line results, but from the scores of personal contacts in the organisation we get a sense of strongly renewed cohesion, and a vibrant energy. One divisional director whom we had earlier interviewed – in a sad meeting that gradually shifted character from interview to counselling – came up to us after the CEO's speech: 'I was blown away. I had never thought that a company like this could change. As I told you then, I was on the verge of leaving. But now I stay!'

The moral of this story: if you want a healthy bottom line, try thinking of something else now and then. Go beyond the base material urges that we find at this energy level. For consultants there is an additional moral: Yes it *is* risky to tell clients that they have their heads up their Root Chakras, but if they listen up and suddenly see the light again you have worked miracles, not just for them, but for all the people whose lives they affect.

ROOT CHAKRA DOMINANT: ARCHETYPE BOB H. – BOOM OR BUST

Bob H. is a trader who alternates between textiles and real estate, with an occasional dabble in office furniture and media production. A casual acquaintance of many years, we occasionally run into him in the lounge of London's City Airport or at a sidewalk café, and bring one another up to date. Originally from Milano where he was known as Roberto, Bob now lives in London, in grand style, drives Aston Martins, mostly dented, and frequently changes address. He is usually installed in a huge loft apartment, ideally in the docklands or some industrial wasteland on the edge of gentrification, but may also take refuge on a floor of his office, or stay with a girlfriend. He speaks of his deals with gusto, speaks with less gusto but without shame of his latest bankruptcy, repeats that one day we should cook up a spectacular project together, and complains about the tax collector, always unfairly claiming millions, and days away from impounding some asset that he needs to move into another shell before Tuesday.

He is ever busy with matter, ever hunting for more, but also lets it go easily, giving generously to girlfriends and any other people he takes a liking to. He once gave a waiter his cashmere jacket, just because the man remarked that it was beautiful – and anyway, Bob said, he had containers full of that stuff.

As Bob H. approaches, the first thing that strikes one is his bloated body shape. Partly because of his overweight he looks older than his 52 years. Chairs groan at the sight of him. His manner of eating appears to have been directed by Fellini, in a scene depicting the cardinal sin of gluttony: sucking on, and slurping around his hot pastrami sandwich, with an unappeasable hunger. He is commonly accompanied by a tasty young thing – okay now darling, go read your maggie for a while, I gotta talk to the gentleman here – and asks for whipped cream on his cappuccino. He goes through life swilling, eating, drinking and fornicating without inhibition.

Ah, what a vitality that boy! And what a might of activity there in that Root Chakra! But let us beware of simplification: no one, not even someone with such an earth-bound nature, is exclusively ruled by one chakra. The Root Chakra may be dominant here, but apparently Bob is also well tuned in to the Sacral Chakra in his lower belly, because he doesn't have these girls around for meditation sessions. His Solar Plexus Chakra is spinning furiously, because as a child he learned that he could have anything he wanted, and if he really wants something he'll break down the door to get it. And his Heart Chakra is wide open, because friends who come asking for help never go home disappointed. You have a serious problem in life, take it to Bob and it will be taken care of. He is a master in the universal system that Americans have such an apt corporate name for. 'What do I owe you?' 'Oh, just make a deposit for me at the favour bank.' Bob discovered the principle early in life, never sinned against it and by mid-life Favour Bank offered him private banking. He appears to have unlimited credit, that he can draw on when needed, for himself or for friends.

What we are seeing here is a pure worldly type, massively geared up for survival and conquest of the outside world, assisted by wonderful relational intelligence, the almost tyrannical will of a child spoiled rotten by his adoring and ever beloved mother, and a warm heart. The throat area suffers from too much smoking and too many untruths, heard and spoken. Where a third eye might be, there is just ruffled forehead, because too much introspection would hurt him. And around the crown of his head, quiet appears to reign eternal. All in all, in its homely simplicity an almost Dürerian archetype, both feet planted solidly on the ground, both hands grabbing what they can of the earth's bounty.

Bob H. is not entirely free of lust for power, a common affliction among those who are ruled by what Freudians would recognise as emblematic of the anal level of consciousness. He indulges in perverted exercise of power, and relishes doing this publicly. He will sit in the clubby airport lounge, send his girlfriend out for drinks, pick up his mobile and call the director of his accountant's firm: 'Hey John, that you? Listen [derogatory term deleted], didn't I tell you that I needed the numbers on that project by Wednesday? It is Thursday morning now, and. ... Yes, but if I can't give the go-ahead by five the whole deal goes bust. Yeah, that would be a shame, indeed – because then I am going to have that whole outfit of yours bought up, and get you kicked out before the ink dries.' John is the managing director of a well reputed accountancy firm, directing many men and women in pin-striped suits, a few perhaps gifts of Bob H., some Cornelianis from an odd lot that passed his hands.

Remarkable is the pulsating character of Bob's Root Chakra – now he is on top of the world, now he lost everything. (He keeps his Astons dented so they are less likely to be impounded.) But whether he is up or down, there is always a lot of energy being expended. Obviously, it would benefit Bob if he didn't put so much pressure on everything he strives for, because that pressure chokes his naturally open Root Chakra. He then corrects by letting go for a while, flying off to Brazil to lie on his back, but comes back more tense than before, raging about all the opportunities for making money that were lost at the poolside.

'Well, you can't have it all,' we once told him.

'You can try like hell, though,' Bob retorted.

So, Bob keeps squeezing his lower chakra till he collapses, then releases his hold, takes a deep breath and goes full steam again. Exciting, but it makes one old before one's years. As for wisdom, we don't push it on him hard. Should his behaviour become less excessive, he might also become less excessively generous. No more cashmere for casual acquaintances. But for old trusted friends?

ROOT CHAKRA DISDAINED:
ARCHETYPE EDWIN D. – THE RETURN TO DUST

Edwin D. is a classic case of disdain for the slime and dirt from which we have all risen, and a study of his development over the years is highly

instructive. He is an erudite man, observant, and an excellent cinematographer, who in his younger years was actively interested in the spiritual, but became less so after he passed the half-way mark.

Because of his life-choice, made in his twenties, never to do any commercial work, he has always had to struggle to make ends meet. Third Eye Chakra (insight, intuition) and Throat Chakra (communication) work as they should, the three below are sort of doing okay, but the Crown Chakra (universal consciousness), which figures prominently in his self-image, is in fact rather dulled, as a result of his disdain for the lowly realm of the Root Chakra. The latter has been frozen for a quarter century, seized up with the notion that money and any other form of material possession other than cameras is filthy lucre, not worth striving for.

As a result of this disdain he makes sadly little money, with the subsequent result that his venerated Crown Chakra gets sadly little attention because his permanent state of financial emergency forces him to peddle and hustle continuously. If the truth be known, he has of late become ever more commercial, to get every extractable penny from his 'non-commercial' projects. It will not be long before the spurned Root Chakra will dominate his everyday existence, at the cost of his spiritual life, for which he is so well equipped. (See also 'Running on all seven' p. 220.)

In refusing to serve, to provide what others would like you to provide to them, there is laudable independence. But we hope that one day Edwin will discover that there is only a fine line between being staunchly independent, or showing pride, with an element of greed – the avarice of not giving enough of yourself. It takes a giving nature to make others appreciate and reward you. The better this is appreciated and practiced, the more readily one can forget about all that material stuff and move on to higher levels of consciousness.

Place on earth: In contrast to the other chakras, which can readily be related to very specific spots where they appear to show themselves in full glory, the Root Chakra is practically everywhere. It is best experienced on very earthy spots – of which there are still very many, though more and more each year are covered with asphalt or concrete. The best places are those where the struggle for life still has the urgency it once had for all, and where we can get a taste of the primordial soup.

The Root Chakra is active everywhere at sea, not just because of the survival element, but because of the connection with the element of which we are all born. Very powerful is the presence of volcanic activity. Anyone who stands at the edge of the Hawaiian Kilauea volcano, watching it throw up magma, or looks down into the flaming and roaring mouth of the Bromo on Java, cannot be but in the thrall of his or her Root Chakra.

An excellent way to experience the force of the Root Chakra is to cultivate the earth, *lavrar a terra*, as Peter's Portuguese neighbours would say, with the element of labour implied in the verb; preferably in rocky, recalcitrant soil, or in mud that sucks at your feet (planting rice being a prime example). Turning the earth with a spade, planting, and weeding all make the Root Chakra bloom, and fill one with primal energy – especially when it isn't about winning the local Gardenia Bowl, but aimed at the production of foodstuff, in a spirit of survival and providing sustenance for loved ones.

Then there is pottery of course, shaping the earth's essence. A classic in meditation sessions is the manipulation of rocks, stones, or large crystals, which strengthens the awareness of our relationship, through this well defined chunk of matter in our hands, with all matter in the universe. The rule here is: the denser the composition of the stone the better. No sediment, but cooled off magma. Relatively young. Basalt, granite, gneiss, and quartz rather than sandstone, slate or marble. What also works, is sitting on rocks or sand in your bare butt, especially when these are cool or moist.

Peter's own primal spot is a spring in the woods near where he grew up, that he discovered himself as a twelve year old, roaming through the forests, pushing through shrub, ranging up and down blueberry covered slopes, slogging through sand dunes. In the middle of a stand of birches he found a small pond, perhaps no more than fifty feet across, where crystal clear water welled up from the silvery sand, the source of a thin little brook, still running today. The small pool of water is ringed with ferns and moss and the silence is complete – was rather, before the construction of the motorway five miles away.

In Peter's words: 'Even as a child I was keenly aware how important this source must have been for the old Saxons who peopled these dry woodlands, and I knew they must have given it some special name. I gave it a name myself, too, as I often did with peculiar spots in the woods that seemed to brim with meaning, like those tiny pools of water, full of life, that one finds up in the trees, in the hollows of branches, minute biotopes, whole little worlds, all your own discovery ... I returned to that spring a few times per year, to that miraculous spot that to me felt like a holy place, which I kept to myself and only once showed a friend – a deeply religious friend, who instantly understood why this place should be kept secret.'[73]

Exercise: Try to assess to what degree your actions are induced by eagerness for material gain, or by fear that you will not be able to achieve any.

Is your score on the high side (more than one-seventh, or around 15 percent), try to determine if you do not focus too forcefully on survival and conquest, whereas, realistically speaking, your survival by now is pretty much assured.

The reason for such a reality check is, that actions springing from the Root Chakra often have an atavistic element, something we inherited from our earliest forebears. That endless plodding on to get ahead, like buffaloes whipped by fate through a swamp of trouble, every God-given day again, year in year out – that got into our genes. You can't help it, we can't help it. But most of us could really do a little less plodding and still survive – with a much better chance to achieve some measure of happiness. Of course we all want to keep driving the class of automobile we are used to, and to step back from Gucci to C&A is rough, but if that frees us from plodding, haven't we gained a fortune?

You would say yes, and you would be right, but this is not an automatic choice. The other day Peter and his wife Ineke were having lunch with friends. He is the former CEO, recently retired, of a multinational health products conglomerate. They are very nice people, have lived everywhere, speak everything, and are free now to enjoy what they have achieved in many years of what he, certainly, has experienced as hard slog. They are not in the least ostentatious, still, hearing what they do and did recently, anyone would deduce within minutes that they are rich.

Peter told him about a street interview he once saw in Cleveland, on local TV. A reporter asking people off the cuff which they would rather be, rich or happy. Astonishingly, 60 percent of the interviewees opted for rich, apparently feeling that happiness would unfailingly follow. One old geezer in a Caterpillar cap said 'Well, I know what money can do for me, but happiness? Maybe it's not all it's cracked up to be.'

The former CEO burst out laughing, interrupted his wife's conversation with Peter's wife and said, 'Darling, answer quickly, which would you rather be: rich or happy?' She looked at him for a while in obvious puzzlement, her brilliant-cut Top Wesselton ear-studs lighting up the room, and answered with some hesitation: 'Well, you do get used to certain things, you know ...'

The gentleman looked at Peter triumphantly. As if her answer had suddenly uncovered the true driving force behind all those years of hard slog. There may be some truth in that, but in fairness to her, he seemed a little too happy to get off that hook: It wasn't me who pissed his life away for filthy lucre, who traded his best years for Jaguars and first class tickets.

So do that little test, then later you can't go around thinking that it wasn't you who got you to do all that chasing after the material, all that plodding. And mind you: best do the test now, and do it again after finishing this book. By then you will have a better idea of the workings of the other chakras, so that you can tell with more exactitude where the accents of your life truly lie.

PARADOX AT THE ROOT LEVEL

Every entrepreneur, since time immemorial, has been in it for the money. (Sure, there is the other 0.0014 per cent.) Money making is the bottom-line of business, the bed rock of enterprise. Yet being only in it for the money is a bad predictor of success. It may work, but usually, other drivers, related to higher energy levels, lead to more long term success. Most of the world's great industrialists had something driving them other than making more money. And often, that something was reconciling their own needs and desires with the needs and desires of others. Seen as 'he has a way with people'. A way to inspire them and make them follow. Leadership. In the classical sense, of showing the way and taking responsibility, but also in the paternalistic sense that involves a caring nature and personal interest.

A fine model is provided by the Tata family of India: great industrialists who employ hundreds of thousands of people, and earlier than many US and European companies started to take care of their people. Started in other words, to move beyond exploitation, the exploitation that was the raw heritage of thousands of years of ruthless rulers.

Some of the world's wealth is made through buying and selling and schlepping stuff around the globe, but most of it is made through the use of human beings. The legal framework for this use is provided by politics, and this is its one and only function. All the refinements of law obfuscate the fact that the main object of law giving is to keep the populace at peace and preserve order, so as not to waste days in bloodshed that might have been better spent creating value for the power elite. For us, say. For readers and authors of books like this, whose honoured duty it is to help organisations survive in their usually highly competitive environments, and create more value.

We are good at this task. In most countries around the developed world physical violence is nowhere near where it was a century ago. The current way to keep labour peace is constructing less abrasive organisations that hurt fewer people, and make them more inclined to truly serve customers and keep the value creation cycle going.

In this use of human beings we have seen manifested varying degrees of gentility. Even today we see brutal examples, such as bonded labour in China[74] and India[75] (there not just bonded, but sometimes also branded,[76] as in Bihar and other backward states), and we see new forms of exploitation of illegal aliens in the US and Europe, but if we take the long view, the trend is up towards more humanity, more care for the other and the environment, more inclusion. Clearly, the election of Barack Obama was a manifestation of this trend. Maybe we are finally arriving at Norbert Wiener's age of 'The Human Use of Human Beings'. Maybe more people these days feel secure enough to feel that they can become more loving? Maybe the human race is slowly – indeed ever so slowly – moving up from the Root Chakra.

Enterprise is wedded to politics and probably always will be. The power elites have traditionally behaved as entrepreneurs, serving the ends of their class and providing stability, the economic backbone, of the country. But paradoxically, being in the game only for the money negatively affects your chances of not just spiritual, but also of material success.

2. SACRAL CHAKRA: RELATIONSHIPS, CREATIVITY

Sanskrit name: Svadisthana Chakra
Aspects: sexuality, emotionality, relationships, creativity
Location: the sacrum, between genitals and navel
Colour: orange
Element: water
Sense: taste
Right: the right to your own feelings
Demon: guilt
Figure: six-petaled lotus
Maslow: level 3, need for love and belonging

Personal Aspects

Favourable development: This is the chakra of (gut-)feeling and relationships. It is also the chakra of sexuality, but various branches of yoga differ in the weight they accord this aspect. Given the importance of sexuality in our society, we tend towards the Tantric interpretation which places great emphasis on the essentially sexual nature of all energy in this realm. This covers the capacity to experience deep emotions, compassion, and the ability to express yourself creatively (an extension of the original creativity in procreation). A wide open Sacral Chakra also provides zest for life, *joi de vivre*, and the art of living, *savoir-vivre*, both of which contribute hugely to the fantasy and inspiration that give rise to creativity.

Unfavourable development: A slide into unrestrained emotionality, defence-lessness, spiritual debauch and guilt – in the Tantric tradition a result of suppressed sexuality.

Corporate Aspects

Favourable development: Warm relationships with co-workers, clients, suppliers, the community, especially on interpersonal level. (The loyalty relationships developed by servant leadership fall in the more elevated realm of the Throat Chakra.) Relationships management, networking: the creation of relationships that serve personal and business interests.

Unfavourable development: Manipulation, the exploitation of others' emotional vulnerability. Shutting people out, or playing one against the other. Killing creativity through the cultivation of envy and the fanning of fear. Generally, playing others' feelings as an instrument for the advancement of one's own ends.

Chief Challenge: To transcend the fear of giving yourself to others.

THE CHAKRA OF CONNECTEDNESS AND CREATION

The Sacral Chakra is located in the lower belly, between the navel and the sacrum.[77] It rules the realm of sexuality, including procreation, creativity (spiritual procreation) and emotions. Through this emotionality it connects us with all others. The name Svadisthana is often said to mean 'seat of vitality', but more literally means 'seat of the self'. (From Sanskrit *sva*, 'self', with an undertone of independence, and *asthana*, 'origin'.) The self is here to be seen in a dual perspective: at once personal, and universal. The individual self as connected with all creation.

The Svadisthana is the chakra of our connectedness with others that grew in the earliest days of mankind, the connectedness with previous generations through the mother, the connectedness with our own corporality. Here lives the primitive man in us, the child in us, the man who remained a child always, the man who knows how to live – and also man as a social being, man who shares life with others. A favourable development of this chakra gives flowing, gracious movement, a rich emotional life, and a flexible manner of dealing with change.

The Sacral Chakra is first and foremost the centre of sexuality. The Root Chakra was all about personal survival, but when this is more or less assured, the attention shifts to procreation: now it is time to think of the survival of the species. This brings a shift of focus from the self to 'the other', in particular to the other of the other sex. This chakra is a powerful source of energy that no suppression however forceful is capable of extinguishing, in many cultures not for lack of trying. This energy hub of the underbelly also rules the realm of intimacy, our capacity to be completely ourselves with others. Because of the interaction it arranges, it is a rich source of fantasy and the urge to create.

The Bulgarian-French sage Omraam Mikhael Aivanhov, who passed away in 1985, had this to say about this urge: 'One of the most stubborn instincts man possesses, is the need to be a creator, and so be at a level with God. If one would not be the creator of children, then at least of sculptures, monuments, dances, songs, poems or music. The existence of art is proof that this desire to be a creator, which is alive in every human being, does not limit itself to the "creation" of children, to simple procreation, preservation of the species, but also manifests the need to go further, to do a little more, and replace the old form by something new, something more beautiful and closer to perfection.'

Man's creative ability needs to be rated well above his normal level of consciousness. It originates from a part of the soul, that has the power of imagination and the ability needed to explore and to observe realities that transcend us, and receive elements of this reality. Creation means to excel oneself, to transcend oneself. (The original German reads, *'über sich hinauszuwachsen'*, literally 'to grow taller than yourself.')[78]

A PROBLEM-CHAKRA *PAR EXCELLENCE*

No other chakra creates so much havoc when blocked or over-stimulated, no other leads to so many social problems. Influences from the social environment, with its powerful excitement and simultaneous moral — where not also judicial — condemnation, assure that in many people this chakra of the lower belly is in a disturbed state. Over the last decades the public stimulation of the sex drive has increased monumentally: sex piped into every living room through cable and broadband, Kama Sutra Shows booking major conference centres, pop music metamorphosed into an artistic excuse for the 24/7 broadcasting of soft porn video clips, public copulation parties on wooded parking lots ... And then there is advertising. Taken in all together, this flood of impulses is like a heavy tome of a book with one single message, hammered in on every page: 'Thou shalt have intercourse.'

Yet we as humans have agreed, by near universal consent, that we shall do this only with our steady partners, preferably sanctioned by marriage, and heterosexual if you please. Other variants are condoned, but a cloud hangs over them. A dark force that grips the chakra in a choking hold. Don't believe everything you heard about the 'sexual revolution' of the 1960s and 70s. To most people, it never happened. In many countries that belong to the West's common cultural homeland, like the Anglo-Saxon states, but also some Mediterranean ones, as in most parts of 'New Europe', the repression is still strong.

Citizens from enlightened countries like the Netherlands, Germany, Spain or Switzerland will find it hard to believe, but in most parts of Europe prostitution is illegal. Portuguese newspapers frequently report police razzias on brothels, complete with arrest and prosecution of the sinners. Across Europe 'deviant' sexual behaviour is truly accepted only in metropolitan areas, in the USA only in a few pockets within such areas. In Poland, police and skinheads collaborate in the persecution of homosexuals. In nearly all states of the USA police actively hunt down prostitutes and clients, routinely destroying the latter's families and careers.

In 2008 New York governor Eliott Spitzer, his being only the most public of many public take-downs, had to resign over entirely consensual sex with prostitutes who had chosen this line of work voluntarily. After the intense flaying by the US media, many Europeans were left with the impression that the American public's indignation mostly fed on the girls being so horrendously expensive. Only a few years ago, in 2003, at the time of the landmark US Supreme Court decision 'Lawrence v. Texas', 14 of the 50 American States and Puerto Rico had laws outlawing sodomy as well as other 'perverted forms of sex' (even when practiced in the privacy of one's own bedroom), punishable by up to 5, 10 and 15 years in Louisiana,

Mississippi, and Michigan respectively; 5 years to life in Idaho. That's a lot of mashed potatoes with cold gravy. Think before you sin.[79]

Due to massive immigration of Muslims into Western Europe the continent now incorporates a foreign, archaic cultural element, and has to deal with a new, even more spasmodic clenching-up of the Sacral Chakra. The European Muslim citizens, male and female alike, also see the sex-boutiques and peep shows, the 'gay pride' parades, the posters for Naked Swingers Nights, the prime time soft porn (unless they quickly switch channels), and as French aspiration consultant Marc Bourgery observed, the bourgeois ladies magazines with free dildos.[80] Yet their own culture prescribes a medieval repression of the sex drive, especially that of the women, and a man-wife relationship marked by differences of authority which does not promote the development of a love union.

The effects of this cultural influx upon the existing culture can be bizarre. Driving back from a seminar recently in the Netherlands with the radio tuned to a news station, we were informed that recent years have seen a steep rise in the percentage of Dutch citizens practicing sodomy, as well as in the incidence of certain gross afflictions of the anus which ten years ago most physicians had regarded as something foreign that one might never encounter in one's life time. The reason for this steep increase is not that many Dutch have discovered a new hobby, but that a high percentage of Moroccan girls are sexually active, and to preserve their virginity, accept anal penetration only.

The effect of all this (not the sodomy, that we have dealt with), is a chakra that is simultaneously stimulated and throttled. This leads to blockage, and impedes the growth of qualities required for leadership. Anyone who wants to go on an inner path needs to have dealt with this issue, before further development can occur.

Important above all, we feel, is to experience one's sexuality in freedom, to accept all related feelings, and in their manifestation to strive for healthy relationships, marked by equality, respect, and an awareness of our relationship within the brotherhood of man. (Any suggestions for a non-gender-specific way to say this?) For those struggling with their sexual drive, Tantra Yoga may be a suitable path.

The intent of any training regarding the Sacral Chakra is to allow it to play its natural unifying role, connecting body, spirit and soul. By freeing up the energy, the lower urges are purified – or sublimated as Freudians call it, an inner process in which the natural expression of a primitive, instinctual impulse is tailored in a socially more desirable manner – so that they may contribute to the development of feelings connected with higher levels of consciousness.

SEXUALITY – SUPPRESSION OR CELEBRATION?

Many classical Indian teaching systems, such as the yoga school, place quite an emphasis on celibacy, the sublimation of sexual powers into spiritual powers – seen as a kind of alchemical secret for access to a higher state. (*Cf.* mandatory celibacy for priests in the Roman Catholic tradition.) People who practice it report that the inner self is enriched by renunciation of bodily pleasures. They would say that, wouldn't they ...?

Whether celibacy is truly necessary for advancement, or even desirable, has been subject of debate ever since man started to look at his urges as something that he might control, rather than the reverse. Our take on it has been affected by the words of the old teacher Ashtavakra:

> *Millions strive for material pleasures, thousands strive for enlightenment, but rare is the wise man who strives for neither and lives with himself in peace.*[81]

As long as you fight your sexual urges you are not living in peace with yourself. Sexuality is something to be enjoyed in any shape or form that does not harm, exploit, demean or otherwise diminish others. To suppress it is to be attached to it, and in a most negative way. Celebrate it, and yes, sublimate it if that is what your heart tells you to do. Indian classical music students are told that they can not advance *and* have lovers, as they can have only one lover, which is their music, physically represented by their instrument, which is to be cherished and venerated and held close at all times.*

---

* Peter's sitar teacher Pandit Shyam Lapitige Don David in the early 1970s used to reprove him for infractions as minor as chatting with a young lady at the vegetable market. 'Why you talk to her? You are not loving your music anymore? The only female shape before your eyes should be our goddess Sarasvati, to whom you owe your talent and the sensual pleasures of exercising it! Now tell me, why are you being unfaithful to her?'

True sublimation requires total transfer of the emotional content to a higher plane. This implies, that any sublimation of our sex-drive must include the vital element of lust. Complete sublimation is rare in all cultures, mostly seen in states of spiritual ecstasy and orgasmic fits of artistic expression. Both come highly recommended. The integration of the aspect of lust creates pleasurable, and therefore nurturing conditions for creative self-fulfilment. In many traditions of inner development, dealing with this issue may take many years.

The sobering reality is, that to most people, sexual energy is not something they can suppress or convert without serious psychological damage – certainly if it is done without competent guidance. Suppressed sexuality creates psychic ulcers which may erupt any day. Hence all those news items about sexual misconduct of priests, preachers and gurus, suddenly exposed. Yes, what else could we expect? Not only are they suppressing one of the most vital urges, the source of unspeakable delight, a celebration of togetherness, sparkling with creativity, they even pledge to maintain this suppression for life – and if that is more than one can take, yes, sooner or later the volcano starts spewing. Many contemporary teachers, both Indian and western, consider the celibacy requirement to be archaic, preaching that in our society, it is preferable for spiritual advancement to have a healthy sex life if you are so inclined.

The underlying reason for this change in teachers' attitude – still not widely understood – is that the sexuality of modern humans, unlike the apes' or our early forebears', is not primarily hormonally driven, but directed by the neocortex, by mental impulses from our outer and inner senses. As the popular saying goes, 'sex is between the ears'. In the time when the old *rishi* of the Baghavad Gita composed their teachings, outer impulses were few and faint. Now they are manifold and forceful, like a bombardment of cosmic rays. The bombardment takes place primarily through the media, and resonates in our personal interaction – showing its effect in tone and intent of conversation, *double entendre*, body language, dress, and every other little detail of the way we communicate with one another. (All this whether we are aware of it, or not.)

This makes sexuality into something that no longer lives just in the underbelly – and because of that into something much harder to sublimate. Dealing with an oncoming hormone rush, as many healthy men need to do several times a day, may be just about manageable in the isolation of a cave in the Himalayas, it is quite a bit more difficult when you're shell-shocked from the bombardment with sexual stimuli already, and that young new eyeful in sales comes parading across the floor again in her clinging outfit.

Women, too, get excited by confrontation with a physically attractive representative of the other sex, but thanks to their slower hormonal build-up, deal with this much more easily than men. They may be safely home kicking off their shoes before it really hits. We are convinced that this is the main reason why most spiritual movements suffer from an overrepresentation of women, usually somewhat older. A few, however, are young and beautiful – which places an almost indecently heavy burden on the spiritual leader who thought he had it all sublimated so beautifully, and is admired for that very sublimation ... Oh yes, guruhood may be full of hidden suffering.

The Sacral Chakra causes more problems than all others combined – or rather, our manner of dealing with its energy does. That is why substantial gains can be realised, simply by learning to recognise its energy, getting familiar with it, and directing its flow into a creative direction. Proper understanding and practice can bring great profit.

Anyone who wants to be able to lead others, needs to teach them to achieve this for themselves, preferably not by instruction but by example. This brings us into the realm of inspiration and passion, to which we return in depth at the sixth and seventh energy level.

FEEL FREE TO FEEL

'You have to learn to control your emotions,' our parents taught us; at least ours did, and they weren't alone in this didactic effort. But it was bad advice, that we better not pass on to our children. Because controlling our emotions is achievable only to a certain extent, and when it leads to suppression, it may cause psychic problems in people who are otherwise healthy. (Note: we are not speaking here of the emotions of the paedophile, the necrophiliac and sufferers of other mental ailments that for reasons of social hygiene are suppressed by law with near universal consensus.)

You never need to feel guilty or ashamed for any anger, sadness or attraction that you feel. *Feelings are intrinsically okay*, and however inconvenient some of them may be socially, there is no need to be apologetic. That is because you cannot keep feelings from welling up, at least not without many years of ascetic training, and so you cannot be held morally responsible for them. We may not refuse to experience them any more than our nose may refuse to itch.

The only freedom we have regarding our feelings, is to act on them or not. Whether we use them as an impulse for action or leave them be is our own choice. No one obliges us to scream back, hit back, hate back. It may seem delightful to touch that man, that woman, and when we do we may indeed be engulfed by wonderful feelings, but we are not obligated to go on and sleep with anyone just because it feels good. When television images of starving children fill us with compassion, we do not have to get up from the couch to transfer money, we have the choice to do nothing and remain seated. What is important here, though aid organisations may see this differently, is that you give your emotions free rein, that you allow yourself to become aware of what flows through you. This is the proper way to deal with emotions: you allow yourself to experience them in all their intensity, then, with the detachment of the inner sage you have in you, you determine whether or not to use them as a source of energy and guiding light for conduct.

DO NOT IDENTIFY WITH YOUR FEELINGS

You are not your feelings. The feelings are yours, but you are not theirs. Let them flow through you, become aware of them. Emotions flow like water, and penetrate everything. But emotions also have the capacity to support you – if you take to them like you take to water, enjoying their sensuality, the bond with the element. In this element, do not move as you would on land, with angularity and resoluteness, but with the flowing grace of a fish. Don't be shy of new emotions, the ocean of feeling covers two-thirds of our being, much of it unexplored. Feel free to go where you have never been before. But don't let yourself be sucked into any maelstroms, because before you know you're at a depth from which there is no recovery.

People who identify with their feelings become enslaved by them. For example: the addictions, common in nearly all cultures, to gambling and sensual indulgence. In most countries these used to be the preserve of the feudal elite, becoming available to the middle-class of the developed world in the 19th century, and in the 20th to the masses. This downward expansion along class lines is a remarkable social phenomenon, the more so as it is also spreading geographically, now leaving untouched only the world's least evolved nations. We are not judging this phenomenon, just registering it for the benefit of our research.

Children in the US, Europe and Asia drink more alcohol than any generation before them and start drinking younger; prostitution and porn production are multi-billion industries, daily advertised in the media; the use of recreational drugs is so common for so many millions that calls for legalisation become ever harder to suppress; and many young people are so obese that life expectations for their generation will need to be adjusted downward. 'Oh great, chocolate mousse! What a wonderful feeling in my mouth! Let me have another one!'

This is the message of this chakra: 'Detach yourself from your feelings and before you know you are Master of Chocolate Mousse.'

EMOTIONALITY AS CHOCOLATE MOUSSE

The problem, of course, is that we are very fond of chocolate mousse. And many of us gorge on our emotions. 'Oh, I don't know why, but I feel so sad, I can't stop crying' – that is chocolate mousse. 'Oh, I am so happy that John is back, I am singing all day long' – that too is chocolate mousse. 'Oh, the way she played that adagio … You have a tissue?' – chocolate mousse. 'If I see that guy parked in my space again I'll kick a dent in his door' – chocolate mousse.

But some of us have been made afraid of our own feelings ('Naughty child, you have to control your emotions!'), so that in self-defence they are silenced, denied, declared null and void, and never mentioned, even to ourselves. In such cases the chocolate mousse is not consumed, and collapses into a sludge that after a few more days in the fridge is dumped in the can. That is not good either, because it leaves you with an unstilled yearning. A yearning for your own emotions, that keep getting thrown out with the potato peels.

Allow yourself to experience all your emotions, everything that flows through you. But do not act on all of it. Moderation, we are afraid, is the key. The same holds true for our relationship to others: anyone who identifies with other people's feelings, becomes enslaved to them. 'Doing this, do I make my mother happy?' Later to be followed by: 'Doing this, do I make my husband/wife happy?' Legitimate questions, but not if they lead to an exclusive focus on the other, and dependency on other people's feelings.

You are not responsible for the feelings of others. Should you be so afflicted, let go of that identification. This allows the Sacral Chakra to do what it is supposed to do, and allows you to be supported by your emotional life, rather than having to struggle with it like a swimmer in a breaking surf. When you experience a feeling that bothers you, or that you do not know how to take, say to yourself, preferably aloud: 'I am not my emotions.' Repeat a few times, and remark how much more easily you will deal with them.

The Zen poet would say: 'I swim like a fish in my feelings.'

ALL GREAT ART COMES FROM THE GUT

Apart from being the cause of many social problems, the Sacral Chakra also deserves our attention as the source of a great part of our cultural wealth, and certainly of its highest expressions. All truly great art – not the clever 'project' – comes from down here: not from the head, not from the heart, but from the gut. Art that comes from the head usually does not survive its maker for very long. Art that comes from the heart stands a better chance to charm or fire future generations, but charm and passion alone are not enough to floor us. Art that comes from the gut however, has the capacity to bowl us over, and will continue to have that capacity for thousands of years.

Examples from literature: Borges, Musil and Cheever come from the head, Shelley and Mahfouz from the heart, Shakespeare, Conrad, Céline and Grass from the gut. Examples from the visual arts: Mondrian and Seurat come from the head, Renoir and Gauguin from the heart; El Greco, Van Gogh and Bacon from the gut. Examples from music: Bartók comes from the head, Rossini and Schumann from the heart, Beethoven and Rachmaninov from the gut. Examples from the art of politics: Chirac and Blair (remember them?) come from the head, Mandela from the heart, Reagan, Bush and Ahmedinejad from the gut. Putin pretends to work from his head, but in reality operates from his gut.

Whether we approve of it or not, power is always held most firmly, not by clever schemers, not by baby-kissers, but by men who go by their gut feeling. The world would be best served if power came to rest in the hands of men or women who have all seven energy centres wide open, including the highest. But before this has been achieved, many great works of enlightenment are yet to be completed.

Place on earth: The earth's underbelly is found in the rainforests, those steaming cauldrons brimming with life. We are all deeply connected with its daily cycle of evaporation and rainfall, warming and cooling down, an eternal process of birth and death and rebirth. All of the jungle is one great uterus, one connected mass of guts, one sexual organ with daily orgasms, one large underbelly to which all life traces its origin. The day begins clear, not a cloud in the sky, in a damp heat that keeps a shirt dry half an hour at best, and stays clear till evaporation has created enough clouds for the daily round of rainfall. It starts pouring around three, and usually continues till a little before sunset, but may also continue through the night. Every day again, all that lives is nurtured. And all around you hear, feel and see living creatures – to which the moisture in the atmosphere intimately connects you.

Moisture conducts, and not just heat. In weak moments (and those are often the most enlightening) you experience the saturated atmosphere as a kind of soup in which you float about like a lump of more or less congealed jelly. Other lumps of jelly are floating about nearby. Almost everything around is amorphous, ephemeral, everything can be different tomorrow. No house older than a few decades, everything rots away in your hands, or is eaten by termites and boring beetles. The course of the river may shift overnight, roads and paths collapse, and clothes decompose as you wear them. Nothing is written down, and the little that does get written down bleeds across the pages and decays. There is no certainty in life anywhere, except in that steady rhythm of sunshine and rain, the certainty of moist heat for ever and ever. Those who are not now reminded of life in the womb are lacking in imagination or were plucked from the cabbage field.

For a sensational experience of the Sacral Chakra in all its glory, the knowledgeable recommend sex in a rainforest – an uncommonly deep experience that, much more readily than sex in an urban environment, can lead to orgasm at the highest level (orgasm as mystical experience), in which union with the partner widens into an experience of universal connectedness.

Exercise 1: Try to imagine where the water molecules in your body have been before they came to be part of your body, and where they were before then... Don't go back all the way to the Big Bang.

Exercise 2: Create your own list of corporate or political leaders and their dominant chakras – leaders who, as you see it, work from their head, their heart, or their gut. Then, and best write this down: how do you see yourself? Thirdly: are you happy with your own rating, or would you rather be different? (The ideal is to have all chakras wide open, free to receive and expend energy, none receiving emphasis at the expense of others.)

MARKS OF A HEALTHY SACRAL CHAKRA
• zest for life
• fertility
• rich emotional life
• warm relationships with others
• open to intimacy
• satisfying sex-life
• lively, dynamic presence
• creativity, especially where it actually involves creating
• enjoying movement in all its aspects
• flexible response to change
• excitable, passionate nature.

SYMPTOMS OF A BLOCKED SACRAL CHAKRA
• shallow emotions
• low emotional intelligence
• social dysfunctionality

- sexual inhibitions, sexual frustration, frigidity
- over-indulgence in passions
- sexual abstinence, anhedonia (fear of enjoyment)
- condemnation of lust, whether or not reflected in behaviour
- perversion, addiction to sex
- enslavement to other people's emotions
- incapacity to achieve much in the world, to exteriorise inner content successfully
- loss of vitality, spleen
- not really living, just going through the motions.

COMPETING FOR BEST COOPERATION

Many people refrain from giving themselves to others, sharing their inner riches, because they fear losing something in the process – either a benefit they enjoy, or a sense of self that is highly individual. The enlightened leader knows that connecting with others and keeping one's own identity is a false dichotomy. The real art is to nurture individuals while leading individuals to serve groups, a process which Adam Brandenberger and Barry Nalebuff have called co-opetition, for 'cooperative competition'.[82] It represents a high level of reconciliation at the Sacral Chakra. An interesting example of well reconciled relational issues is Motorola's Total Customer Satisfaction competition. Teams which have 'totally satisfied' Motorola customers in any part of the world gather together the evidence of their success and enter a world-wide competition in which they present their solution on stage, backed up with the results achieved.

The contests teach members how to compete fiercely – but the criterion by which they are judged is the degree of success achieved in cooperation, both with customers and fellow team members. This is 'collaborative competition', or co-opetition. Important deliverables of this competition are not just the relational learnings, but also the hundreds of winning practical solutions that surface, to be studied and disseminated by Motorola University. Competing differentiates ideas. Cooperating integrates them. In the same vein, truly innovative executives have finely differentiated, well integrated strategic maps of their terrains. And the most effective also have well integrated maps of their inner terrain: their aspirations, their emotional needs, their intuitions and their energy distribution.

Consider the concerted attempts to regain an innovative culture in the US semi-conductor industry. Sematech (acronym for Semiconductor Manufacturing Technology) is a non-profit consortium that performs basic research into semiconductor manufacturing. Conceived in 1986, it began operating in 1988 as a partnership between the United States government and 14 US based semiconductor manufacturers to solve common manufacturing problems and restore competitiveness to the US semiconductor industry – which, to America's horror, had been surpassed by Japanese industry in the mid-1980s. It was a true shocker, that unsettled the very foundations of America's belief in its superiority. Asian effectiveness forced a complete industry to the brink of collapse.

To counter this national threat, the American Ministry of Defence founded Sematech. Its sole aim was to ensure that American chip manufacturers and their suppliers dramatically improved their cooperation, so as to make them more capable competitors. Thanks to this government inspired and government sponsored model the whole industry made an unprecedented comeback. The story of Sematech is a classic example of co-opetition: 'cooperate to compete'. All relational issues are fully reconciled. In the future we shall surely see more of these: competitive organisations which purposely come together to discuss and develop new standards and create a level playing field – on which to compete happily ever after.

Cartels are well-known examples of companies working together in order to limit competition. In contrast, co-opetition focuses on cooperation between companies in imperfectly competitive markets. Examples of co-opetition include Apple and Microsoft building closer ties on software development, Sony and Philips jointly setting the new standards for DVD players and the cooperation between Peugeot and Toyota on a new city car for Europe in 2005. Other examples are Free and Open Source Software companies: They all contribute to the production of a software pool that anyone is free to further develop, and which anyone can use as a base for their own business model. The whole Linux world is based on it.

Teaching the process of co-opetition is crucial in the creation of innovative teams. Yes, individuals are the main source of invention. Their autonomy and free thinking stimulate creativity. But if their thinking is unconnected to the larger environment, be it the team or the organisation, it remains an invention that will never go into manufacturing and is never launched onto the market. In our consulting practice we have often encountered reward systems, both formal and informal, material and immaterial, that unintentionally jeopardise the innovation process by promoting individualism through highly variable pay for individual performance.

WHAT ROLE FOR RELATIONSHIPS?

Most Western reward systems are predicated on the basic assumption that one has to motivate the individual. This assumption is not often challenged, and when it is, emotions can run high. We recently met the American HR director of a global company who claimed to have developed the ideal reward system, which he was well into implementing world wide. Where permitted by law, all fixed salaries were converted into 50% fixed and 50% variable, taking the previous year's performance as a benchmark. As a result, employees who improved their performance by say 30% would see a 15% hike in pay. Half of the variable part consisted of options on company stock that could be cashed only after three years of service. An avid reader of Fons' books, he rather proudly explained that in this approach of his, short and long term thinking were particularly well reconciled. His employees were highly motivated, because they saw a direct relationship between their individual work and their remuneration, while recognising how the system benefited the performance of the organisation as a whole, on the stock of which they had options. He had to admit, however, that the new approach had met with much resistance in Europe and Asia. 'Could it be culture?', he wondered.

Obviously, his system was designed for a highly individualistic culture, where relationships with others may be cherished, but not necessarily to the point of sharing income. Joe makes the deal, Joe gets the percentage. Anyone else who claims a share of his percentage is suicidal; either that or a communist. This focus on the individual is also reflected in other aspects of management: when operating in an individualistic society, it pays to give proper attention to 'knowledge management', as sharing of information is foreign to the culture.

Conversely, in most communitarian cultures we see some degree of immaterial pressure, often quite strong, to conform to the larger group: to subordinate personal ambitions and personal gain to the greater goal of collective advancement. The end result, all too frequently, is that no-one dares to stick his neck out. And here too, the group focus is reflected in other aspects of management: when operating in a communitarian society it pays to give proper attention to 'creativity management', as striving for individual excellence and creativity are foreign to the culture.

The problem in designing remuneration systems for innovative global companies is that neither individual incentives, nor group incentives support the innovative powers of teams across all cultures. The solution can be quite straightforward. If you are operating in America, reward individuals. In Asia, reward the team. In Europe, design fiscally clever packages. This approach is simple and effective, and it will work for any multi-local organisation. However, in a truly global firm, characterised by numerous multi-cultural teams comprised of people from different cultural backgrounds and with different motivations, more innovative reward systems may need to be invented, such as rewarding individuals for team spirit or customer focus.

As an example, take the advice that the consultant Gallway gave to IBM's sales force. The legacy system had been quite aggressive, simply granting bonuses to those who sold the most personal computers, which placed stress on both the sales people and their clients, and by consequence was quite horrendous from a relational perspective. The Sacral Chakra was highly active, but in a cramped way. Gallway suggested a smoother alternative. All the sales people were instructed to prepare a presentation each quarter on what they had learned from their customers. Bonuses were awarded based on the relevance and practicality of the learnings. Sales figures rose by 25%, information exchange between the sales staff increased sharply, and clients indicated improved satisfaction. This also is co-opetition: competing for optimal cooperation with clients. It is a highly relational way of working, which aims to meld creative individuals into teams that surpass themselves. Solutions of this genre lead to great innovation by not replacing one cultural logic by another but by creation of a new logic that reconciles both.

GUT FEELING

Of all the things that help business leaders bring mergers and acquisitions to a good end, the most powerful (and the most reliable indicator of success) is not shrewdness of strategy, nor cleverness of organisation. It is the ability to connect to people on an emotional level. This manifests itself not just in corporate life, but on all levels of existence. The guy who touches people in the realm of the Sacral Chakra creates success after success, the gal who does the same risks being accused of using her female charms, but is likewise unstoppable. There are hairdressers, male and female, living in villas on Majorca, simply because they managed to connect; greengrocers and masseuses with palaces in Marrakech.

And if we turn our view up to the world of high culture: there are artists who produce the same mediocrities that thousands of colleagues turn out, but manage to turn them into objects of great value simply by connecting with people on a gut level. It's either that or styling yourself as a demigod who despises his or her admirers, another act that goes down well in the upper middle-class, always desperate for status. Someone who can afford to look down on everyone else must be an inordinately great being, and to be associating with him or her must confer great status. We see this manifested most vividly in Hollywood, that living caricature of contemporary mores. There are any number of good actors out there, and George Clooney is certainly one of them. But is Clooney as great as his fame? Is he so much better than others in delivery, expression, presence? Clearly, what helps him to the top of the popularity pack is not just his sexy looks and acting skills, both of which are entry level requirements in the movie industry, but his masterful ability to connect at a gut level.

George Clooney[83] is *likeable*, because he makes us feel no distance, he makes us feel that if we should run into him somewhere, he would turn out to be one hell of a guy. He wears the golden aura of one who really cares. When Clooney was interviewed for a *Time* cover story in 2008, instead of routinely doing the interview at the agent's or some public place, the journalist had the chutzpah to invite the star over for a pasta dinner at his home. The reporter awaited the arrival nervously, weighing how modest his place was compared to his guest's multiple mansions, but Clooney turned out to be as pleasant, as natural and unassuming as if he were a neighbour. The two hit it off so well that, really, this seemed the wrong time to do an interview. They jointly fussed over the pasta sauce, Clooney stirring the pot, had dinner and drank one bottle of wine after another, having a great time till close before dawn. What we take away from the *Time* piece is far more powerful than a standard interview would have been, and does more for Clooney than a nicely styled Q&A. It shows him as a man who is comfortable with himself, and for that reason connects easily. There is no need to pretend or prove anything, so he can give himself to strangers, be open and share – and get juiced with them in full confidence.

Now, a word about getting juiced. But first a disclaimer from our lawyers: 'The following is not to be read as a plea for ad libitum alcohol consumption.' Alcohol is an accredited tool of the trade not just in journalism, but also in politics and business, as it has a powerful effect on the Sacral Chakra. It affects our sense of connectedness through the mother with all humanity, and reinforces or awakes feelings of camaraderie and welcome towards our fellow men and women, serving us up deep draughts from the emotional vat that is the common patrimony of 'the Family of Man'. It increases our enjoyment of shared sense impressions, heightens sexual responses and loosens inhibition. Quite a package. And then there is the heightened creativity that moderate use may facilitate by allowing greater access to the subconscious, to deeper knowledge of ourselves, particularly at this level. But enough about booze. It's not about what you take or abstain from, but about awareness of, and access to energy.

Connecting at gut level is the hidden key that the wise use to unlock secrets. The most important element of trust and likeability is absence of fear. And it is this, that the sensitive (the traveller, the author, the trader, the student of human nature in general) becomes aware of instantly upon meeting – at least rarely with much delay. At times indeed there *is* a delay, because crooks, who for their livelihood rely on acute insight into human nature, intentionally try to mask their fear of losing control, of getting caught, getting hurt, forfeiting freedom. They know that if they show the slightest discomfort, or the emotional coldness that their profession requires, the more sensitive among their marks will sense it. This has forced them to developed great acting skills, though that causal order is sometimes reversed. For that reason, getting your feelings right in an encounter sometimes takes a shift away from the perceived set of signals, the construct, rich as it is with studied expression and cleverly added emotional content, to an underlying reality which, fortunately, to the trained eye always remains visible, in the way that the snake seen in a root across our path, to the alert wanderer never quite negates the reality of the root.

Great leaders develop this ability – if they are not born with it. This leads to an argument we should stay away from, because no definite answer will ever be found, between those who think that leadership can be taught and those who think that it is inborn, and most likely inbred. Our experience teaches us that some are naturally gifted in the use of their sacral energy and connect with people from all walks of life without plan or prodding, others need to work at this faculty. To them, people are an acquired taste. This may happen if you grew up as an only child, or read too many books by Jean-Paul 'Hell is other people' Sartre, though for the younger generation of leaders the latter risk is much diminished. In that case, yes, by all means work at it. Try to connect. Try to feel where the other is, emotionally. You will notice results more quickly than from any management or leadership course you may take.

CREATIVE SPARKLE

While of course any M&A integration programme should be predicated on operational compatibility, much more attention and resources need to be given to managing the cultural disparity between the new partners. Relational problems such as censure of the other party's way of doing things, ridicule, condescension, and lack of trust are so common as to almost seem the rule. This is even more striking when we realise that building trust is a cultural challenge in itself. Lack of trust is often caused by different views of what constitutes a trustworthy partner. In addition, most intercultural alliances involve differences in corporate cultures as well as national cultures. Problems at the level of the Sacral Chakra can be due to more or less 'objective' cultural differences, but also to mutual perceptions, highly subjective, including perceptions of corporate culture and national culture. To deal with this in an adequate manner, consideration must be given to leadership styles, management profiles, organisation structures, working practices, and a wide range of perceptions.

Ten years ago Peter was retained by a large advertising agency that somehow had lost its sparkle – and with that its aura, several large clients, and most of its top creatives. The only way to get back all of those was to, well, sparkle. A textbook example (so far of course there is only one such textbook) of issues at the level of the Sacral Chakra, which governs relationships and creativity. Unfortunately, after three months he was taken off the job when the CEO who had retained him left to set up an agency of his own, and the new appointee, true to tradition, brought in a friend. However Peter did learn something of interest. The agency had brought in several other consultants before, who introduced a variety of measures and programmes, none of which had made so much as a splutter.

But something had happened, largely inadvertently, which 10 out of 30 interviewees spontaneously mentioned as the best that had happened in the company, the one thing that had temporarily restored the spirit and go of the agency. The CEO had taken the whole agency on an outing that involved a short sea voyage: a four hour ferry crossing, scheduled to land them before midnight. They spent the evening wining and dining, and wining again – and then the ship's engines stopped.

Progress was halted, there was no indication if and when the ship's engineers would be able to get the engine going, but the PA messages from the captain stressed that continuation of the journey was not imminent. Apology was offered, patience requested. The CEO ordered more drinks: as long as we're stuck here we might as well enjoy ourselves! Half an hour later new refreshments were urgently called for. They all ended up getting high and drunk, bringing the gently rolling house down with their laughter and creative eruptions. The repair took many hours. Even the believers in moderation who normally might have left it at one or two glasses, now gave in to the aqueous ambience and let it flow. By the time the ferry arrived, at the break of dawn, they were stupidly drunk, tumbling down the steep steel stairs to the car deck, shrieking with laughter. They piled into the buses, many on one another's lap, and partied on during the one hour drive to the hotel where they all crashed out wherever and with whom they liked – most probably in their own beds, except the creatives who had kept up an after-party with some girls from traffic to help them through to daybreak. This event, by all accounts, this impulsive celebration of the Sacral Chakra, had been the best that had happened to the company for as long as anyone could remember.

What to advise? How to improve on this? Organise orgies? Fortunately, just then fate intervened and the new guy shunted Peter off the case, giving him the consolation prize of deep insight into the powerful energies of the Sacral Chakra. Energy at this level is very visceral, it is emotional, and deeply bonding. To connect with people at this level is very powerful, because it turns people into associates, in the most literal sense the Romans would have used it, someone with whom we are deeply bonded through trust and mutuality of interest. Trust, while it requires the higher energies of the Third Eye Chakra and the Crown Chakra to reach full bloom, has its foundation in the Sacral Chakra, in gut feeling. If that gut feeling isn't good, don't go for it. That goes for actions, that goes for people.

What we call gut feeling is a powerful sense that tells us whether to trust or not. It is the first thing explorers need, and traveller – and leaders, particularly when they are on unknown terrain. All other aspects of a situation or a person that we take into consideration, that whole amalgam of analyses of cues and prejudices and basic assumptions, fade away into insignificance compared with the judgement we make at the sacral level. Does it feel good? If it feels good, do it!

But not everyone is capable of doing this, of operating effectively at this energy level. Some people are far better at responding to their feelings than others. Many in the corporate corridors, in the rarefied air of top story offices, are not good at it at all. One can't blame them for it, by the way, as they have been told to mistrust their feelings all their working lives, and usually well before in school. Go by reason and reason alone. In most jobs you can't say, 'Oh I don't know why, I just had a good feeling about it,' or 'I didn't feel good about it'. Well, you *can* if you happen to be the owner, but other than that, if you have others to report to, talking about your deeper feelings will not do you any good. This has been hammered into professionals ever since the onset of Enlightenment. Most forcefully, and unambiguously, it was hammered in through business courses teaching people organisational skills, and that throughout most of the twentieth century.

Unfortunately, reason has been over-promoted by all those high IQ types. It has been promoted to an extent where great numbers of business leaders have lost trust in their deeper feelings. By repeated disregard for their feelings they gradually lost touch with themselves. They dissociated themselves almost entirely from their feelings – which they remained vaguely aware of, as a kind of parallel lives veiled by mist. Contemporary versions of the parallel moralities that Albert Carr saw as essential to maintaining one's sanity in a duplicitous business world. Here it is not morality that subjects take leave of through dissociation, but their feelings.

SACRAL CHAKRA WIDE OPEN: ARCHETYPE FRANCIS W. – BELOVED BY ALL

Francis W. is the head of an important governmental body, a position he has held for many years – king of his own domain. The work of his organisation is of a highly technical nature, but Francis himself is not. He did major in something related, without excelling in it, and did little to stay abreast of developments in his field. Yet his leadership is never in question, because he always manages to build warm, trusting relationships both with the consecutive ministers in charge and his staff. Subordinates gladly spend a weekend writing a report for him, because they know that he will show his gratitude – and promote them when an opening occurs. Francis has been asked to join the cabinet on several occasions, but prefers the warm, embedded sense of an appreciative organisation over the snake pit of politics. Next week he turns sixty. He says he wants no grand affair, just a modest celebration. His wife expects three hundred people.

Now, let no one get the impression that in Francis W., the Sacral Chakra is the only one working properly. His wide-open Third Eye Chakra gives him unfailing intuition, his Root Chakra keeps both his feet firmly on the ground, which happens to be the field that the work of his organisation directly acts upon, and the glowing of his Heart Chakra is immediately apparent. Should you wish to meet Francis off-duty, your best chance is at rallies for better invalid care.

Remarkably, his unfavourable qualities also lie in the realm of the Sacral Chakra. He is sexually over-active, visibly greedy for young and pretty, and runs a serious risk of scandal. Our take on it is that he is protected by his almost childish spontaneity. As his grey-haired secretary once remarked: 'Every woman here knows that it isn't meant personal. Physical contact is as natural to him as eating and drinking.' We don't think she believed that herself, but she *was* protecting him, that says it.

SACRAL CHAKRA DOMINANT:
ARCHETYPE CARLO F. – CHARMING TILL THE GRAVE

Carlo F. is a charming man with a handsome face, well groomed, in his early fifties. The type of man that women find attractive, and men as well like to have in their company. In his twenties he founded a trading agency in Argentina for medical equipment, a company that he rapidly built up to international proportions. His firm is one of South America's largest by now, with representation of various leading brands, in several countries as sole agent. He has a few hundred employees, who find him a nice guy, and work so hard for him that he doesn't need to do much himself anymore besides keeping his body in shape by regular massages and the odd botox job. The term 'playboy' was invented for Carlo.

The relational sphere is Carlo's great strength. Thanks to his charm, his interested attitude, and the glad warmth that he manages to bring to every meeting, he can get almost anybody to do anything for him. Exclusive representation on markets people kill for, the best stands on trade fairs, a better purchase price than his competitors – and almost every woman he ever wanted. This has led him to develop what *de facto* amounts to three parallel lives, with three different women, in three different countries. The three, one of whom he married, do not know of each other's existence.

How he manages this, is anybody's guess. Even his best friends are baffled. Part of the system is telephonic: he has separate ring tones for all three women, so that he never picks up the wrong call at the wrong moment. Still, life with the trinity is not ideal, because Carlo's beloved younger brother, Eduardo, is starting to feel awkward about the arrangement. Specifically, he starts to tire of having Carlo over for vacations in his Chilean mountain chalet, now with the Uruguayan, then with the Brazilian life partner – while he, as a gracious host, has to pretend not to know of any other women.

The other day, Carlo asked Eduardo if it was okay that next time he bring his new Venezuelan sweetheart, but now Eduardo is coming to the end of his tether. Frankly speaking he is coming to the end of Carlo as well, but because he has always loved his elder brother despite his weaknesses, he does not want to tell Carlo. Moreover, a certain pity is developing. The last few years Carlo has suffered several minor heart attacks. It would be hard to prove a causal relationship with his life style, but in confidence, Eduardo does speculate that such a relationship might exist. It appears that usurpation of the energy in his lower belly has taken a heavy toll on Carlo, sapping his strength. But business is still booming. You cannot get operated on in South America, die, or get born, without making him even richer.

Question: Should his next stroke be worse, which of the three women will get the privilege of caring for Carlo? And where will he say that he is to the other two? In a private clinic so private that they are not allowed entry?

3. SOLAR PLEXUS CHAKRA: RESPECT, WILLPOWER

Sanskrit name: Manipura Chakra
Aspects: willpower, respect, sense of self-worth, autonomy
Location: the solar plexus (in front of the spine, level with the navel)
Colour: yellow
Element: fire
Sense: sight
Right: the right to act
Demon: shame
Figure: ten-petaled lotus
Maslow: level 4, need for esteem

Personal Aspects

Favourable development: This is the chakra of inner force, called the chakra of respect, or the chakra of the will – the will in that deeper sense of the philosopher Schopenhauer, as the directive force that shapes our existence here on earth. The Solar Plexus Chakra is the seat of our inner sun. Here the great power is generated for our 'conquest' of the world. It is also the seat of our need to be respected for what we contribute.

In an emergency, a properly functioning Solar Plexus Chakra can make us explode in effective violence. A mother protecting her child from an attacker, a soldier fighting to hold an untenable position in the defence of the fatherland – their unstoppable violence comes straight from the solar plexus. In peaceful times, the Solar Plexus Chakra purrs on without attracting notice, like a ship's engine at cruising speed, but should the need arise, its huge reserve of power can be called upon instantly.

Unfavourable development: Dependence on other people's opinion of oneself, disappointment in self and others, shame, blind rage. Enlargement of the ego, in extreme cases (not rare in the corporate world, probably rather over-represented) to the point of egomania. In cases of very weak activity of this chakra we see lack of direction, docility, living at other people's leash, silliness and futility. Incompatible with leadership. Occasionally found in positions where leadership would normally be expected, because people with these qualities have one advantage: they will do as told, so others can exert power through them, while staying in the background.

Corporate Aspects

Favourable development: This is the chakra of energy and ambition, the drive to make your mark on the world, to do better in every sense. It is like a power plant that, when no extreme demands are made on it, is a durable source of energy. It is also the chakra of professionalism – especially in the sense of craftsmanship, respectable performance, best practices, but also in the sense of efficiency, productivity, quality control systems, ISO 9001.

Unfavourable development: Lust for power, severity, authoritarian conduct, bureaucracy, hardening of emotions, rage-fed destruction.

Chief Challenge: To make your mark without overpowering others.

THE CHAKRA GOVERNING MANIFESTATION OF OUR WILL

The Solar Plexus Chakra lies below the diaphragm, roughly level with the navel but more towards the back, just in front of the spine. The physical organ it corresponds with is the solar plexus, one of the largest autonomic nerve centres in our body. Rich in ganglia and interconnected neurons, it controls many vital functions such as adrenal secretion and intestinal contraction. It is a specific target for boxers: a blow to the solar plexus is not merely very painful, but potentially incapacitating. (This just to underscore the importance of this area.)

According to several authors the name Manipura means something like 'lotus jewel', but that cannot be but western fantasy, because *mani* means 'holy' and *pura* is 'town' – almost every Indian state has one or two Manipurs. Intended, clearly, is the inner holy town: the centre where energies from all parts of the personality combine into a powerful motive force, like pilgrims flowing into a holy town, fully charged and eager to be given direction. In the town the amalgamated energy of the masses is overpowering, dissolving individuality – the ideal preparation for collective ceremonies geared to create a new sense of unity and joint purpose. The successful pilgrim returns with strengthened willpower, increased vigour, and the sense that he/she can tackle the world and come out winning.

The Solar Plexus Chakra determines the capacity we have to act in the world, the firmness of our stance, our assertivity and effectiveness, our power. At a spiritual level this is the chakra of our Schopenhauerian *Wille*, the expression of our deepest being. We could visualise this will, charged as it is with awareness of the energy reserves it can call upon, as a conscious and forceful projection of ourselves outward, with a single-minded intensity directed at concretisation and realisation. Energy from other chakras, notably the one below and the one above, here gets the spark that initiates action and blasts through obstacles.

The Solar Plexus Chakra helps us to 'manage' our sense impressions, determining what to allow into our consciousness and what to ignore – filling that huge recycling bin of our subconscious from which hardly anything ever escapes[84] – the primordial neural processing which manifests our will and our autonomy. In the earliest phase of our life we are dependent on the will of others: parents, teachers and other authorities, who usually (except in more enlightened families and educational facilities) attempt to keep imposing their will upon the young one well into adulthood. For the young it is important to develop resistance to this imposed external will during puberty, in order to develop their own will and attain the independence required for adulthood.

During the development of this period of growing self-confidence we acquire the habit of seeing and hearing only that which we really like to see and hear, and focus all our attention on it exclusively. 'Well, yes, I do notice that something over there is not going the way it should, but I choose not to pay attention to it for a while, as it distracts me from my chief interest here.' 'Sure, I do know that glittering new opportunities appear left and right, trying to lure me into another direction, but the world is full of lures and glitter. For now I stick to ...' Discipline, one-pointedness, that is the Solar Plexus Chakra in action, that is a grown man shaping his life.

We see the Solar Plexus Chakra light up, figuratively speaking, when we withdraw from chatting and gossip, avoid talk shows and amusement, horror movies and other sick pulp, turn down the social knob a bit, muffle our inner chatterbox; when we seek the silence that allows us to hear our inner voice, or the darkness that lights up our inner nature, and dedicate our energy to that which we deem vital, and which we will pursue to the exclusion of anything else.

Discipline may be an effect of a properly functioning Solar Plexus Chakra, conversely it is also true that discipline is required to keep it functioning properly. When you deal with it in a positive manner, the rotation of this chakra has the character of a virtuous circle: the happier you make it by disciplining yourself, the easier it makes it for you. And yes, of course, it works the other way around as well. But I don't need to explain the vicious circle, because we all know how easily loss of discipline can make one slide into a state where even doing the dishes becomes a major challenge, especially by the time they are yesterday's dishes. You end up not tying your shoelaces because you'd have to untie them again at night.

When we work on strengthening the will, it is important to make sure that it does not overpower the other aspects of the personality, because it has that tendency by nature. People who rely too much on self-consciousness and willpower, sometimes fail to pay attention to matters that touch the heart and the under-belly. When the Solar Plexus Chakra outshines its neighbours, none of that focused attention and iron achieves anything, because no one around will support is. Real willpower is achieved most easily for causes worth willing, if only because it finds the most willing support.

POWER AND HOW TO APPLY IT

In the relational field of the Sacral Chakra, the one below the Solar Plexus Chakra, the exchange of energy between individuals creates patterns of power – some people happen to be more forceful than others, and everywhere on earth, except in some remote jungle tribes living happily ever after, the powerful dominate the less powerful. The Swiss businessman, philosopher and founder of the Red Cross, Henri Dunant, wrote on this subject that we celebrate the combination of 'freedom, equality and brotherhood' as ideal, but that in reality the first two are mutually exclusive, so that the third is rarely achieved.[85] Only one good look around in the world makes clear that his observation is correct. Because:

- The more freedom you give a population, the more drastic becomes the exploitation of the weak by the strong. (*Cf.* Brazil, USA, Montenegro, UK.)
- To achieve equality, a phenomenon not found in nature, it needs to be imposed by force, with the result that freedom is dead. (*Cf.* all communist regimes, from Stalin and Mao, to Castro and Pot.)

All of world history may be seen as a continuous battle between the forces promoting freedom and the forces promoting equality: it's all about power, all about the functioning of this well connected energy node. That may not be ideal, but it is a biological, social-psychological and historical fact. For that reason, a proper functioning of this energy centre – not hyper-charged, but also not too reticent – is of great importance. A clenching up of this chakra can lead to perversion of the will, and as a consequence to a destructive influence on others. Attenuation of this chakra leads to lack of direction, a life directed by other people's will, be it the steady life partner, a sequence of changing partners, or even total strangers.

WOMEN'S WEAK SPOT

In many women the Solar Plexus Chakra manifests itself in rather subdued fashion, because it has never been stimulated, or was intentionally suppressed, which inevitably leads to a dependent attitude, resulting in underdevelopment of talents and even exploitation. (See above, *re* freedom and equality.) No one will deny that some women are endowed with formidable willpower. From Jeanne d'Arc and Florence Nightingale to that great heroine of our days, ocean sailor Ellen McArthur, we have seen women whose willpower reduced the tallest standing men to wimps. But perhaps they speak to our imagination so forcefully especially because they are such spectacular exceptions.

Most women are taught from an early age, that they are here on earth to do as others tell them: first the parents and their proxies, then the husband. Many emancipated women will break up laughing about this image of the docile little woman, and some men will join in the merriment, but the truth is, that in most marriages and other man-woman partnerships, and even in gay couples, the male has the last word in the weighty choices on which the family's stability depends: source of income, place of residence, care for old age, and size of the video screen.

When women want more influence, they are usually well advised to try to exert it in the periphery of men's field of view, or, preferably, well outside it. That is how daddy's little sweetheart can go out with that boy he has told her to stop seeing. That is how, after long deliberation, the living room gets painted just a little warmer than the sample he thought they'd finally agreed on. That is how the cheaper holiday package happens to be sold out, sorry love, so now there is no choice but the deluxe package with free beautician's sessions. And that is how it can occur that my espresso-loving friend David B., who has both a weak heart and a hard head, doesn't know that at home he has been drinking decaf – 'Oh, that despicable stuff!' – for the last five years.

WOMEN'S SPECIAL GIFT

The most important thing that women can do, is to increase their independence. Not necessarily by making their own money, although that can work wonders, but to develop their own interests and their own passions – whatever hubby may think of it. Many women get to this point after the kids have left the house, which is nice, but sadly late. Whatever occupation you then pursue, is entered short twenty years of experience, twenty years of networking, twenty years of building up a reputation. When you find yourself in a situation like this, do not consider just practical activities (everything from sports to business to work for charities), but also look at areas where you have *not* stood still: emotional life, insight in people, intuition, bond with nature and attention to health.

For example: anyone who survives motherhood can readily transform the caring attitude into a coaching attitude – which in fact is much easier because you don't sit there all tangled up in an umbilical cord. You care for your coachees, of course, but if at forty they still turn out to have the maturity of a six year old, you don't go for the Prozac, but hand them a tissue so they can blow their own nose, and tell them to continue their growing up in the next session.

Women who do develop their will, and most female readers of this book probably did, can sometimes acquire a level of power beyond that of males in their class, because they developed not just their Solar Plexus Chakra, but also the chakras below and above – underbelly and heart. Take relational strength, add the passion of the heart and a steeled will, and you have a powerhouse that can change the world.

Another positive note, is that slightly more women than men develop the higher energy centres – though men who do are more likely to be noticed, perhaps for their relative rarity, or because they have more power, and can thus make more of a difference more rapidly. But still, only about half of all men show much development above the third chakra.[86] Most, above all, want to remain *men*, preferably men in power, and they will harden their hearts to achieve this. Unfortunately – for them that is – it seems very likely that in the coming years development of higher energy levels will be a requirement for all leadership positions.

This leads to a piece of practical advice for men in a mid-life crisis: think twice about leaving your wife, because in the coming years she could teach you a lot. And a motivational hint for women in mid-life, crisis or not: you have always known that you were the more mature, but now comes the time when he, too, may realise this.

MARKS OF A HEALTHY SOLAR PLEXUS CHAKRA
- powerful, but not overpowering personality
- independence
- balance in action
- leadership qualities
- perseverance
- self-discipline

- firm, but humane grip on the organisation
- resilience, quick recovery from misfortune
- humour.

SYMPTOMS OF A BLOCKED SOLAR PLEXUS CHAKRA
- lack of willpower
- low self-esteem, shame
- allowing oneself to be manipulated, living on other people's leash
- blaming others, victimhood
- irresponsible conduct
- refusal to take ownership, lack of perseverance, failing to finish the job
- staying stuck in conceptual phase, no energy for implementation
- Peter Pan syndrome
- lack of humour
- stubbornness
- aggression.

Place on earth: New York City. No other place on earth is such a palpable manifestation of the will. The construction of the new World Trade Centre is a fine demonstration of the city's willpower and resilience, should any be required. This very aspect is the main reason why so many people get a kick out of New York: because here, *things get done*. New York is willpower turned to steel, to concrete, to glass, to canvas, words on paper. And last but not least, to money. It can make newcomers feel like they are living in a pinball machine. The whole day they are bounced back and forth by the flippers of other people's will. Until you figure out how the game works and start your own pinball machine, keeping the balls high up there where the scoring is good, making them hit one bumper after another, so in no time you are rich beyond your dreams. If you want it, go for it! That is the spirit of the Solar Plexus Chakra.

Other places of this nature are all those that show a powerful manifestation of the will, and demand respect for what has been accomplished there. Brasilia, the Dutch Delta Works, the Palm Islands of Dubai, and any really tall buildings. Go stand in front of one of them, with your back to the entrance, so that you can feel but not see the towering shape behind you, and try to imagine that there is nothing there behind you, just vast emptiness. You then concentrate on that energy centre at your solar plexus, that golden ball of power in your mid-section. See how it glows and grows, fanning desire to bring your will into play. Now you let the tower rise in your mind, floor by floor, as if pushing it out of the ground with your sheer will. Once you are done erecting it in your mind, turn around, and prepare to be stunned to see what willpower can achieve. This effect, more than efficiency, is the main reason why great corporate leaders tend to prefer soaring buildings.

Exercise: Become aware that your whole being, your whole life up to this moment is the expression of your will, in the Schopenhauerian sense of the directive force that manifests itself in the world through you, and shapes your existence. Identify yourself with that will that has made you into what you are today. Do not deny your relationship to it, but shoulder it. Take ownership of who and what your are, because you have willed it this way. Not your ego willed it this way, but that unknown force that directs your life and is wholly your own. (Schopenhauer was one of the first western philosophers to absorb the classic Indian wisdom of the Vedas and the Upanishads, so any resemblance to the law of *karma* is probably not coincidental.) Go stand in front of a mirror, look at yourself, keep looking till you really see yourself, and say: 'This is how I willed you to be.'

'This is how I willed you boy, this is how I willed you gal. ...' That identification with the cosmic will that flows through you as you stand staring yourself in the face, will lift you right out of the role of victim (should that be your trouble), and gives a tremendous sensation of power. Bringing back the memory of that moment of great power can invigorate you at crucial moments when willpower makes the difference.

WILLPOWER AND HOW TO GAIN RESPECT

We have yet to see a merger, acquisition, or other intentional corporate change of substantial consequence where the will does not play a very important part. But as the above Chief Challenge indicates, the crux is to not let it become dominant and suppress all other levels of energy. The will is our power to manifest ourselves, to make our mark, to create the world we live in, to shape our destinies. It supports our efforts to secure the foundations of our life, material and relational, but finds its most powerful expression when it supports the higher energy levels.

Ideally, the will serves as a source of energy that can be tapped into by needs on all levels, with no preference of its own for any of them. In this respect the will, properly managed, should always be subservient. This may seem paradoxical, but it is not. Where it is regarded as paradoxical, there is a misunderstanding of the true nature of the will. The will is at its most powerful when it is employed in the service of a great ideal, in the pursuit of a noble – or at least not blatantly ignoble – purpose. This is the realm of the servant leader, who has subjugated his or her will to the needs of others, and is the more powerful for it.

The last few years we have found ourselves disseminating the concept of the 'Servant Leader', first articulated by the celebrated Robert K. Greenleaf, who was inspired by the German-Swiss poet philosopher Hermann Hesse, who in his turn was inspired by Eastern philosophy, in particular Vedanta and Buddhism. The idea of the servant as leader came to him from reading Hesse's *Journey to the East*, which must have resonated with him deeply because he himself travelled to India six times. In Hesse's story we see a band of intelligent and sensitive men on a mythical journey. The central figure is Leo, who accompanies the party in the capacity of servant while keeping up their spirits and inspiring them with song. He is a character of extraordinary presence, and well liked. The journey goes well until one day Leo disappears. The group unravels, abandons its goal and disbands. Clearly, they cannot succeed without Leo. After years of wandering the narrator stumbles upon Leo, who then turns out to be the head of the spiritual order that has initiated the journey. The man whom he had known only as the group's *servant*, was in fact its guiding spirit, a truly great and noble *leader*.

In essence, servant leadership means subjugating your will to the needs of others: using your will to serve their needs. This is a powerful concept of leadership, and one of the few that gives a very straightforward answer to that famous question asked before: 'Why on earth would anyone be led by you?' 'Could it be because I am out there, not for me, but for them?' Greenleaf: 'The servant-leader is servant first. It begins with the natural feeling that one wants to serve. Then conscious choice brings one to aspire to lead. The best test is: do those served grow as persons; do they, while being served, become healthier, wiser, freer, more autonomous, more likely themselves to become servants?'[87]

The seminal research of Jim Collins reported in *Good to Great*,[88] has shown that for an organisation to gain sustainable profitable growth it needs to reconcile the more 'harsh' 'envisioned future' comprising a bold mission (or Big Hairy Audacious Goal) with a core ideology, comprising its core values and purpose. After putting 1,435 good companies through a rigorous performance analysis, Collins discovered that only 11 were truly great – defined by him as consistently outperforming the index for 30 consecutive years.* These organisations had two main characteristics. They were value driven, and their CEOs were relatively unknown, not particularly charismatic. Most of these what he called 'Level 5 leaders', showed up two striking characteristics: they demonstrated highly developed willpower – and were very humble. In our terms they had radiant Solar Plexus Chakras. Their willpower was full on, with none of that craving for respect (the main demon at this energy level) that brings lesser characters to their knees, be it through exhaustion or self-worship. These Level 5 leaders have harnessed their energy at this level, which is so deeply linked to respect, and sublimated its potentially negative forces into humility, a trait that brings respect without asking.

INNER-DIRECTED PUSH OR OUTER-DIRECTED PULL

Another area where we see the Solar Plexus Chakra in action at the corporate level is in the inclination to either shape or be shaped. Do we respond to market pull, or create markets for what we push? The major issue at stake is to connect an internally controlled culture, leading to technology push, with the externally controlled world of market pull in order to achieve a culture of inventiveness. Take a company like Philips; nobody will deny its technological prowess and inventiveness, nor the quality of its marketing staff. The problem the company faced for decades was that its two major functional areas didn't seem to communicate. The success of an organisation is dependent on the integration of both areas. The push of technology should help you decide what markets you want to be pulled by. The pull of the market should help you decide what technologies to push.

A core quality of today's enlightened leaders is the competence to marry the feedback from the market with the technological advances

---

* One may wonder if this definition is not too materialistic. But it has one great advantage: in terms of building a business case for a particular type of leadership it is hard to beat, because for most people in corporate environments bottom-line performance is the only valid yardstick.

developed in the organisation. To reconcile inner and outer directed manifestations of will power. The modern leader knows that constant hammering on technology push will eventually lead the company into the ultimate niche market, the part of the market with zero customers. Conversely, a monomaniac focus on the market will leave the leader at the mercy of clients.

Our thinking is that truly creative leaders *combine* values: they create zero-emission sports cars that don't pollute (like the Ferrari beating Tesla), delicious stuff that doesn't make you fat, a life insurance that doesn't kill you. A computer capable of complex operations can also be user friendly, though you wouldn't think so living in the world of Windows. Where there is creativity, particularly when supported by willpower, there is hope. Nobody claims that combining values is easy, but it is possible. The challenges abound.

Challenges are the true stuff of Solar Plexus Chakra energy, because they invoke the will. Do we really want this? Are we ready to commit the energy of the chakras that are subordinate to it, do we find support from above, from the heart for instance, or the higher mind? If so, the powerhouse of the solar plexus region can be fired up and relied on, providing plentiful energy year on year.

Laurent Beaudoin, president of Bombardier, skilfully reconciled the inner and outer directed aspects of corporate willpower. This reconciliation probably accounted for much of Bombardier's success. Any strategy focused on serial acquisition is an advanced form of outer-direction with powerful motives, steered from within. Beaudoin has created a company that looked for the rare and valuable. Now of course many companies and individuals are looking for the rare and valuable. But when they find it, what will they do with it? Will they hold and cherish it? Too often, acquisition hungry executives crush their treasures like children capturing butterflies.

AN ENLIGHTENING INTERMEZZO

Recently, an American colleague told us about a case that we find fascinating, because it so fittingly illustrates the point we are trying to make here, and because we once experienced something rather similar in our own firm – not so strange, because things like these happen all the time, which is why they are so immediately recognisable and make such powerful illustrations. The protagonist of the story was a middle aged man we shall name Max Hartman, founder-owner of Keep the Change, a successful Californian consultancy firm in the field of change management. A company builder by trade, who had been in giftshops and computer rental before, Max hit upon consulting in the course of post-divorce recovery. His wife told him to take a fresh look at himself and suggested an intensive at Esalen, the mother of all self-discovery institutes. When he came out, Max was a New Man, so he announced, with new priorities in life. He set up a management consultancy firm in San Diego and in a short time managed to generate much wealth by the preaching of friendship, coupled with application of a deep immersion consulting approach (the 'Embrace') which required hordes of consultants, all of them young, half of them female, most of them pretty, to swoop down at the clients' like a flight of sparrows and stay there for a long time. Clients loved the chatter, though there were some moanings that Max was turning Keep the Change into a sect, complete with monthly sessions called 'Maxing Out', where he was pontificating on friendship, authenticity and purpose to his adoring young employees.

Wishing to attain higher rank in the global pecking order of consultancies, Max decided to use his stash of holy loot to buy another consultancy firm of much higher standing, let's call it Norton Consulting, led by the venerable John Norton, who taught at Harvard Business School and served on the board of several global companies. Negotiations went well, a deal was concluded and put on paper, with a few details yet to be finalised, including final valuation. As he would have done in any change process, Max Hartman let his young people swoop down on his acquisition. These initially inspired the Norton staff by their youthful energies and optimistic views, but their almost paranoid loyalty to their boss soon started to grate. It transpired that anything people said to Hartman's birds was instantly transmitted to him. If any scepticism about his intentions or method of integration was expressed, or even hinted at, Hartman was on the phone to the person involved sometimes within minutes, to demand explanation or suggest correction.

In the meantime Hartman announced the acquisition to his staff and clients, indicating that the future name of the company was as yet undecided, though he rather favoured 'Hartman & Norton Consulting'.

At Norton's one day, walking through the offices, he instructed John Norton's PA to start redecorating the offices by taking away the austere, stainless steel Mies van der Rohe chairs and replace them with orange, pillow strewn sofas, to match Keep the Change's look and feel. Perhaps it was this orange that switched the alarm phase at Norton's to a higher level.

In the classic tradition of rapacious conquest, Hartman fired the CFO and CIO and brought in replacements from his own firm, young lads who could not believe their luck at the career jump they were making. A classic Machiavellian tactic: first of all get rid of the conquered princes' most trusted advisors, and replace them with people deeply beholden to you. His next move was to tell Norton's consultants that he would give them a new conceptual framework, teach them his views on leadership, and generally whip them into shape for today's world. They would no longer operate as lone rangers (though most of them were on the road seventy percent of the time), but as a unified flock, one in soul, spirit and body.

Unfortunately, though rather predictably, Norton's consultants did not like to be told what to do. Also, they were quite happy to be lone rangers, connected across the continent by a shared love of challenges, common tools, and a readiness to help one another at the first call. Norton being a straight up guy who spoke his mind and liked his people to do likewise, the consultants told Hartman that he was abusing his acquisition, showing as little respect for his 'conquest' as a rapist for his victim. (Respect, that core issue at the level of the Solar Plexus Chakra, so intimately connected with willpower in all manifestations.)

Hartman appeared to be seeking a way out for weeks, allowing, perhaps unconsciously forcing, minor disagreements to escalate into shouting matches that usually ended up with him threatening Norton's people that he would call off the whole acquisition if they did not comply. 'And I assure you, John is not going to be pleased!'

Soon, the promise this threat implied became a reason in itself for Norton's people to annoy him. In the end Max Hartman freed himself through clever use of a technicality: rejection of the Norton pension plan, so much more lavish than his own, which had a lightness commensurate with the frivolity of his staff. John Norton, who had been looking forward to the creation of serious old age provisions for himself, but by then had become deeply distressed by the massive unhappiness of his staff, and was infuriated by the mere idea that his name might ever have to take second place to Hartman's, did not give an inch. Within 24 hours, Hartman managed to escalate the disagreement into a barrage of mutual accusations, and the deal was off – to the delight of the Norton staff, who pulled out the Champagne that had lain ready to celebrate the merger, but could now be put to better use.

The effect of all this on Norton was highly positive. The staff found a new level of awareness of what connected them, and the spirit was better than ever before. John Norton had no regrets and moved on with his life with more zest for life than he had shown during the months of the stifling 'Embrace' by Max Hartman. A year later he sold half of his company to a large professional services firm that was eager to integrate his methodologies and mature consultants.

To Hartman it was a hard blow to the body. Straight to the solar plexus, that most vulnerable spot. He had to tell his Keep the Change staff that they were not, after all, to become associated with the illustrious John Norton and his team of highly regarded professionals. He also had to tell his clients, and, one presumes, himself. He lost the respect of his management team and flock of young believers, muddled on for a few months, then quickly arranged a management buy-out so he could move to a small town in Colorado and lick his wounds in peace. The whole spectacle, from beginning to end, took six months.

This illustrates how an unfavourably developed Solar Plexus Chakra can damage organisations, the people that work for them, and the people that own them. If you ever contemplate imposing your will on an organisation, instead of inducing the people to follow you, think of Max Hartman, and the iron fist of willpower in which he caught his precious butterfly.

Laurent Beaudoin to the contrary (let's snap back to Bombardier and the bright side of life after this endarkened intermezzo), skilfully reconciled his dilemmas at the level of the Solar Plexus Chakra. Like Keeper, he was always looking for the rare and valuable. But he did not crush his butterflies. Instead he showed a remarkable capacity to reconcile the inner-directed strategy of bold new acquisitions with the outer-directed policy of respecting the integrity of acquired companies. Beaudoin used humility, listening and patience to learn about the companies that

Bombardier acquired. He let the leader of the companies he bought share their dreams, so he could understand what they thought possible, and of how much they were capable. There should be a word for this particular leadership talent: a capacity and readiness to understand, acknowledge and respond productively to the value-creating capacity of another system outside yourself.

Pairing these contrasting abilities, hitting the acquisition trail hard and studying respectfully what you acquire, is the way of 'The Acquiring Scholar'. He or she makes a mark without overpowering others.

IMPOSITION VERSUS ATTRACTION

British and American companies in the role of buying party have long had a tendency to rigorously export and implement their culture – though some of the more advanced, banks among them, are now changing this attitude as they become more global. Willpower based power structures work best within limited geographical areas, less well in dispersion, and hardly at all within networked environments across large geographical footprints that rely on remote management. We encourage all clients with such profiles to ease up on directive management and bring it down to the people: look at what energises them and then channel their energies in a way that matches the corporate purpose.

The traditional Anglo-Saxon model is driven by a strong Solar Plexus Chakra. It largely depends on willpower, whereas the European model has to some extent made willpower an instrument of the higher order energies represented by the Heart and Throat Chakras, and perhaps even the Third Eye and Crown Chakras. Crudely put, the European model has a higher measure of civilisation – if we define civilisation as the degree to which one takes into account the needs of others. The European model taps into higher levels of energy than the Anglo-Saxon model, which allows a harsher degree of exploitation.* As Jeremy Rifkin has brought to our attention in *The European Dream*, Europe is the first large empire created not by domination and imposition, by raw application of willpower, but by attraction; based on respect for its institutions and way

---

* *Vide:* Great Britain's refusal to sign up to the European social laws, because it would cost companies, and therefore shareholders, too much money.

of life. Keep this in mind for your next career planning phase: willpower expressed with humility evokes respect and attraction.

SOLAR PLEXUS CHAKRA NEVER WOKE UP: ARCHETYPE WILLIAM D. – THE HANDICAP OF COMFORT

William D. grew up in an entrepreneurial family, the eldest of three sons. His father had a cattle feed business that grandfather started in the late 19th century, and by means of hard work, seven days a week, had managed to survive the Depression of the 1930s. William's father began helping out in the warehouse when he was seventeen, and jointly father and son kept the company sort of alive right through World War II – financially weakened, but with a solid reputation. Shortly after the war William's dad – who had then just become a father – took over the helm. The company benefited from the post-war recovery, and was fattened by decades of European agricultural policies providing guaranteed income for all customers with dairy cattle. Most years, the business grew ten to twelve percent without any special effort – though William's father continued going to the office at 7 AM each morning to keep up the employees' spirit.

From a very early age, William was given to understand that in due course he would take over the business. No one informed him about the size of the family capital, but by the time he was sixteen years old, it had become apparent to him that there was enough money to provide a life of leisure, not just for his ageing parents, himself and his brothers, but for a next generation as well. He studied a little here and there, had a few jobs at attractive places in Europe, and in his early twenties married a girl from a similar background. When the time came to take over the family business and buy out his parents and brothers – for a decent price, not too generous, and not too mean – he did this in the anticipation of constant growth which required no effort on his part other than leaning back in his chair and see it happen, not necessarily from early in the morning either.

He gave himself a fat salary, bought a nice house and a nice car, and played CEO. But the employees appeared to find it hard to see him in that capacity. He kept having run-ins with sales managers and floor managers who claimed to know better, and developed the odious habit of reminding him of his exemplary father. He found it hard to pin down exactly what irked him in their attitude, but he clearly felt a lack of respect, and started avoiding the office – never mind the warehouses and logistics departments.

In the 1990s the European authorities began weaning the dairy farmers off their subsidies, not scrapping them altogether, but still, quite troubling for an industry that had money coming in like milk from that huge udder in Brussels. Falling milk prices, quota, farmers going bankrupt ... And worst of all, suddenly there appeared a new class of competitors: Americans, who did business in entirely different, cut-throat ways. William's profits diminished, he broke even for a year, then saw two consecutive years of losses, and before things could get any worse he sold the whole lot to a Belgian competitor who had been stealing clients from him for years.

Now William D. could have just leant back and enjoyed his money, and he did entertain the idea of retirement for a while, but in the end he did not embrace it – if only because he knew that his mother, who was still alive, had never forgiven him the sale of the company, and that she would never respect him if he did not create something of substance with his own hands. That was when he was approached by a head-hunter, who managed to place him at ABC Corp., a multinational agro-business that he now runs as general manager – something his ninety year old mom is not necessarily proud of, but accepts as a lesser evil, although she fails to see why ABC might want to employ him. Because mom knows one thing: he may be a nice boy, with lots of friends ready to spend spare time with him, but willpower William never had. The unfortunate ABC Corp. will probably take some time to find out, because lack of willpower is easily masked by introducing some sweeping changes. It takes time before it becomes apparent that there is no real drive behind it, and no real direction. But who knows, by that time maybe his mother has gone to greener pastures, so he can finally kick back and relax.

When we spoke to him last month, William complained of not being shown enough respect by his managers, something that troubles him deeply, because that is the one thing he lacks. Everything else he has. All he still craves is respect. And then to be shown such patent lack of respect by his own people ... It's as if the employees know, as if they smell it. In fact William exudes that deep down inside the only thing he stands for is his own comfort. To discern this, no higher insight or special psychological gifts are required. How your chakras are doing is plain for everyone to see: all people need to do is be open to the energy, to feel where you are at.

SOLAR PLEXUS CHAKRA DOMINANT: ARCHETYPE ROGER T. – WILLPOWER MASQUERADING AS DETACHMENT

Roger T. is a colleague on the public speaking circuit, where he is beginning to establish a reputation for inspiring talks on themes like authentic leadership. (For the protection of the party concerned this case history has been heavily edited; yet in its essence it is entirely truthful.) He has a background in management consulting, and for many years has practiced yoga, meditation and intuition development. A few times a year he organises leadership courses targeted at corporate and governmental decision makers around the theme of 'detachment' – because as Roger T. explains, it is only through detachment that the inner leader can free himself and step forward.

Once in a speech Peter also referred to the importance of this detachment – Jim Dreaver's 'Being present without agenda' – and this motivated someone in the audience to put him and Roger T. in touch, thinking that maybe they could offer a course together some time. They agreed to meet at the Canary Wharf offices of a corporation that Peter at the time was serving in an advisory capacity. The appointment was for 1 PM and he arranged a swanky room on the executive floor, with superb views over London, costly abstract expressionist paintings and cream leather easy chairs. They sat down, partook from the welcoming array of coffee, tea, fruit and cookies, and Peter opened the conversation. But before he could finish his first sentence, he was interrupted: 'Listen, I haven't eaten yet, and eh …'

Oh gee, lunch time, of course …

'I often skip lunch, or just have some fruit,' Peter explained, vaguely hoping that his guest, too, might be on a light diet, but Roger's features hardened, making it instantly clear that for him skipping lunch was no option. Peter apologised and led the way to the executive dining room. It was busy and lively, and the buffet looked excellent. He asked the manager if there was a table left for them.

'Not in the dining room itself, but I could lay a table for you in that niche around the corner.'

'Oh that's fine, thanks.'

They sat down, and within minutes the table was laid and they were both served a generous plate of sandwiches and various tasty looking morsels. Roger looked at the offerings and froze: 'Gee sorry, but I am vegetarian of course, and –'

'Oh, no problem sir, then we'll get you something else.'

'I can also go get some myself from the buffet.'

'Don't bother sir, we have vegetarian plates all prepared.'

Roger gave in, after a fleeting, but noticeable moment of resistance. Finally they could begin their conversation. After some ten minutes a pretty young girl in black and white appeared with a beautifully arranged vegetarian plate. Roger scanned the offerings and recoiled in his seat, as if he feared that something on the plate would jump at his throat. 'At the buffet I also noticed [...],' he said hesitatingly. There is no record of what else he noticed at the buffet, but clearly something was badly amiss.

'No problem, feel free to come and get some any time,' the young lady said with a detached air. This did not appear to satisfy Roger entirely, but at least now he tucked in, so that the obligatory item of the feeding could be moved off the agenda. Roger picked at his food and the exchange was a conversational parallel of the nutritional proceedings. After about ten minutes Roger dropped his cutlery. 'I am going to get something from the buffet,' he said. Peter had seen it coming, so he ate on unperturbedly. Lamb carpaccio on a toasted focaccia bun with rucola and capers. It made him think that he should have lunch more often. Roger came back with his booty on a plate, moved the other plate aside resolutely and began eating in earnest.

When Roger was ready, they could finally come to the point. One of the two hours planned for the meeting was over. But still, one hour of face time in peaceful surroundings can mean a lot for two people who connect on content. Peter brought up the idea of the joint course that their *postillion d'amour* had conceived.

'Yes, splendid idea,' Roger said, 'we should certainly do that.' It was just that the course title Peter proposed was not something he could live with. Other than that, perfect, absolutely. Except the location – that really had to be the location where Roger used to do his courses, otherwise what he had to offer would not have its proper supportive atmosphere, and didn't Peter agree that it was actually an ideal location: so plain and simple and yet so elegant?

In the same vein they discussed a few more aspects of the joint programme, but every idea Peter served up was sent back to the kitchen, invariably preceded by a brief irritated sniffing – a tic that he had not noticed previously, but that now, with so much repetition, became conspicuous. When Roger returned from a private little expedition to the buffet for pudding, Peter had had his dessert already. His dessert was detachment from any notion of collaboration with Roger T., and its taste brought a warm, charitable smile to his lips. A smile which widened to a grin when Roger sent back the decaf espresso – because in the meantime, noticing that it was also on offer, he preferred to have herbal tea. Oh, never to need to witness this again, what bliss!

And the funniest thing is, that many people swallow it whole. They really think that Roger T. is a very detached person, because he is a vegetarian and drinks herbal tea – there you go.

4. HEART CHAKRA: LOVE

Sanskrit name: Anahata Chakra
Aspects: balance, love, learning, transformation.
Location: heart area (middle position of seven chakras)
Colour: green
Element: air
Sense: feeling
Right: the right to be loved
Demon: grief
Figure: twelve-petaled lotus
Maslow: most correspondence with level 3

Personal Aspects

Favourable development: This is the chakra of balance, but also the chakra of connection at the heart level, of love. It is the chakra of people with a big heart, of people who know how to give – acceptance, trust, compassion, support. We are all born with the Heart Chakra wide open, but as a result of unfavourable development of the personality, it can get severely squeezed, particularly when greed combines with societal (read 'corporate') pressures to negate feeling. Whatever its previous condition, the Heart Chakra normally jumps to life at the birth of one's first child, but that child may also be figurative – the same energy boost is obtained by shouldering any enterprise that transcends narrow self-interest. This transformational aspect can manifest itself dramatically in people of mature age who start to question what they have really done with their lives so far – then discover that their Heart Chakra is next to extinguished, and turn their lives around.

Unfavourable development: This energy centre can suffer badly when ego holds it in an iron grip, and in such case offers spectacular potential for positive change. Symptoms are heartlessness, callousness, heart disease. (This is not to suggest a causal link between afflictions of the heart and evil intent, because there are many darling people who get sick to the heart – from grief for instance, or genetic predisposition – but there does exist an associative link, in the sense that heartlessness is not doing the heart any good.) Other marks can be lack of social acceptance and ostracism, practiced or endured.

Corporate Aspects

Favourable development: Growth by giving expression to widely held values, by the establishment of loyalty relationships with employees, clients and suppliers, 'soft power'. As a speaker dear to us recently expressed it at a seminar: 'All things grow when you give them love.' Balance and harmony. Openness to change, increased capacity for self-renewal, transformation.

Unfavourable development: Fake humanity, isolation, loss of trust base in the organisation, respectively loss of trust of the organisation in the community. Disintegration, or better yet decomposition of the organisation as a result of lack of vitality.

> **Chief Challenge:** Letting the heart rule in harmony with lower and higher levels.

This is a key issue, which we will review in more depth in the chapter How
hallowed is the highest? *(Page 217.) It boils down to the wisdom that only
those who manage to maintain inner balance can achieve successful transformation – be it of self or organisation. Failing that inner balance you will
not bring transformation, just (self)destruction. A one-sided focus on one
particular aspect of one's own, or of corporate behaviour, however noble it
may be (e.g. more warmth, more room for learning, increased contribution
to general well-being) can block achievement of fundamental change. A truly
enlightened leader sees the needs of his organisation on all energy
levels.*

THE CHAKRA OF THE HEART – IN ALL CONNOTATIONS

The Heart Chakra, at the heart of a range of seven, is seated deep in the
chest, just in front of the spinal column, level with the physical heart.
The Sanskrit word *anahata* means 'unstruck', 'not produced' – in the sense
of existing in the inner world, not the outer.* This endows it with an
aspect of purity – the purity of love, devotion (pledged life energy) and
unselfish application.

This energy centre in the heart region is also the node in which all
opposites merge: body and spirit, man and women, higher and lower self,
inner world and outer world, beautiful and ugly, good and evil. The Heart
Chakra's principal attribute of 'love' brings forth self-acceptance, and
helps reconcile differences – both in one's make-up, and between one's
own and others'. Love is the great merging force, the Great Merger,
helping us to not just recognise, respect and reconcile differences, but to
transcend them; inspired by love, by the striving for a shared passion, a
common ideal. This is the essence of all true romance – it is also the
essence of what the corporate world needs to learn, to adapt to the chang-

* The first time Peter heard this word, was when his Indian music teacher, quoted in a previous
footnote, explained to him that you could not just sit down, pick up your sitar and start playing.
No, first one had to appreciate the difference between *ahat nada*, struck sound, such as produced
with instrument or vocal cords, and *anahat nada*, the unstruck sound that is heard in one's mind.
In the study of Indian classical music, which springs from meditation, from silence, the student
is taught to first hear the inner music, then go out into the physical world and produce it. This
is the transformational moment at which the spiritual descends into the material. As a result of
these teachings, the term *anahat* for him has become synonymous with 'done from within', 'done
from the purity of your heart'. It originates in the spiritual realm, and you, messenger of the gods,
carry it out into the world.

ing reality of a shrinking world, where, going beyond 'diversity', differences need to be *celebrated* to stimulate further growth.

Warning: Activation of the Heart Chakra can have far-reaching consequences, which tend to be irreversible. We are concerned here with processes beyond the control of logic, hard to manage by traditional means. A thorough understanding of the heart's unmanageable workings is essential for anyone going through major changes, or directing such changes in others.

A FORCE FOR THE GOOD

The Heart Chakra is the energy centre where we receive and radiate love. Proper functioning awards tremendous power, because love makes everything possible – at least nearly everything. Love is the Great Empowerer, *and* the Great Merger. It makes people perform the most altruistic deeds, to the point of sacrificing their own lives for others. Living in love is empowering because we feel supported, carried aloft by our loved ones – and even by total strangers who manage to make a connection at the heart level, often in the first split-second of meeting. This instant connection is manifested in mutual trust, acceptance, empathy, and the deep-felt wish that the other may do well. Recognition of this mutuality tends to come with smiles ready to break through, first betrayed by the corners of the eyes. It is found in all cultures that we have come across, from the most advanced to the most primitive.

The most empowering aspect of love is the sacrificial. Hence the heart's traditional association with courage. A man driven by love goes through fire. So does a woman of course, and there are no reliable statistics as to which sex scores better in the sacrifice department, though many women would not want to even argue the point. They feel that self-sacrifice in men is widely celebrated (hero worship) only because it is so rare. Certainly, many of women's greatest achievements have come from this hugely powerful energy source. They have fought battles that would have exhausted their men, because they were fired by that greatest of all powers, as yet little tapped in the corporate world, the power of the heart.

Leaders who manage to develop this aspect of their personalities, can attain pretty much anything they set their mind to, because their will-driven energy of the Solar Plexus Chakra is subordinated to the higher level force of the Heart Chakra. As a result, the willpower is given a clear direction: not downward towards the lower chakras with their reproduction and survival issues, but upwards, towards self-realisation, and beyond that to a self-image that comprises the whole universe, and may lead to devotion to a higher purpose.

When the Heart Chakra is not doing much, or not enough to make a difference, it may be subtly opened by the development of tolerance – the warm acceptance of people as they are, and events as they occur. An acceptance, it should be mentioned, preached by Buddha 2500 years ago, several of his contemporaries, and by many spiritual leaders since. Its essence is the acceptance of all that occurs, all waves and wavelets in the river of life, without any attempt at valuation, leave alone emotional reaction. (The growth step here is to go from conditional to unconditional love of the universe we find ourselves in.)

When the Heart Chakra is fully open, there is all-encompassing love, productive of a deep serenity – even at moments of great upheaval, in acute danger, and under conditions of general panic. The serenity springs from the realisation that beyond giving yourself entirely, there is nothing you can do. It endows people in leadership positions with an empowering realisation of the ancient rule: 'all work done for others, is work well done'.

The natural feeling at the heart level is a radiating warmth. When we open ourselves to the heart force and feel its warming, nurturing glow in our chest, then we are united with the source of all life. This sense of union in love produces happiness, and the courage to shoulder challenging undertakings. We feel peaceful and fortified, and go out into the world to manifest ourselves as a force for the good.

THE CHAKRA OF INSIGHT INTO HUMAN NATURE

The Heart Chakra is also the seat of our insight into human nature. It instantly senses the heart energy of others, and rates it. Failing a specific terminology for chakra energy, we settle for the approximation of temperature: 'Ah, great!' we feel, 'someone with a warm heart!' Or the opposite: 'Oh boy, what a cold-hearted fellow!' This sensing of heart 'temperature' is one of a range of communicative phenomena that we collectively call intuition.

Every energy centre makes its own contributions to our intuitive capacity. We have the Root Chakra's presentiment of life-threatening events, proven by thousands of documented cases; the widely acclaimed gut-feeling of the Sacral Chakra; the lucid moments and stunning epiphanies of the Third Eye Chakra; the Throat Chakra's instinctive appreciation of truth in speech and conduct, with instant detection whether something is spoken (or done) in truth or not; and the Crown Chakra's sensitivity to inner peace or lack of it in others.

There is a potential weakness at this energy level for people who have spent much of their lives in environments where impulses from the heart are not generally valued, or even considered a proper subject for discussion. Allowing for possible exceptions that we can't think of right now, one does not gain insight into human nature by treating humans like resources, like units of production, animals, tools, robots or furniture – none of which unheard of in corporate environments, be it in business, politics, armed forces, health care or even organised charity. Instead of providing insight, such conduct makes us callous; it creates a tough, resilient layer around the heart which prevents it from receiving and radiating warmth. For people in a position to lead others, full restoration of the innate intuitive faculty at the heart level, which in the course of a hard fought career may have been dulled by years of discounting, is of great importance.

Some of the most restorative activities one can undertake are travel through unknown parts, preferably under more primitive conditions than we are used to, and reading the great masterworks of literature, ideally of course during such travel. Much of the world's enduring literature – even when written from the gut – deals with the realm of this chakra, in recognition of the fact that matters of the heart tend to touch us deeply. Other chakras too play their parts on life's stage, but generally the heart has the leading role.

Contemporary bestsellers like Houellebecq, Nobel laureate Jelinek, Easton Ellis and others of the Brat Pack, who write the heart out of the script, deny it its ruling position or display downright cynicism about love, still shock us (after all these years …), and typically enjoy their success largely on the strength of this capacity to shock, *vide* Jelinek. By their denial of love as the ruling force of the universe, they figuratively stab us in the heart – cleverly hooking into the epidemic of adrenalin addiction of our society. But they leave readers with a hollow feeling, a perverse excitement that is hard to put to gainful use, or disgust with the human race.

Few people are happy to have sadness, depression, disgust and nihilism poured into them on a regular basis – and those who do should seriously consider therapy. It is hard therefore to see how heartless literature can endure, because what shocks today, no longer shocks tomorrow, and in fifty years it is likely to ring hollow, devoid of that force to grab the whole of us, starting with the heart, that the great masters developed thousands of years ago, when the great stories of mankind first began to be written.

Anyone who would like to increase his or her insight into human nature can start right there, with the *Gilgamesh Epos* and the *Ramayana*, move on to the *Odyssey*, to *Layla and Majnoun*, the *Tale of Genji* and work his way up to *Anna Karenina* and *Pride and Prejudice*. The alternative is to jump right into Dostoyevsky, in whose oeuvre all human types are represented – with rich and merciless detailing, drawn with a burin as fine as Albrecht Dürer's, showing every wrinkle, dimple or twinkle – plus the dramatic consequences of bringing such types together in various constellations.

The phenomenon is wider than just literature of course. Again with some provision for exceptions, it is fair to say that all great art touches the heart. Works that do not are rarely more than intellectual tours-de-force, stylistic exercises, or fashion statements, their cunning creators performing variations of Tom Wolfe's Boho Dance (the phenomenon he ridiculed in *The Painted Word*,[89] a biting critique on soulless art), 'in which the artist shows his stuff within the circles, coteries, movements, isms, of the home neighbourhood'. Purely cerebral art, like Vasarely's geometrical studies that were all the rage in corporate offices in the 1980s, are striking at first sight, but emotionally sterile – soon leading to indifference. Bartók's piano sonatas may excel at making neurons spark, but few will shed a tear over them, feel lifted to seventh heaven, or have them on that famous pack list for a deserted island.

But when we hear Mozart or Dvorák, who poured out their hearts, when we read Claus, the Flemish giant who appears to have lived through every heartache and celebration of his characters (and would have had the Nobel Prize ages ago if selecting him weren't potentially divisive in a country locked in a language struggle), or when we see *Gone with the Wind* on the big screen – oh yes! Anyone seen the tissues? Unlike art that provides a mere intellectual spark (temporarily useful to impress others in conversation) the effect of art with heart persists, often for a lifetime.

This is why millions attended the funeral of Oum Khalsoum, the legendary star of Cairo whose songs laid bare the heart of her people, her suppressed and suffering people, her proud and strong and loving people. You don't have to know much Arabic to realise that in the end *love* is all she sings about: '*Habeeb* ...!' This is also why similar crowds blocked Lisbon to see Amália Rodrigues to her grave, the singer who had poured out the Portuguese heart during its time of oppression; and why Amsterdam Arena overflowed to send off André Hazes, singer of popular laments, no voice, but all heart. Artists with similar vocal cords but no such heart are lucky if at the end enough people show up to fill the first three rows in the chapel.

THE CHAKRA OF TURNAROUND

Every great leader is also an artist, in the sense that – as Obama does so effectively – he has to transport us, take us to a higher level, make us see the world with new eyes, give us new energy to face the world and shape it. Art for that reason is highly relevant to our subject. The art forms most topical for our study of enlightened leadership, are those depicting a transformation – a process that takes place in the realm of the Heart Chakra. This is the energy centre of love, but by extension also of turn- around – which takes place as the heart is discovered, freed to operate to full capacity, and begins to inform the personality, dictating new conduct.

Countless memorable art works have been created on the basis of these simple but ever so powerful psychodynamics, and many moving movies. Hard, calloused protagonist finds, or is made to find his heart, and turns his life around, leading to happiness ever after. Or, at the very least, he is found to be not so bad after all, a person with many shortcomings, but not heartless. (Women too play such parts, but there are not many of them, perhaps because few women – not a derogation but a compliment – can credibly portray someone bereft of feeling.) But few of such magnificent stories of transformation are set in the corporate world. An exception is the movie *Jerry Maguire*, with Tom Cruise and Cuba Gooding Jr, whose characters both, in each in his own way, learn to live from the heart: 'Show me the money, baby!' Why is this theme so popular? Because deep down inside we all hope that it will happen to us: that something will give us such a staggering jolt that we burst out of our armoured shell, and allow our oppressed heart to take over our lives.

Fortunately, there are numerous indications that in the corporate world something is changing which may reduce the thickness of armour people go to work in. Thousands of men and women in leadership positions are now discovering that life in heartless environments – such as created in the Age of Endarkenment when we allowed ourselves to be led by prophets Taylor, Friedman, and Carr – leaves one bitterly cold, and ultimately unsatisfied. Many others who are still satisfied perpetuating cold-bloodedness (business is business), and seek instead to warm themselves at the bonfire of profit share and bonus, are bound to discover that in the near future, in which talent will be so scarce that you have to pray for it on your knees,[90] heartlessness is likely to become a disqualifying handicap for all senior positions.

Even the *Economist*, not a breeding ground of softies, in a special report on the scarcity and thus value of talent, noted the need for heart, though from a rather pragmatic impulse. Towards the end of the lead article: 'And the talented would do well to intervene in this debate on the side of the disadvantaged. [...] Most societies will tolerate the idea of well-rewarded winners, as long as there is equality of opportunity and the losers also clearly gain something from the system.'[91] A missed opportunity to speak from the heart? Or an editor, editor-in-chief John Micklethwait presumably, speaking from the heart under the guise of pragmatic advice? If so, let us join the chorus. Where corporate self-interest helps promote the human cause, we are all for it.

Now let's look at some common scripts in which the Heart Chakra plays a central role:

- *The Hard Nut To Crack*
  In this scenario someone makes an emotional turnaround, usually precipitated by a crisis. Ogre turns into loving guy, miser becomes generous, envious person kindness herself. And the rule is: the hardest nuts crack the loudest. See for instance the pathologically selfish bad

apple portrayed by Jack Nicholson in the movie *As Good As It Gets*, whose heart is melted by a little dog dropped on him under threat, and does well in secret. Or the hard-nosed airport manager in *Terminal*, who, after weeks of iron protocol-upholding and badgering, for one crucial moment opens his heart just a crack, and lets the stateless traveller played by Tom Hanks escape from limbo to the jazzy New York that the poor man has set his heart on.

- *Courage on Land, at Sea and in the Air*
Sacrificing oneself for some ideal or other – or just for an idea. Note: whether or not the ideal in question is benign or malign is not at issue. Thousands have been praised for their valour in mass murder. Think of the highly decorated leaders of the German *Sonderkommandos* who braved killing frost and their own disgust following the front eastwards to exterminate the Jews; think of the equally awarded French, Dutch and Portuguese officers who lost their limbs in the colonial wars of oppression; the Japanese kamikaze pilots; the lauded heroes of the Vietnam war; or, from the hard-line Islamic perspective, the unsung heroes who flew into the Twin Towers. Leaders often stimulate the Heart Chakra while firing up their men. Acute problems arise when victims do the same: 'Please, if you have a heart, spare my wife and children. ...'

- *Complete Devotion*
Often found in situations where the female element predominates. Mother love, sister love, the daughter who gives up all chances of happiness to care for a sick mother. But devotion is found among men as well, as unforgettably told in Tolstoy's story *Master and Man*. A rich man and his servant are travelling by sleigh in pursuit of a business interest that the master feels strongly about. So strongly, that when the weather worsens, he presses his man to keep going, straight into a snowstorm, which soon overwhelms them. While they are freezing to death in the sleigh, the master, in a redemptive act of devotion, covers his man's body with his own, and dies saving his life.

- *The Ruin of the Heartless*
The slow, but inexorable demise of people without heart is a common theme in world literature. A magisterial example is Stendhal's *Scarlet and Black*, where a woman gives her heart to a man who does not deserve it. His life ends in ruin, his high hopes for advancement by

cunning unfulfilled. Llosa's *Feast of the Goat*, is a thrilling tale of the downfall of the Dominican tyrant Trujillo, a heartless monster: men out for revenge creeping up on him out of the pools of spilled blood, brothers of tortured ministers, fathers of raped virgins, till no one can be trusted anymore, and victimhood becomes inevitable.

- *Living on with Bleeding Heart*
  Sometimes people get maimed so badly that the hurt never stops and the Heart Chakra no longer functions. This usually leads to tragic collapse, but in stories with a happy end someone will appear on the stage who gives so much love, so unselfishly, that the attenuated energy centre revives. In life this is more rare than in the arts.

A PRIVATE EXAMPLE

Peter says: 'Because I work mostly in countries other than where I live, I need to take many flights. To deal with this necessary evil, I early on accustomed myself to a purely functional attitude: I am here at the airport to have my body transported, and that's it. Living cargo, a suitcase that doesn't go on the belt, but moves by itself. Like most other business travellers I spin myself into a cocoon, and spend the waiting time reading; brilliant stuff preferably, but anything really, even a *Daily Mail* left on some seat – just so I won't have to be where I am, and can gracefully avoid contact with all those other people milling around me, not even being aware of them, ideally.'

'All over the world businessmen and businesswomen scurry around airports in the same way, self-contained parcels of vitality trying to make their way between the hordes of tourists as efficiently as possible, while struggling to keep up the spirit. The most extreme form of this encapsulation is probably found on the New York subway: 'thousands of people tightly packed together, all carrying an invisible DO NOT DISTURB sign, radiating dissociation from reality and their own humanity, their beings veiled by a grey, silky film of tough fibre. "If you strip it all away, yes I am human underneath, but for the moment let's keep pretending I am not."'

'It is a token of my own urgent need to open up the heart that I fell to such behaviour as well. But one day something odd happened, without any apparent cause or reason, which taught me a valuable lesson. I came to the gate, saw that we were delayed half an hour, found a seat and was about to unfold my newspaper, when instead I looked around me at the other waiting passengers – mostly tourists on their way home – and suddenly became intensely aware of their humanity. All brothers and sisters, deeply related with me through time, and through our struggle for survival, our need for safety and belonging, and so on up the pyramid. Most appeared to be tired. Fatigued by the days of compressed happiness, though still enjoying the afterglow; or tired with that profound exhaustion caused by a bleak life, from which a temporary escape had been bought, but which would be lying in wait for them upon return.'

'I opened myself to them, emotionally as well as mentally, and couldn't help entering into the intimate arrangements and the nitty-gritty of their lives. There was an old English couple, longing to go back home, knitting their hands as they sat waiting. I saw them in their draughty council flat, knelt in front of the gas meter, and dropping in a coin – their last one, going by the mood. A young couple lay sprawled across a bench, resolute to maintain the libido level built up on the beach, though I noticed part of him slip off already, eager to mount his Kawasaki instead.'

'Then there was the old man next to them, still gasping for breath from the exertion of getting his belt looped after he had to take it off for the security check. I had a vision of him lying in a hospital bed, all rigged up with tubes and wires, and felt sure that he was having the same vision. When he met my eyes he realised that I saw into his fear, into the very depth of it, and turned away beaten. Knowing he would look again, I tried to radiate peace, acceptance. When he did I gave him a slight nod of confirmation: "Yes, I am aware of your condition and prospects. Perhaps it helps you to know that you are not alone." The old man looked at me puzzled, but somehow relieved.'

'Next to him sat a woman with slightly bulging eyes, who appeared engrossed in a crossword puzzle but never wrote a word. I saw her standing before a window high up in a towering building, in the same flowery dress, staring into space, and sinking into inconsolable sadness. I became engulfed by something akin to compassion, but closer to concern, combining an acute consciousness of the others' pain and a readiness to share it, though as yet no urge to come forward.'

'I suddenly noticed that I felt much better than before. There was no longer that haste to escape from an ordeal. And everything went much smoother than normal: during boarding everyone was friendly and considerate, there was a lot of eye contact, smiles passed all around, there was patience with one another ... Transformed, I sank into my 1C. On arrival, in the train to Amsterdam Central Station, the warm glow endured, and at the taxi stand where you'd normally have to fight through a gang of North-African hustlers eager to stuff you into a car with a buddy who will rip you off, the first driver I gave the nod was willing to go where I wanted, and go on the meter. The heart had been opened, and life was good ...'

Many of us have moments like these, at least we suspect so. (The cynic will say, 'Yeah sure, we all get sentimental at times.') Ideally of course we should be like this all the time. But our society has many sharp corners, rough at the edges, so that we often tend to open our hearts less than would be desirable for a more humane world. That is why it is of such great importance to work towards a world with softer edges – a more loving world, if that word is allowed one more time – because the softer the world we find ourselves in, the easier it becomes to open up our hearts and contribute our own love.

We believe we are now seeing the contours of such a world being drawn. It is exciting to note that many leadership thinkers and corporate leaders from all over the world are contributing to the development of a new outlook and a new business model in which money is no longer the absolute monarch, and the heart ascends the throne (or at least isn't kicked out of court, as business gurus of old advised).

Call us idealists if you want, we can take it. Because even seeing our own, in our case severe, shortcomings, we remain optimistic that, finally outgrowing the cave-dweller's mindset, our race is currently entering an upward spiral towards more recognisably human shape. And by the way: like us, many of these thinkers, dreamers and planners are convinced that this model will prove much more profitable than the old.

LEADERSHIP WITH HEART POWER

Any leaders who operate with the Heart Chakra wide open have a significant advantage over others who do not: people follow them much more willingly than someone in whom they don't feel any warmth. You can be ever so brilliant or charismatic, if people do not feel that you are there for them, they will not lift a finger for you – at least not without threat, coercion or pay rise.

A striking example of leadership with Heart Power is provided by our friend John K., who runs a division of a high-tech company that outperforms other divisions year on year, serving blue-chip accounts that stay with him forever. People often think that John must be a really smart cookie to be always involved in such super deals, but the secret of his success lies not in his smarts. John is successful simply because he is such a truly nice guy – especially towards his employees, always supportive and mindful of their needs. As a result they support him with all their hearts, and compete as to who can serve his clients better.

Much of our work is aimed at promoting such leadership – and we have found that the best way of doing that, is to present its business case: *why does it make business sense?* We hope that this book will serve that purpose, and we say that with a sense of urgency. Let us repeat therefore:

The chief challenge for corporate leaders in this day and age of globalisation and diversification is to recognise, respect and utilise the power of the heart, because as human beings we are becoming ever closer to one another, both physically and in terms of knowledge and shared (media) experience, and cannot therefore keep our hearts closed to others without causing conflict, disruption and impoverishment.

If this challenge is met, the power of the heart can be the driving engine of a new phase of human development. After thousands of years of negation, suppression and manipulation in the market place, love is still out there, ready to empower those individuals and organisations who have the courage to accord it its deserved place in their lives.

MARKS OF A HEALTHY HEART CHAKRA
- compassion
- empathy
- altruism, charity
- the ability to forgive
- the ability to forgive oneself
- courage

- focus, not on confrontation, but on harmony
- reliability.

SYMPTOMS OF A BLOCKED HEART CHAKRA

- heartlessness in feeling, thought and action
- remoteness, coldness, arrogance
- shyness
- incapacity to forgive, remorse
- difficulties in dealing with grief: clinging to it, wallowing in it
- selfishness
- jealousy
- conditional love
- uncontrolled outbursts (such as raging at employees)
- breach of trust
- emotional dependency, leeching off others' emotions, clinging
- sentimentality (indulgence in cheap warm feelings without attendant commitment).

Place on earth: The Heart Chakra is very alive in places 'with a heart' – cities like Paris and Rome, Porto and Cairo, Bombay and Rio de Janeiro, New Orleans before Katrina, Venice before mass tourism. Communities that are spiced with a vital, crude type of humour that helps people to reconcile themselves with their fates, and where laughter and popular songs ring out in the streets, albeit drowned out these days by the claxons of taxis. Old cities most of them, ideally older than time, like Benares, where for thousands of years an endless chain of generations has lived and loved; where blood and sweat have drenched the flagstones, people of all ages have laughed and cried and gone stark raving mad; where the struggle for life with bosses and landlords was fought from decrepit tenements; where robbery was done from hunger and murder committed from passion; where all forms of lust have been indulged in and all senses explored; where insanity grew like mould on the walls, genius blossomed in quiet courtyards and poetic minds took flight from rooftop terraces; where mothers pushed and shoved to get the best for their children, and children took pride in supporting their parents in every deed and endeavour, legal or otherwise; where hope and despair knew each other intimately, and friends and foes embraced on meeting; where between all the fighting, envy and hate, the love grew that makes people pay a fortune to live there. Places one can leave only at the cost of deep nostalgia, at unguarded moments delivering a stab in the chest that brings tears to our eyes. Such are places of the heart.

Exercise: Go among people you would not normally seek the company of, and try to experience their humanity; try to feel the beating of their hearts, and open yourself to the feeling they invoke in you. Go amble beside a garbage truck for a while and try not to block impressions that you find disagreeable: the smells, the rough menial labour, the workers' poverty, transparent from their need to do this kind of work. Or go stand in a commuter train or rush-hour city bus without secreting yourself in a cocoon of disinterest. Make the whole bus your cocoon, and feel your connectedness with all the other living cells in it. (When doing this exercise on the Paris *metro* near Gare du Nord, or a Line 3 streetcar in Amsterdam, keep a hand on your wallet, because a big heart does not need to make you into a sucker.)

Other suitable locations are large railway stations and airports, preferably during the holiday season. Also all places where masses gather with which you have no intrinsic connection (such as shared background, shared purpose, shared taste). So when you are a sports fan, this exercise will not work during the game, as you sit huddled up with buddies, surrounded by people wearing the same colours – but so much the better after the match, ideally after a home field drubbing, while going out the gate mixed with supporters of the winning team. Open your heart to the humanity of these cheering losers and give them the love you give your own relatives and buddies. If this works, congratulations, your Heart Chakra is running at top capacity.

But seriously, if you really manage this opening of the heart towards utter strangers from many layers of society, you are patently gifted with great energy at this crucial middle level – a great indicator of success. Others who are similarly endowed will notice this heart force in you, and give you their own in support.

COURAGE AND CAUTION, PASSION AND CONTROL

A word about the Chief Challenge, above. The risk of using the almost inevitable word balance, on account of its allusion to scales, is that we revert back to the linear paradigm that the enlightened leader has put behind him or her – or tries to put behind, because there are trapdoors of the ego at all levels. He or she does not think or feel that if one thing comes up another needs to go down, as literal interpretation would suggest. We use the word balance here in the larger sense of full reconciliation. The enlightened leader pours out the inner feelings of his or her heart while at the same time checking it with all the other energy centres.

We have seen where courage leads when it is not integrated with a dose of caution. Bush with great display of valour invaded Iraq, blaming his political friends Chirac and Schroeder that they were too cautious. Too much caution and too little courage and nothing happens for years. Too much courage and too little caution and you annihilate one tyrant, but create ten new ones in the process. When you climb a tree to relieve a ball for your child, you show courage by the mere onset of the action, and enlightenment by doing it so cautiously as to not fall down and break your neck.

Success comes from a harmonious interplay involving all seven notes of the scale, all subtly tuned to resonate with one another like the sympathetic strings, so called, of a sitar. With a properly functioning Heart Chakra, courage is reconciled with reason (in the form of caution), with intuition and with a larger sense of self. Its manifestation is driven by willpower, advanced through relationships, while survival is secured by a well rooted material process: the steady conversion of human energy, social needs and inventiveness into wealth.

Now we might question: is an enlightened leader a passionate person, or rather a person who controls his or her display of emotions? At first sight we recognise two extreme types. Passionate leaders without reason, who are known as neurotics. And overly controlling leaders without emotions, who are known as robots or control freaks. Both types are unsuccessful in a multi-cultural environment. Virgin's Richard Branson, spectacularly successful in such an environment, derives his success from his ability to continuously check his passion with reason, with intuition and gut feeling, with a universal vision, and so on, all along the range of energy levels, full spectrum. And boy, does he make money.

Richard Branson comes across as a near perfect example of the kind of leadership advocated in this book. Though he is a strong personality whose personal reputation is very much the brand, a brand which unites the disparate units of his empire, he remains a strong exponent of participation. Because of his dyslexia he must rely on others to supply skills he lacks, and explain complex operations. He is very much an 'ideas man', yet we find him constantly at the sharp end – on one occasion dressed as a can of Virgin Cola in Tokyo's main railway station. He is a strong exponent of enlightened leadership and when travelling on Virgin Atlantic, he serves meals with the cabin staff instead of relaxing in Upper Class. A great believer in ceaseless innovation, he encourages staff in all his companies to come up with entrepreneurial business ideas, many of which he spins out, using a mixture of his own equity funds and their own.

Branson's motto is 'Have fun!' and business after business is built around colourful ideas like 'Virgin Brides'. He explains that when employees enjoy being with each other, an atmosphere and a culture are created that customers enjoy. He scrupulously avoids bureaucracy by dividing companies that grow too big, and having them compete against each other instead of getting all fat, their arteries clogged up with organisational blubber. He is a great believer in informal, intimate behaviour. He also has a great nose for a narrative or story, whether he is bidding to run Britain's national lottery, fighting against British Airways, or rescuing a BA crew from Kuwait who were trapped by the Iraqi invasion. He devised a plan to blow up land mines using blimps, in honour of Princess Diana's campaign, and defuses criticism by telling hilarious self-deprecating stories, cf. his autobiography *Losing My Virginity*.[92]

Branson deliberately courts controversy and turbulence whether he is aloft in his balloon, or trying to save the Concorde from being mothballed. Again and again he emerges unscathed, even when his bid fails, as did his offer to run the National Lottery at no profit. His big-heartedness wins him much public sympathy. When he found out that shareholders might prevent him from being as generous to employees and customers as he felt appropriate, he bought back the shares and returned his companies to private ownership. That is how the heart does its work. Love may not work wonders, but it works.

Our hero is now about to enter space tourism with his Virgin Galactic, working hand in hand with that other intrepid explorer, Burt Rutan of Scaled Composites, to create commercial space flight for ordinary millionaires – suborbital as yet, but still … Again, there is radiant heart energy in this project, and if you can bring the same amount of heart to what you are doing, you are in great shape.

HEART POWER AND THE LACK OF IT

We recently interviewed higher and middle level managers in a company in a developing country, owned by a giant a continent away, where the local, mostly expat, management complained bitterly that employees were not loyal. 'We train them, invest in them, and as soon as they see an opportunity they skip, preferably to a firm in the developed world.' The country happened to be a dictatorship, universally reviled, and the top of the company was widely regarded as not simply friendly to, but part of the regime. (The government in fact had 51% of the shares, granting its foreign 49% partner just a 15 year licence to operate – a heartless arrangement not uncommon in dictatorships.) We talked to two dozen managers, a quarter of them in one-on-one interviews, some of them in the back of taxis with linguistically challenged drivers. We estimate that about 80% of the managers hated the regime. One exclaimed bitterly: 'It is horrible! We are ruled by our enemies!' The only way out for them was to do so well in their jobs that one day they could get a job abroad. This was their one and only motivation. To illustrate what happened here at heart level: the HR director had a finger printing apparatus sitting on a wing of his desk.[93]

As you roam through the bloodstream of global companies, you run into companies like this sooner or later. The first signal of a serious lack of love may not be gloom and doom. In this particular company, people had a gangy, clubby thing going and celebrated birthdays with huge cakes and plenty of laughter. The first signal of heart problems was the suspicion we felt at the start of the one-on-one interviews, the querying look: what is this guy coming over here for? To check and report on me, or screw with my mind?

If you are okay, the second signal you receive that something is deeply wrong, is the palpable sense of relief when it is established that you can be trusted, that you have a heart, that you are for real. At that blossoming moment the Heart Chakra just flashes, releasing tons of energy. The more the heart is held in the iron grip of tyranny, the more courage enters the blood stream – till you say things to a visitor from afar that could get you hung if a colleague overheard you.

Another third world company we recently visited distributed, let's say, pumps and related equipment. They had been bought by a Qatari conglomerate two years ago. The Qataris felt that the local company was not performing, and were wondering why. Growth was nowhere near as steep as it had been before, and we were to appraise the local company's corporate culture, essentially to see what was needed to inject more energy, to get more employee engagement. We ran a survey asking participants to describe the strengths and weakness of the company in a few keywords. There were many submissions like 'strong', 'leading', and 'powerful' but also quite a few like 'manipulative', 'heartless', 'money oriented'. Several participants had not stuck to keywords but written short phrases like 'financial arrangements', 'no commitment', 'you are merchandise'. We thought they were complaining about the salary level, like others who were doing so explicitly. It was only in the interviews that we found out how bad the situation really was at heart level: everyone we spoke to, including the expat CEO, saw the deal as purely financial, a purchase like so many others, of some money generating and therefore marketable, commodity-like entity, to be sold again any time to a party willing to pay a better price. They were all sure that the new owners would be Chinese, and feared the worst.

Two years ago a colleague told us about his latest assignment at a European frozen foods company. A private equity company, let's call it STI Ltd., had bought the business for under a billion euros, and planned to turn it around by selling off redundant production units, firing 20% of the staff, brushing up the corporate identity, and reselling the lot in three or four years, aiming for a billion two. Top management stood to share a €30 million bonus, a second tier would share a projected €2 million, the rest of the employees could not look forward to any special reward. The bleeding had been taken care of, now it was time to work on vision, mission and values. We questioned the integrity of our colleague's approach: how could he seriously work on 'values' in a company whose sole management aim was to sell out to the highest bidder in four years? Fortunately he forgave us our bluntness.

A year later Trompenaars Hampden-Turner was approached by the directors of STI, asking us to do a management audit of their frozen foods business. Bottom-line results were disappointing and an employee engagement survey had shown up a saddening level of passion for the company. Remembering our colleague's work on values, we asked to what extent STI's plans for the future might be known. 'Oh, everybody knows that, I guess,' STI's managing director said breezily.

'Might there be,' we ventured to ask, 'a causal relationship between your aim to sell and the low employee engagement score?'

The managing director looked at us puzzled.

'You know,' we could not help saying, 'generally, people are more likely to engage with a company whose values they share, than with one whose one avowed aim is to make money out of them ...'

But that was so heartless. One could see them suffering. On the other hand, it was kind of courageous, and as every consultant knows, in the end you make more by telling clients what they *need to know* than by telling them what they *like to hear* – because paradoxically, with all that heart you build up a reputation as a tough one.

HEART CHAKRA WIDE OPEN: ARCHETYPE MANOUS D. – MATERNAL LOVE AND COURAGE

Manous D. is a self-made lady who made good. In her twenties, travelling around India and Nepal for many years with a toddler (who grew up on the road into a wise and streetwise young girl), she displayed both a marked gift for organisation and a big heart, manifested in almost universal hospitality. Whether she settled in Goa, Kathmandu – Pashupatinath of course – or Benares, her house was instantly transformed into the local meeting place for travellers; because Manous' was where a doctor would be found if you needed one urgently, where the parties were held that everyone went to, and where, if you were alone and strung out, you would find motherly care and a place to sleep, if only on the veranda if you came in peak season.

In those days, Manous was chronically low on money, but it was common knowledge among even the poorer travellers, some of them flagrant leeches, that under Manous' roof you might have to learn Tibetan Buddhist meditation, but at least you would not starve to death. And should you be interested in road stories, Manous herself could give you an earful, because everything you had done, she had done – but further, higher, and more solitary. (Like a six week crossing through the Himalayas from Lahul Spiti to Ladakh during which she rarely dipped below 16,000 feet, all with that toddler.) Though she might at first glance come across like just a winning girl, blond and bouncy and with radiant smiles, anyone observing her a little closer would see a full-grown woman, ready to make her contribution to the world.

In her thirties, still in India, Manous organised cooperatives of village women to produce, after her own design, highly labour intensive clothing – with sequins, appliqué, embroidery, weavings with supplementary weft in silver or gold – which she sold to boutiques in Paris, London and Los Angeles for serious money; so serious that she could pay her workers extremely well for local standards and still come out ahead.

She now runs a fashion house in Paris, built up in the '80s and '90s from a back room in a *souterrain*, to an entire floor off Avenue Montaigne, serving a world-wide clientele. A large part of her business grew from her big heart. Both buyers and suppliers know that Manous always gives them a good deal. Still, the business doesn't make her as rich as could be expected. Partly because of those generous deals, leaving only a small margin for profit, partly because her payment terms are almost criminally soft (if you consistently don't pay, shipments will ultimately stop, but that can take a year) and employees who do not perform can hang in there forever as long as they have a good yarn or manage to invite pity. As a leader, she is both inspiring and demoti-vating: always brimming with ideas, but if you do not feel like execut-ing them, it is ultimately up to you, she'll just ask someone else. She is loved by her employees, in a selfish sort of way, but insufficiently respected.

The fact that Manous still manages to get so much done, is not just achieved by the power of her wide open Heart Chakra, but also by her Sacral Chakra: her embeddedness in a network of personal contacts span-ning numerous countries, both developed and developing; people who may come in the door any day with an idea, an order, a crazy new fabric, another contact. And then there is her Root Chakra: many corporate leaders could benefit from a study of the way she manages to keep upright, all alone under constantly changing conditions, often very tough, and from her capacity to survive on nothing but her own physical strength, endurance and toughness of spirit.

Yes, Manous is a true survivor, but her definition of survival lies at rock bottom level (in her case found at 16,000 feet), so that she is not highly motivated to make more and more money, leave alone chase it. This gives her a high degree of inner peace, and an unstoppable strength – resulting in double digit growth year on year. In her little niche of highly labour intensive fashion creations, Manous D. by now is the largest in the world.

HEART CHAKRA SEIZED UP:
ARCHETYPE JOHN D. – THE POVERTY OF CUNNING

John D. is the CEO of a young IT-company, all of nine years old, in which he reigns supreme as last remaining founder. He has surrounded himself with half a dozen eager young hounds, specifically charged with achieving a turnaround after a recent crash in turnover followed by a disastrous reorganisation. The other two founders left when the going was good and are living in peace and wealth somewhere in Southern Europe. In truth they didn't so much leave as get shunted out by John, who was continuously picking quarrels with them, meanwhile keeping files on the exchanges, so that, should it come to litigation, if he couldn't prove negligence on the part of his partners, at least he would be able to show that the relationship had become irremediably unworkable.

John had simply wanted to be the boss, period. *And* he had wanted the largest slice of what he saw as an ever-growing pie. His partners' families suffered from the constant fights and tensions, not least of which the continual threat of an eruption which could mean the end of the business, and the end of the family income. John knew this, but kept up his scheming and haranguing, because the goal appeared to be in sight. When a foreign buyer showed up who liked the firm, but wanted to thin out the overhead – a profit enhancing move that John himself had vaguely hinted at during the negotiations – he 'resigned' to staying on board singly for the required five years, hanging on to half of his original one-third of the shares. Those shares, John figured, could easily gain 1000 percent over the period of his contract. A year later the dotcom-bubble burst. John D. took quick and, what he considered effective, measures. He cut fully one half of the 300 staff and hired the above-mentioned young managers.

Now the job is to make those shares of his worth something again. The hunting dogs smell the lack of loyalty which pervades the air-conditioned air of the office tower, and adapt to the atmosphere. They are going for number one 24/7. In everything they do for John's company, they keep an eye out for better options, like a switch of sides. ... Some are giving his customers such sweet deals that he wonders if they aren't working for them already. He also keeps having very different opinions about strategy than the bright young managers that he has brought on board as directors, and worries that they are consciously preparing to ruin him. But okay, as long as they manage to bring enough cash flow to keep paying the banks ...

John D. now invites a top-shelf consultant to speak about a possible assignment, in order to pick his mind for free during the first meeting, in which he outlines the problems to be dealt with – 'and how would you deal with those, from your specific perspective? Well, I don't mean in detail, but in global terms, say a set of steps to be taken?' During this fishing expedition he omits a few crucial details, which obviates any possibility he might have had of obtaining useful information. He says the firm is doing rather nicely. But the market is not really going his way, and as the consultant knows, it can't be very sympathetic to a company which dumped half of its employees without even thinking. John knows that IT is a tough business, in which money speaks louder than anything, but he does not seem to know that even the toughest business still needs to be *granted* to you, to be *given*. And he may be respected in his field of business, with his Bentley Cabrio and all, but as 'The Man of Half Measures' he is hardly beloved.

Even as he speaks, familiarising the consultant with the company's ostensible condition, he is fully cognisant that the firm, all his 16.5 per cent of it, is tottering at the edge of the abyss. When he stands up and looks down from his rented twelfth floor on to the parking lot, perhaps to cast a loving glance on his gleaming vehicle, he sees the full depth of the abyss. By common accounting standards the value of his assets is down to practically zero. The consultant suspects that deep in his frozen heart John D. knows that zero is all he deserves.

5. THROAT CHAKRA: COMMUNICATION

Sanskrit name: Vishuddha Chakra
Aspects: communication, purity, community spirit
Location: throat, neck plexus, thyroid gland
Colour: blue
Element: ether
Sense: hearing
Right: the right to speak and be heard
Demon: lying
Figure: sixteen-petaled lotus
Maslow: level 5, need for self-realisation, integrating the levels 6
  and 7 defined in his later works

Personal Aspects

Favourable development: This is the chakra of communication, with purity as the underlying notion. In the Nada Yoga philosophy that has inspired the Chakras of Leadership, expression is called for only once purity has been achieved. A more profane equivalent is found in the popular expression; 'Oh Lord, please help me keep my big mouth shut till I know what I am talking about.' While reading this chapter keep in mind that in the philosophy which informs it, human beings are seen as godly in nature, and that therefore, with the exception of the mentally and socially deranged, expressing oneself, sharing one's inner wealth, is a good thing *per se.*

Purity, in Indian thinking, is never a given condition, such as the purity of a diamond, but always the result of an action: purification, the core of most Hindu, Jain and Parsee rituals. To achieve purity, *effort* needs to be made, often involving outward activities such as pilgrimage, baths, and rituals, but essentially an inner process directed at the removal of impurities, just as a dutiful housewife purifies the *ghee* (clarified butter) by spotting tiny particles and fishing them out. Another metaphor that recurs in classical descriptions of the Vishudda, is that of neutralising the effect of a poison with an antidote; all poisonous thoughts are absorbed and converted into positive, life-giving energy.

Purification at the level of communication is achieved by the development of an honest voice. Express all your emotions, values and ideas carefully, airing them consciously with your vocal cords. Do not be afraid to experience your inner content to the full, *and share it* to the full, including less 'noble' sentiments and ideas. Listen closely to your inner voice and learn to express it as well. Develop an intimate communication with yourself, in which you guide yourself to higher levels of consciousness.

In the ideal case, this cleansing process leads to an elevated state, so pure and delightful, so *shudda*, and so charged with energy, that we long to communicate it – with the ultimate goal of sharing this state of bliss with others, a hyper-charged form of communication generally known as evangelising.

Unfavourable development: This chakra gets choked by lying. The resultant effect is loss of communicative power. A most striking example, which rapidly acquired cult status, was created by the English actor Ricky Gervais in *The Office* series for the BBC: the self-seeking, self-defeating manager who cannot say a word without being disingenuous. As in: 'People look at me, they say he's tough, he was in the army, he's gonna be hard, by the book. But I am caring, and sensitive. Isn't Schindler's list a brilliant film?' Brilliant, indeed, as is Gervais' new awards-amassing series *Extras*. The same total choking of the Throat Chakra, which makes every word come out false.

Corporate Aspects

Favourable development: On a primal level, the Throat Chakra is the energy centre that determines how well we communicate. Speech is our dominant form of self-expression, and because man is a social animal, success in business, politics and many other fields of endeavour largely depends on our communicative powers. Highly talented people with weak communication skills rarely manage to make the most of their talents, whereas people with average endowment who are verbally gifted, often outperform early expectations.

On a higher level, the Throat Chakra may be seen as the nexus where a connection is made between our pure inner self and our physical body. The Throat Chakra is responsible for our desire to be a force for the good: to express values that transcend the fulfilment of personal needs and personal recognition and make a substantial contribution to society. This desire manifests itself in a drive to make the world a better place; the development of relational strength on the basis of content; community building; and internal cohesion.

Whenever we speak of our need for a sense of purpose, of our desire to make, through our daily work, a contribution to general well-being, we are sharing with the world a beautifully open Throat Chakra. This aspect plays a crucial role in the development of enlightened leadership.

In organisations, a properly functioning Throat Chakra is manifested in a positive, winning corporate personality, and a corporate culture based on shared values and vision.

Unfavourable development: As above. Lying chokes off this chakra. The resultant effect is loss of communicative power. This also applies to organisations – and in this age of transparency can have ruinous consequences.

> **Chief Challenge:** To master your own inner content and its expression in the outer world.

An inseparably related challenge is, to transpose the energy of the Heart Chakra to a higher level, at which work becomes an expression of inner growth.

THE CHAKRA OF A YEARNING FOR PURITY

The Throat Chakra is located in the throat, at the level of the neck plexus and the thyroid gland; close to the brainstem, our 'reptile brain'. The name stands for 'purification', a word that in Sanskrit has a very special place, because all Hindus, Jains and many Sikhs are obsessed with purity. To every Indian who has the least pretence of spirituality, or even just a nice bourgeois sense of self-worth, the morning and evening baths are holy rituals. And anyone who goes to the market to buy *ghee*, be it for the altar or for the kitchen, is interested, more even than in the taste, in the question if it is *shuddha*. (It is thinkable that this keen focus is maintained, not because purity is so central in Indian inner life, but because no country in the world has so much food adulteration.)

The multinational guru Bhagwan Shri Rajneesh, by all appearances not very pure himself, but a rich fount of traditional wisdom, has a beautiful explanation of the Throat Chakra in the hierarchy of seven: '... after love has happened there is purity and innocence – never before it. Only love purifies and only love – nothing else purifies. Even the ugliest person in love becomes beautiful.'[94]

THE CHAKRA OF COMMUNICATION – VERBAL AND NON-VERBAL

The Throat Chakra is also the chakra of the ears, both of the physical organs, and of our inner ear, our capacity to 'hear' what others are conveying without saying anything: what they think, feel, and try to communicate to us non-verbally. A properly working energy centre at the throat level improves this inner hearing, attenuation makes deaf or tone-deaf. Meditation on the Throat Chakra cleanses the mind of thinking, making it still and pure. Its energy source is our deep longing to receive and transmit universal values – to hear, speak, and be understood.

An Indian guru once told Peter, in the days when portable radios started to become popular in his country: 'Vishuddha is like a transistor radio which allows us to tune in to the thoughts of others, both up close and faraway.' Modern Indian masters' predilection for such utterances has not served them well, because many people take their words literally, and discard them as nonsense. No, you cannot sit down and meditate on your Throat Chakra, and just tune in to the thoughts of others by turning some inner dial. What *does* happen, at least to people who have their Throat Chakra wide open, is an awareness of feelings, thoughts and intentions before they are communicated.

'Very useful around the office,' our friend Robert said tauntingly, as we discussed this chapter over lunch. But we ended up agreeing that it is infinitely more valuable even in intimate relationships, and that such relationships themselves are the finishing schools for these very capacities. 'I don't even need to begin to tell Carla a story,' Robert said, 'because before I have spoken the first word, she knows that that is what it is, just a story. In the first few years sometimes I would go ahead and tell it anyway, but it was too depressing to see her amusement.' We wondered aloud if she might be telling *him* stories. 'Absolutely, and I love her for it. Because she can't do it without her please-forgive-me look, meaning I can get anything I want.'

The reason why Carla and Robert can 'hear' the true story, is that at the same time they are communing at a non-verbal level, a primal human capacity. Recent research makes scientists question if *Homo neanderthalensis*, that related species which modern man lived side by side with for a long time, and appears to have driven out of existence as little as 30,000 years ago – had speech at all. A definitive answer is expected from DNA research; facial features suggest that they did not. But surely, judging by the complexity of their social arrangements, like all proto-linguistic early humans they must have had a fairly effective way of communicating non-verbally before they developed speech, because (unknown to some evolutionary retarded specimens of *Homo sapiens* of the 'boss' variety) there is only so much that you can communicate with grunts and shrieks.

There is no reason to believe that our branch of the family of man lost its primal capacity to communicate without speaking, but every reason to believe that we pay it little attention, because speech is all the rage in our species. A properly functioning Throat Chakra keeps open the original channel, and during speech restores some of the content that gets lost in verbalisation. Vishuddha gives words their true force of expression, adding all of the unspeakable content that tends to disappear in the summarising, abstracting and inherently reductive process of verbalisation. Just as a poet evokes ideas and feelings in us without mentioning them by name, the Throat Chakra evokes a deeper understanding for the true content of what is being communicated.

NEXUS WHERE INNER AND OUTER WORLD MEET

The Throat Chakra is the connection between our inner being and the outside world. In the hierarchy of seven chakras it stands for the first level of consciousness that brings awareness of a higher intelligence, and of our interaction with this intelligence. It is the nexus where the physical world and the metaphysical world meet. (Should you be troubled by the notion of a metaphysical world, then just see the Throat Chakra as the place where your ideas meet the physical world.)

The Throat Chakra is the energy centre where the focus is effected that makes us into who we are, a cloud of atoms that hang out together for a while, united around a core of consciousness without which we would not be cognisant of these atoms, nor of anything else for that matter, animated by another sort of cloud or energy field: the one that keeps all those atoms from drifting apart, but which, in deference to materialists, we do not necessarily need to name.

A proper functioning of the Throat Chakra is of vital importance for success in life – particularly for success in terms of self-realisation, but also in the more mundane terms of 'doing well'. Communicative ability is a core requirement for success in almost any kind of endeavour that involves cooperation with others. So apart from writing books and sailing solo around the world, there aren't many ways to get ahead that do not wholly rely on the ability to understand others, and make yourself understood.

When Peter returned to Europe in the early 1970s after a long time in India, and found employment as a copywriter in an advertising agency, he heard someone remark admiringly about a colleague that she had a very big mouth, linking that anatomic feature directly to income: 'The bigger mouth takes the bigger bite.' This kept spinning around in his head for weeks, because he wondered a) whether it was true, and b) if it was desirable that someone with a big mouth amassed a lot of money, irrespective of what that mouth uttered. He had seen that happen in India as well, but not as a general rule, just as individual excesses; exceptions confirming the rule that to be able to be respected and heard, you need to be a master of silence. Most of the truly powerful Indians are soft-spoken. Need God raise his voice?

But in Western societies, the naive returnee found out, there indeed exists a strong correlation: all else being equal, the one with the biggest mouth does have the most influence, and consequently the greatest access to financial means. And as for the second question: no, this is not neces-sarily desirable. We would all be better off if most attention would generally go to individuals with plans that truly benefit the community, irrespective of the force of their voice, and that they would get preferred access to the material resources needed to implement their intentions. But alas… The creator really messed up here – perhaps to make life more thrilling.

The result of this screw-up is that many people, out of sheer opportun-ism, talk too loud and too insistently, so that words of wisdom spoken at a lower voice get drowned out. The enlightened leader develops a capacity to plug the ears for verbal violence (about as effective as Boules Quies; nice, but don't expect too much), and open his or her mind to more subtle voices and more subtle forms of communication.

During this process of opening up, known in many schools of inner growth, aspirants also get in touch with their inner voice, and experience the Throat Chakra in its most luminous capacity, as the centre where our spiritual selves inform our physical selves. Allowing this process to run its course has a transformational effect on the vocally handicapped, as the voice produced by the vocal cords now becomes an instrument of the inner voice. A very powerful voice, raised or otherwise, because it says, not what is convenient or expedient, but what the speaker (informed by her or his sense of connectedness, empathy, care, love) feels urged to say. It is a clean, pure voice, which rings clear because – unlike in dissimulation and other forms of messing about with the truth – the mind does not need to scheme and work overtime as the speaking is going on, but can devote itself entirely to optimally externalising the inner content. No voice fed only on the pursuit of personal benefit ever has that kind of force.*

Acquiring this kind of deeper voice predisposes one for a superb career. Truth-speaking is a capacity which any leadership worthy of the epithet 'enlightened' needs to embody, and those that practice it will come in ever greater demand, even in circles such as accounting and banking where various forms of deception, usually for the purpose of tax evasion or other fiddling (think due diligence), have traditionally been pervasive. Opportunists are herewith alerted: integrity is the new buzz-word.

A fundamental principle of enlightened leadership is the idea that man is good by nature, at least not thoroughly rotten. In fact, in the philosophy underlying the Chakras of Leadership human beings are seen as godly in nature – part of a universal force that is all-powerful. From this perspective (excepting the mentally and socially deranged), expressing oneself is a good thing *per se*. As we have seen, the problem with endarkened leadership was that inner goodness was repressed – muted, to stay with the throat metaphor – in the service of ego-needs. Deep down inside

---

* Except, alas, when energised by psychopathy, when it turns into the kind of power that leads people into war.

we know exactly how best to apply our talents, but we block this knowledge because we perversely fear that living by it will limit our opportunities for financial gain, make us lose respect in the corporate community on account of what is seen as too soft an attitude, and so on.

The battle against our own endarkenment largely comes down to opening wide that Throat Chakra waiting to be heard, because it brings us in touch more intimately with our pure higher self, which goes through life basking in light, untouched and unpolluted by our worldly doings, just waiting to be tapped into. With all the defects we two have, like a love for the material (we both have a weakness for fine cars), we have the one advantage that we have been writing all our lives – and have therefore met both our higher and our lower selves on a daily basis. In a book like this, not a page can be written without deep involvement of the higher self, and frequent distraction and detraction by the lower self, particularly in the form of challenges: 'Oh come on, like you are such a great communicator ...!' Or worse: 'Oh really, dedicating yourself to some cause that transcends your own interest, that is the secret? Then what do *you* do on that score? Ah you write books, books with a message ... Right, of course, what unselfish dedication! Sorry I didn't immediately get the altruism.'

One might conclude that this would bring us to inner standstill, but that is not the case. We are just growing very slowly, from one phase to another. The net effect must in the end be uplifting, so we have figured, because the more you identify with the higher self in thought, speech (writing) and action, the less attractive the lower self's seductions appear; whereas, if you identify with your lower self, your higher self will appear as attractive as ever.

We do not feel compelled to provide an exposé here of our own inner struggles and provide a kind of public accounting of our spiritual state. *Chacun son gouffre...* The only thing we do feel compelled to, is to use our talents at least partly in an effort to strengthen the positive tendencies in human beings, starting with ourselves, and perhaps as a consequence also affecting others.

Connecting the inner and the outer world ... After the above exposé only the most cursory reader could fail to discover that the authors – like any author – are mostly writing about themselves. But before misunderstandings arise: we do not see it as the writer's duty to improve the world.

His only task is to externalise his inner being, to communicate it in all authenticity and fullness. To gutter-dwelling poet Bukovski, author of *These Words I Write Keep Me From Total Madness*, and *Junkie* author Burroughs, this meant exposing their desperate struggles with addictions, sexual perversions and other obscene weaknesses. Their unique quality lay in opening the throat wide and pouring out their inner selves without any inhibition, distortion or embellishment. (It doesn't have to be pretty to be great.) To us, at this moment, it means exposing our struggle with this theme of enlightenment: what it means to us, and what any enlightenment on our part could mean to the world.

Having said this, we shall retreat into the text again, remaining in the shadow of the letters, in the white spaces between the words, because in effect this is not about us, but about you – you who read this and may be right in the middle of your own struggle to be who you really are.

MARKS OF A HEALTHY THROAT CHAKRA
- truth speaking
- capacity to listen
- clarity of communication in speech and writing
- clarity in action (action in agreement with what others intuit about the inner being of the person performing the action)
- a powerful voice, well articulated speech
- the power to touch others in speech or writing
- musicality
- an aversion to chit-chat and pulp media.

SYMPTOMS OF A BLOCKED THROAT CHAKRA
- inability to express oneself adequately, introversion
- vocal dominance (speaking too much or too loud)
- vocal retention (speaking too soft, too timidly)
- lying and other manifestations of failing self-discipline
- troubled or poisoned inner life
- excessive secrecy about private matters, or breach of trust regarding secrecy promised others about private matters
- an uninspired life with little creativity
- little or no musicality, inability to be moved by music

- production of verbal muzak (babbling on, in a vain hope to suggest that there is a deeper connection)
- production of claptrap, twaddle, drivel and gossip.

Place on earth: To Peter, the Throat Chakra is intimately linked to a hill in Southern Portugal that we shall climb in another chapter. One of its striking features is a deep fold between two ridges, where the winter rains create hundreds of tiny rivulets, millions of litres gushing and gurgling down the hillsides. A few years ago he had a dam constructed in the bottom of that fold, to create an artificial V-shaped lake, and conserve as much as possible of that precious water. The reservoir is a refreshing addition to the dry interior. It sustains a fair number of frogs, which presumably boosted the snake population, which is good for the eagles, and so on. The partridge families love the convenience of a water source closer to home, and tortoises, who can smell water from miles away, are probably there already, waiting to be detected. The muddy bank between the bushes at the far end, rapidly became a favourite mud-bathing spot for the area's wild boar. With one earthmoving operation a whole little biotope was created, which, like the many other reservoirs in the area that farmers have built over the years, will gradually get integrated in the larger biotope of the foothills of the Monchique.

Around the little lake, an equally V-shaped road was bulldozed, so that now there is easy access to the innermost point of the fold, which formerly could be reached only by hazardous climbing. In Peter's words: 'I often go over to that spot in the still of night, to stand at the head of that silent little valley, shielded from the wind, and invisible to the world, but with a clear view of that world, lit by moonlight or starlight: a fertile river valley with orchards and fields and some widely set farmhouses, their white walls silvery in the cosmic light. As I stand there in the dark, the steep hillsides curve behind my back like a huge upturned collar, and on both sides they extend forward, sloping down away from me till the height of the dam near the bottom, enclosing the little lake like something precious. It is as if I have two huge arms that hold up a black mirror to the starry sky, or, when the moon is out, a glistening tray, to present to the world some glorious bounty, presumably the water itself.'

'At times, between the chirping of crickets, sounds the windblown bark of a dog, ragged and faded by its passage across the fields, then the screech of an owl or the rush of air under its wings. Sometimes when I stand there at the head of that still fold in the hills, with that collar of bushy slopes curved tight around me, I say to myself: "Do nothing." Repeat: "Do nothing." This to imprint on my mind that there is no need to meditate – or do anything for that matter. Just standing here, listening to the sound of the cosmos, is enough. When the urge overwhelms me I may chant the *mantra* "Om" (pronounced "Aum") that primal sound that the yogi uses to make his connection with the universal. Long and drawn out: "Auuuuummmmmmm." I hear the hillsides carry my voice outward, hear it strike the water and bounce off into the world. At this moment my inner voice and my vocal cords are speaking the same language. It brings with it a lucidity in which my consciousness is seen as a membrane that both separates and unites inner and outer.'

Exercise: The best place on earth to become more aware of your Throat Chakra, is your own body – if only because you have it with you at all times. So, whenever you are ready … The only thing you need to do, is to become conscious of your role as the actor who manifests your inner self in the outer world. From that consciousness flows a strong, clear manner of speaking: the voice of someone who says what he or she means, and *is* as he or she seems: what you see is what you get. Begin, therefore, by writing down some fundamental truths in the first person – a short list of statements you can back up to the hilt: 'I love chocolate', 'I am a writer', 'I broke my nose when I was sixteen …' (Just as when you are introduced to a lie detector, but this works the other way around, and is more reliable.)

   Start with simple things that you have no doubt about at all, and speak those lines out loud, ideally in front of a mirror, looking yourself in the eyes attentively. Check all your pronouncements: whether or not they feel good, and when one doesn't, strike it. Now go a little further and try statements like 'I always have the best interests of my co-workers at heart', 'I am a shining example to my peers', and 'People can trust me and do right by following me'. Again check how this feels. Then, after some fine-tuning (purifying the *ghee*), try to come to three fundamental statements about yourself that are rich in meaning and one hundred percent pure; three clear truths that connect your inner self with the persona that you exhibit to the world.

Now pronounce those three true statements to yourself once every day for a month, preferably in the morning and eye to eye in the mirror. This activates the Throat Chakra and strengthens your communicative abilities – and, quite a boon from a career perspective, your ability to apply your inner strength in the outside world.

THE PATH OF INTEGRITY

The varied work we do as a corporate culture consultants, which includes (re)definition of purpose, vision and mission, management auditing, and in-depth studies of individual corporate cultures that we undertake as part of an M&A process, usually combines interviews with on-line surveys charting the values distribution in the two legacy organisations, often involving hundreds, or thousands of people. This gives us a broad view checked by a deep view – and many surprises. Over the last few years we notice a striking rise in the score of 'integrity' among the top five desirable values. The attraction of this value is broad based. We find 'integrity' scoring well in all globally active organisations, wherever they may be headquartered, in Edinburgh, Jamshedpur, Johannesburg or Seattle.

Banks as a group have a high Integrity Quotient in terms of espoused values. A participant at one of our CultureLabs, mentioned that once in a rural American bank's headquarters he saw Integrity chiselled into the granite wall of the lobby. Clearly, at the time it was chiselled into the wall, integrity had not yet become a basic assumption. For a bank this is worrying. If you need to profess integrity or trustworthiness of any kind, you may not have it. 'Trust me, I am not trying to take your watch,' the pickpocket said as he filched the wallet.

Now we are not accusing this particular bank of anything, nothing at least beyond dim-witted marketing. They are probably as honest as the next bank, if that reassures you. Deviations from the path of integrity are hugely more risky than they were a few decades ago, not just on the corporate level, but also on the personal level. This negative motivation to be honest, when paired with the positive motivation that in the long run integrity tends to have the better pay-off, forms a powerful incentive for integrity in thought, speech and conduct.

Also very noticeable is many employees' insistence that any espoused integrity be actually lived, and the emotionally charged rejection of declarations of integrity that merely serve as a marketing ploy, a sop to the HR people and other 'softies that are taking over the world'. A year ago, a French consultant familiar with our methodology from past association with THT related a case involving a former client of hers (discreetly masking its identity), that had Integrity as one of its seven stated values. The job at hand was the integration of a company it had just acquired, with eight country operations in Western Europe involving five thousand people. She started work within weeks after the takeover. When she ran workshops for higher management in the acquired countries, she asked the two hundred participants in the various countries our standard opening questions about the espoused values of the company they now belonged to:

- How important do you find this value?
- To what extent is this value being lived?

The value Integrity scored an average of 93%. Far higher than any of the other four values. But when she asked to what extent the participants saw it being lived, the average came no higher than 32%, with one country scoring only 5%. Many of the participants were quite appalled by the profession of Integrity by a company that had created much wealth from its operations in countries like Romania, Bulgaria, Belarus and Uzbekistan, and was widely suspected of lining local rulers' pockets. The majority of the employees were very unhappy about their integration in the buying company. Some felt that they had been sold down the river, their reputations blemished. Many were looking for the exits. Their anger was not always of a moral nature. The marketing director was mostly appalled by the company's stupidity of mentioning the one aspect of its corporate personality that was widely suspected. 'They should have used Courage or something like this,' the expert said. 'That they do have.' When we contacted our colleague to verify our telling of her story, we learned that after much bleeding, the company was recently bought up itself, for less than it paid for its string of acquisitions only a few years ago.

A LOOK IN THE MIRROR

Of course one could wonder if we should have taken this job. The truth is that many of our assignments are of a very urgent nature, so that we do not always know our clients well before we start. We do some basic homework, but often need to learn on the job what a client is like. Would we have worked for this company if we had known who they were, and how little integrity they probably had?

We feel that the decision should depend on how much of an opportunity there is to be a force for the good. In this case we managed to shock the management of the acquiring company into reflection on its priorities and working methods. They could not afford to lose all the talented people in the operations they bought, scores of whom had already left by the time we presented our report, some five weeks later. Top management realised that if they wanted to actually enter Western Europe, their whole corporate being needed to change. It was a hard slog, but it worked, as far we can tell. We could not have foreseen this outcome. Had we known the acquiring company better and rejected the job because of their dubious backgrounds, the opportunity would not have presented itself.

We often discuss such issues within the company. Should we work for tobacco companies, for arms manufacturers? Or for liquor brands, junk food, stuff that makes your hair fall out, leads to useless expense, or contains more than three suspected carcinogens? And what about food companies owned by tobacco companies? Aircraft builders that also built rockets? Beverage companies that give kids ADHD? But we only ever manage to come up with another question, by now as familiar as the carpet: where do you draw the line?

In our view the enlightened way to deal with such core issues of integrity is not to think in terms of *exclusion* (we don't work for A, B, C, etc.), but of *inclusion*. When in doubt – in the as yet merely theoretical cases where a client's personality seems less than laudable, but the job appeals to professional hunger – we shall try to judge if the opportunity to be a force for the good presents itself. In practice our focus on inclusion is mostly realised by a concerted effort to strengthen our relationships with organisations that share our values. This is put into practice by means of a simple expedient: we go out of our way to serve the clients we truly admire and are well rewarded for this dedication, preventing temptation to attend to the needs of those we don't admire from even arising.

One of those we do truly admire is Johnson & Johnson, a fine example of a truth-speaking organisation. It derives a great deal of its strength from its well developed Throat Chakra. A co-passenger on an intercontinental flight told one of us in a night-long conversation on corporate culture: 'I have worked for Johnson & Johnson for twelve years, and I have never had to lie.' A memorable endorsement, and one that carries well from mouth to mouth, in workshops, lectures and general conversation. Imagine what this does to Johnson & Johnson's retention record – and for the quality of candidates vying to work for them.

In Johnson & Johnson's credo,[95] essentially a statement of what the company considers its responsibilities, it first describes its responsibilities towards doctors, nurses and patients, mothers and fathers; next come its responsibilities towards employees, followed by those towards communities. It is only in the last lines that shareholders are mentioned, declaring that they should enjoy 'a fair return'. What makes this such a suitable illustration for positive development at this energy level is not just the text, because there are plenty of good copywriters out there. What makes Johnson & Johnson such an exemplary company, is that it actually lives by this credo, creating an environment which attracts and nurtures enlightened leaders.

THROAT CHAKRA IN CLINCH:
ARCHETYPE AGNES W. – STRAINED VOICE OVER-USED

Agnes W. heads a US government directorate in the field of education. Her life pattern is shaped by properly functioning lower chakras, a fairly open Heart and Third Eye Chakra, a weak Solar Plexus and Crown Chakra, and an unusually stressed Throat Chakra. Though a non-smoker, she has a rough, husky voice that is often one of the first things people notice about her – the more so as she verbalises frequently, often with endless meandering while maintaining a tiring intensity. After a time the veins in her neck swell from the effort.

What strikes the observer is Agnes' powerful urge to communicate, continually stifled by something that grabs her by the throat, as if she has to force the inner content out through enormous resistance. When she gets very worked up, as in an argument, her speech sounds like the last words of someone being choked. One gets the impression that she has applied the will of her Solar Plexus Chakra to the throat area with all its might. Sometimes it is unclear if she truly speaks to express content, or whether all this verbal violence springs from a craving to assert herself. As a child she suffered from whooping cough, which brought her to the edge of death several times. This probably caused both the incorrect use of the vocal cords, and her deep need to assert herself, to be heard and understood, which in her work is manifested in a tendency to micromanagement. Her staff do like her, but wish she would take life a little easier, and cut down on her use of speech.

Since a few months, Agnes W. has taken up a meditative type of singing lessons. (In fact the chanting of the Indian *mantras* that represent the different chakras — a subject beyond the framework of this book.) Through the chanting, gently welling up from silence, she is taught to use her vocals cords differently, and to use her voice consciously to connect her inner being with the outside world. People in her immediate vicinity say that she appears to become more at ease with herself, and at the same time more determined. This is a hopeful sign. If she manages to wrench her willpower away from its compulsive focus on her throat area, she will become more determined on other energy levels, and achieve better overall results.

THROAT CHAKRA WIDE OPEN:
ARCHETYPE NORBERT G. – MISSION DRIVEN VOICE

Norbert G., manufacturer of suspended ceiling systems, used to be a fairly reticent person. Not shy or socially handicapped, to the contrary rather, but simply not someone with a lot of text. When public speaking for the company was required, he was glad to have people do it for him. His grandest speech ever, for the jubilee of a foreman hired by his father forty years ago, had amounted to a full hundred words and was generally considered to have been a miracle. His business was doing quite well, thanks to Norbert's gifts as employer, buyer and salesman, the wide open Sacral Chakra which helped him build a huge network, and a resolute focus on the bottom line. Then, in 2005, his newly hired 25 year old head of HR, female, and very bright, persuaded him to attend the 'Be the Change Conference' in London, and something in him awakened. One day a man came onto the podium who strongly reminded Norbert of his late father, both in bearing and occupation: Ray Anderson of Interface Inc., manufacturer of carpeting. Like himself and his father before him, Anderson owned and ran a manufacturing company using a lot of man-made materials. Anderson told the audience his story, by now legendary, of how one day a journalist appeared to write a background piece about his company. 'Now tell me,' the reporter asked after jotting down the essence of Anderson's promotional presentation, 'what you do for the environment?'

'What I do for the environment ...?'

Anderson stared at the newsman with open mouth and realised that there was a gaping hole in his corporate policy – a hole that could be the subject of highly embarrassing questions. 'Come back in two weeks,' Raymond said, 'and I will tell you in detail.'

In two weeks of very long days Ray Anderson let his staff chart all possibilities to change the production process so as to do less damage to the environment. A year later he had retooled his company to such extent that the environmental impact was minimal – an example not just for his specific sector, but for all companies that work with man-made materials. Anderson became so enthused about this clean-up of his manufacturing process that he began doing the rounds of the sustainability forums, spreading the word like a missionary. A very effective missionary, in the case of Norbert G., who came out of the session in a state of great excitement.

The fact that Norbert's young HR manager was on his side may well have been an additional motive force. This is said in all purity of spirit. Conferences like these tend to make one more sensitive, more ready to admit feelings perhaps than on routine business days. Under these emotional conditions Norbert must have been intensely aware how happy it would make his young HR manager if the event that she invited him to should indeed lead to fundamental change. He may also have been aware of who was leading who. If so, it is proof of his maturity that he allowed the reversal. Only truly great leaders have the capacity to follow other leaders.

Afterwards Norbert mingled with the coffee and juice drinking crowd, joined a 'World Café' and heard himself quacking some banalities at strangers who seemed at a much lower level of awareness, bringing him down to argumentation and polite discourse. He stared at the roster of workshops for the rest of the day, and suddenly realised that he did not want to talk, listen, confer, or be facilitated any more. He told his companion to stay and pay attention, took a taxi to the airport and went back to work – to retool his whole operation the same way Ray Anderson had done. And suddenly, Norbert's formerly dozing Throat Chakra is up and running full force. He has created a video outlining his method, the successful *Throw Out the Waste*, and teamed up with a reputable consultancy firm as external consultant, to share his insights on a very pragmatic level, helping other manufacturers make more money by wasting less. His latest aim for his own company: zero negative impact on the environment by 2020 – as it happens the same target Ray Anderson sets for his company.[96]

Norbert's transformation at the throat level works out so well, not thanks to his increased attention to active communication per se, but to the fact that now his words connect his inner and his outer world. Norbert's bottom line looks better than ever; not just because of all the savings that result from the prevention of waste and garbage creation, valuable bonuses for his environmental efforts, but also because of his new reputation as a leader who stands for something and does what he believes in.

6. THIRD EYE CHAKRA: INSIGHT, INTUITION

Sanskrit name: Ajna Chakra
Aspects: insight, self-knowledge, intuition, devotion
Location: above the bridge of the nose, pineal gland
Colour: purple
Element: light
Sense: sight, sixth sense
Right: the right to see
Demon: illusion
Figure: two-petaled lotus
Maslow: the transcendental aspect of levels 6 and 7, defined in his later works

Personal Aspects

Favourable development: People with a well developed Third Eye Chakra have powerful intuition that they learn to rely on in every day life. They also have excellent self-knowledge, so that they stand on solid ground, and get easy access to their energy sources.

For the religious among us: intuition is our inner hearing of God's voice. For the universalists: intuition is the voice of the universe resounding within us. For materialists: intuition is cognisance of what is to happen before it does, arrived at without direct input from the senses, a stunning demonstration of the enormous computing power of our brain, which correlates all the data garnered from our whole life so far, scanning our huge internal hard disk with inerasable, burnt-in data, and on the basis of analysis and extrapolation comes up with a fitting prediction.

Now what spoils the case for the materialist view, is that young children often have far better intuition than grown-ups, at least until such day as those grown-ups become like children once more and regain what they lost in this area. Many kinds of animals as well appear to have powers of intuition, and to be aware of events at a distance. Much research has been done into these phenomena, for instance with whales, those sensitive and highly gifted creatures.

The French philosopher of consciousness, Henri Bergson, in the 1920s posited that, like all animals, we are all telepathically gifted, but that this faculty is suppressed by our uniquely developed brain, which elects to pass on only those impulses that it deems important for our vital functioning,[97] a selection process that, as we developed our humanness, of course has become lorded over by the ego: 'Hey you, don't let that enter your awareness! Ignore it. Believe me, it's not important for you ...' What mankind has done, with its spectacular development of the neo-cortex and concomitant focus on thinking and verbal communication, is to neglect and even negate our innate talents for non-verbal communication, to the point where most people no longer hear anything that doesn't come from the ears or their own mouth.

Restoration of the powers of intuition is a beautiful and important challenge for all leaders in the 21st century. And this challenge is not limited to the restoration of intuitive powers in the leaders themselves, important as that step is. The challenge extends beyond them to the people that have accepted them as their leaders: how do you help them to develop their intuition?

The most important thing here is to help people rid themselves of their fear of *trusting* their intuition — the fear, instilled in all corporate environments of going by something non-empirical, non-measurable, non-quantifiable and of unproven worth. Allow people room for error in reading their own minds, and they will soon get to know it. Keep in mind: anyone who restores something to others that they lost, has enriched him or herself immensely.

Unfavourable development: An unfavourable development of this chakra usually has consequences in the area of narrow-mindedness, in all its connotations. It is manifested in a 'small' concept of the world one lives in, and a clinging to notions that are regarded as objective truths, such as 'good' and 'evil' – or, in the absence of such notions, a strong yearning for them. The most common symptom is a refusal to admit to consciousness information that is, or is feared to be, conflicting with what is regarded as established truth or fact. Variations on the near hysterical reaction of some children who are told that Santa Claus does not exist: 'No, you are lying! Santa *does* exist!'

For some people Santa Claus keeps existing all their lives, and when they ever need to accept that some of their notions do not mesh with reality (such as the notion that there exists something like objective reality, tangible and measurable, or objective truth, the same for everyone), they become distraught, angry or even venomous. Because of this Santa Claus phenomenon, which is far more common than educated people tend to think – particularly in the USA, where 20% of the population believes that the sun revolves around the earth[98] – it is taking ages for concepts like Heisenberg's Uncertainty Principle, formulated in 1927, to start influencing the philosophy of even one percent of the general population. That is because few are given the openness of mind of the Dalai Lama, who preaches: 'I have often said that if science proves facts that conflict with Buddhist understanding, Buddhism must change accordingly.'[99]

Another consequence of unfavourable development of the Third Eye Chakra is confusion: lack of clarity about one's own place in the world, and continual surprises by what are seen as unpredictable turns of fate.

Corporate Aspects

Over the last few years we have seen growing acknowledgment that intuition is more important for effective decision-making than the much vaunted rational weighing of information. Malcolm Gladwell's *Blink, The Power of Thinking Without Thinking*, a catchy survey of studies into the result of going by split-second impressions, gave this acknowledgement an extra push, though its effect will probably be as ephemeral as its subject.[100] More solid proof of the rising recognition of intuition, is that highly reputed management training institutes such as the Centre for Creative Leadership, ranked 5th worldwide in the *Financial Times* executive education survey, offer courses specifically to strengthen leaders' intuitive capabilities.

Anyone undertaking such work on his/her own may be helped by CCL faculty member Talula Cartwright's reader *Developing Your Intuition: A Guide to Reflective Practice*.[101] For those wishing to delve deeper, Gay Hendricks and Kate Ludeman wrote *The Corporate Mystic: A Guidebook for Visionaries with Their Feet on the Ground*[102] which, among other salient points, stresses the importance of integrity for the development of intuitive powers. In case the link is not directly apparent: loss of integrity corrodes the intuition.

When you repeatedly act contrary to what your inner voice recommends, that voice is slowly but surely muted. If you continue doing this year in, year out, you may only hear it occasionally, usually on days that are somehow milestones: birthday, Christmas, an anniversary of marriage or divorce, or that day when you quit your job in disgust, without knowing exactly why. The reverse is also true: when you start to maintain your integrity, your inner voice slowly recovers, so that after time it once again becomes a reliable decision-making instrument.

In corporate environments a properly functioning Third Eye Chakra manifests itself in a focus on higher purpose: a desire (ideally realised at least in part) to contribute something of value to society at large. This variously takes the form of loyalty relationships with employees, co-creation with clients and suppliers, co-operation with the community, environmental stewardship, alliances, and the shouldering of a leadership role.

Unfavourable development: Leaders with a closed Third Eye Chakra, or one that is dusted or misted over, confuse not just themselves, but also their organisations, by the creation of a worldview that does not match everyday reality – such as General Motors' view, espoused until recently, and in its heart of hearts still not quite abandoned, that (allow us to paraphrase) 'within five years all that whining about climate change is over and then we, who have always kept making seven litre engines, will be in the front of the field.'

Such leaders brake the development of their organisations by clinging to a worldview that is no longer valid: 'Whatever happens, people will always keep wearing spectacles (read newspapers, drink milk, and so on and so forth, the endless litany of unperceived, denied, and ignored major changes)'. The people they are supposed to lead will generally experience them as a massive block that they either smack into or have to work around carefully. Their only advantage, in the eyes of their subordinates, is that they are neither very observant, nor intuitively astute, so that it is relatively easy to fool them. Staff pretend to do as told, but in fact do it their own way. Or, behind an intricate screen of compliance, do something entirely different.

Chief Challenge: Pairing intuition with sensing.

THE CHAKRA FOR CONTACT WITH THE HIGHER SELF

The Third Eye Chakra lies low in the forehead, just above the bridge of the nose — a spot that many Indians mark daily with a *tilak*, a dot of carmine that designates connectedness with the inner, the universal, the divine, the sublime. It is the seat of the mystical organ of sense that is commonly called the 'third eye' — with which we practice introspection and intuitive sensing. This invisible organ plays an important role in the process of raising consciousness, more important than all other sense organs combined. Because what we 'see' within is more important than the information obtained by the physical sense organs.

And it is not just about answers at this level, but equally about questions. How do we interpret experience? How do we envisage our own development? How indeed our relationship with everything that surrounds us? What is spirituality and how does it relate to the material? Is there something to strive for? Or is truth found in acceptance? In non-attachment? In transcendence of all opposites by seeing them as the dual aspects of one and the same? Or is it all just about living in peace with ourselves?

An open Third Eye Chakra makes us reflect on such themes and start seeking – or, as in many mystic traditions such as Buddhism, Sufism and Vedanta, give up seeking because the searching makes the finding impossible. The Zen master says: 'What is the sound of one hand clapping?' The Sufi Master says: 'Why should I go to the mosque and perform prayer ritual to search for that which is in my own heart?' The Vedanta master says: 'Observing all the various practices of yogis and popular rituals of devotees, the wise man is content to do nothing special, and lives with himself in peace.' In Sarah Maha-Siddha's *Treasury of Songs*:

Mantras and tantras, meditation and concentration, all cause self-delusion.
Do not pollute by these works that which is pure in its own nature,
Stop tormenting yourself and abide in the bliss of peaceful awareness.[103]

Freely flowing energy on this level gives strong conceptual powers and rich ideation, opening the door to the development of a coherent personal philosophy. It allows the creation of imaginary universes, fantasy worlds, and complex works of art and architecture. It keeps us aware of the fact that even such an icon of trust in objective truth as solid matter, is alternately particle and wave, and that nothing in this world is stable or well-defined. The practical advantage of such realisations is that they impart a high tolerance to uncertainty and ambiguity: when you don't expect certainty, you are not threatened by its absence. And to stay on the pragmatic level: a well developed Third Eye Chakra also provides awareness of systemic changes in the world and major shifts in common thinking.

Most delightfully of all these gifts, the Third Eye Chakra enriches one with a sensitivity to philosophy and mystical poetry such as given above and these lines from the 11th C. Sufi poet Sheikh Ansari:

Any eye filled with the vision of this world
cannot see the attributes of Heaven.
Any eye filled with the attributes of Heaven
would be deprived of the Beauty of Divine Oneness.[104]

THE THIRD EYE HELPS SEE MORE DIMENSIONS

At a strictly practical level the Third Eye Chakra stimulates analysis and synthesis: what happens when we combine concept A with concept B (or even, imagine, with concept Z)? And it challenges our conceptual strength: can you think not only horizontally, vertically, and laterally, but multi-dimensionally as well? Or in spiralling dimensions, like fractals, fanning out into infinity while endlessly withdrawing into themselves? Can you conceive of toroidal universes, exploding and imploding simultaneously? People who indulge in this kind of fun have a Third Eye Chakra running on meth.

At an even more pragmatic level we get paradigm shifting questions such as: 'How would things look for our company if we no longer conceived of ourselves as an outsourcer, but turned into an insourcer, offering our services as marketing partner to producers abroad?' Or, a thought we keep seeding: 'How would it be if I used the great power of the organisation I lead to be a force for the good – and have myself paid royally to do it?' (All this without mentioning, of course, the hermit sage who looks down on our work in the garden from his cave and asks: 'Does striving to be good really matter in a world of apparent duality where good and evil are always in balance?' Nihilism is for saints, the rest of us need the inspiration of noble goals and its attendant passions.)

The realm of the Third Eye Chakra covers as well all that is referred to by the term extra-sensory perception, and all events and activities that involve the use of psychic energy, such as the frequent experience of striking coincidences – and with frequent we mean once or twice a year, because running into a neighbour at the supermarket while grabbing for the same bottle of Chardonnay does not count. Anyone interested in coincidences should get a copy of Arthur Koestler's *The Roots of Coincidence*.[105]

THE THIRD EYE AND THE PINEAL GLAND

In many forms of meditation attention is focused on the third eye, because activating this energy centre is essential for the development of inner life. On most sculptures of the Buddha, Bodhisattvas, Jain saints, and deities from the Hindu pantheon, the third eye is depicted prominently – as a little nub, lozenge or a rosette. There is an intriguing correlation with a physical organ, the pineal gland, which lies in the same cranial location, though in humans somewhat retracted, deeply embedded between the frontal lobes of the brain. In some species of iguana, lampreys and several birds, the pineal gland still has a function in 'normal', outer-directed vision. Peter stumbled upon this as a student – at roughly the same time that his interest in the other kind of third eye awakened. He dug into the hard science as best as he could, because the implication was very exciting: the third eye of the pineal gland in fact represents evolution's earlier approach to photoreception.

The human fascination with the third eye, which is thousands of years old, may be the result of genetic knowledge of this original function of the pineal as a sense organ in aid of outer vision. By now there is an extensive literature on this subject. In much of it biological facts and mystical ideas are hard to separate – perhaps because they are in fact intimately connected.[106]

INTUITIVE LEADERSHIP – WHEN TO BRING INTO PLAY?

Intuitive leadership is of vital importance in situations like these:

- There are insufficient data in the process' *Umfeld* to come to a rational evaluation.
- There is no time to collect input for rational evaluation because a decision needs to be taken right this minute.
- There are too many data, or they are contradictory.
- The data are open to multiple interpretation or support multiple options equally.
- A new idea is being launched, the full ramifications of which are not immediately clear, leave alone chartable, but about which a decision needs to be taken at very short notice to pre-empt competition.
- Certain staff members function sub-optimally, without any apparent obstacle to their optimal functioning.
- There is no clear vision/mission or existing vision/mission statements are outdated.
- There is something wrong, but no one knows what is the matter.

The observant reader will have noticed that these are all completely ordinary, everyday situations – situations where analytical evaluations simply don't cut it, and there seems no way to arrive at logical conclusions. At those moments a happily spinning energy centre at this level can save the day. When the going gets tough, the tough look inside.

With the caveat that as a corporate leader you can't always admit that this is what you are doing, as the *intellect* rules in your world. Any understanding beyond the five senses is highly suspect and best kept to oneself, like adultery and masturbation. 'I just had the impulse that I should go for X,' doesn't come across right, especially when afterwards the choice proves unfortunate or mediocre. Naturally, if things did go well you can tell everyone that the idea was whispered into your ear by a drunk gnome, and no one will think the less of you. But oh boy, if your choice proves to be a bummer, and you have nothing better to offer than 'I went by my intuition', you are in very rough weather.

Many highly successful people have claimed that they took the most important decisions of their lives on the basis of intuition. To take one example of many: Steve Jobs, CEO of both Apple and Pixar, who never studied at any university, in his commencement address at Stanford University, entitled *You've got to find what you love*, spoke the following words:

'Your time is limited, so don't waste it living someone else's life. Don't be trapped by dogma – which is living with the results of other people's thinking. Don't let the noise of other's opinions drown out your own inner voice. And most important, have the courage to follow your heart and intuition. They somehow already know what you truly want to become. Everything else is secondary. [...] And much of what I stumbled into by following my curiosity and intuition turned out to be priceless later on.'[107]

HOW TO STRENGTHEN YOUR INTUITION

Intuition is a capability like many others, comparable in a sense to artistic sensitivity and creativity – you've got to have the gift, but almost everyone has it to a certain extent, and all talents can be developed by being open to them and using them. It is related to extra-sensory perception, telepathy and other branches of human activity that belong to the realm of parapsychology and therefore in a realm that 'serious scientists' consider dubious at best – although, partly thanks to work at Stanford and Princeton referred to below, this may well change in the near future. It is not easy to write a curriculum for developing intuition, but these three simple steps should be in 101.

1. *Suspend disbelief*

The biggest problems with intuition occur when the phenomenon as such is not taken seriously. The first thing you need to do, if you are intuitively handicapped, is to stop thinking that intuition is nonsense, useless or ridiculous. Topical advice is provided by Joseph W. McMoneagle, who devotes himself to 'remote viewing', in other words clairvoyance; work that many put down as weird or occult and reject out of hand, but that he was paid to do for twenty-one years by the CIA, a company not given to superstition, racking up 2000 missions. His advice: *suspend disbelief*. Stop rejecting information of a kind that you are not used to.[108]

McMoneagle's accounts can be rejected out of hand as easily as stories about kidnapping by UFOs or mysteriously appearing crop circles, because we have no way of verifying the facts. But it is less easy to reject reports of someone like Hall E. Puthoff, Ph.D., connected to the Stanford Research Institute for many years, who delved into recently declassified material about long-term research with clairvoyants by both the CIA and its military counterpart, the Defence Intelligence Agency, in co-operation with his institute. Puthoff shows, with stunning images, that clairvoyants regularly proved capable of detailed description of specific installations thousands of miles away, in remote parts of the Soviet Union that they had never seen, nor could have seen, and that even the researchers who conducted the double-blind research, had never seen either in real life or in images.[109] Just suspend disbelief for a moment – stop rejecting information of a kind that you are not used to ...

A curious, and highly pertinent detail is the correlation with literary theory. When we start reading a novel, we know that what is described did not actually happen – but the novel 'works' for us only if we manage to ignore this. The same applies to intuitive and related capabilities: they only work when we suspend disbelief.

This is not easy, least of all for people with a scientific background, or with the respect for verifiable facts which dominates corporate environments. Not easy, but still, it may have to be done. Brenda J. Dunne and Robert G. Jahn, of Princeton University's Engineering Anomalies Research Institute, for 25 years conducted extra-sensory perception experiments, particularly focused on remote perception.

They not only found frequent occurrence, with far greater degree of reliability than could have been the result of mere chance, but also noticed that the 'perception' often took place *before* the specifications had even been passed to the 'sending' subjects. Speaking of intuition ...

In their study 'Information and Uncertainty in Remote Perception Research' Dunne and Jahn state: 'The possibility that ordinary individuals can acquire information about distant events by these inexplicable means, even before they take place, challenges some of the most fundamental premises of the prevailing scientific worldview.'[110] They don't say it in exactly the words that McMoneagle used, but the message is similar: suspend disbelief and take note of what is happening.

We are particularly struck by their observation that subjects performed better as the set-up of the tests emanated less scepsis. One of Peter's earliest essays, in fact his second published piece, concerned exactly the same issue. It unravelled a doctoral thesis on experiments involving drug induced heightened suggestibility, which showed many people developing psychosis-like symptoms, while ignoring the fact that the setting, a psychiatric clinic, suggested pathology. Had the same experiments been done in a temple, most subjects would have had blissful experiences. How we experience things is not just determined by our own mental set, but equally by the setting. Therefore, if you want to develop your intuition don't spend too much time in environments where it is not valued.

2. *Be more open to subtle impulses*
Intuition takes place in a field of subtle forces, usually shouted out by coarser ones. If your intuition is not naturally strong, learn to become more aware of it. Go sit somewhere quietly, preferably when you will not be disturbed, and relax. Free yourself from all that occupies your mind, emptying it by any way you know. Then, after these moments of deep relaxation, let the various aspects of the matter at hand pass before your eyes, and take note of your reactions: of the emotions they invoke in you and the ideas they engender.

3. *Let experience strengthen your gift.*
As a child Peter conducted his first experiments with extra-sensory experiments without being aware of doing anything unusual. When he was around fourteen, his neighbour, a mysterious, robe-clad lady

of mixed European-Asian descent, often invited him over to play cards. One day she said: 'Let's try a new game.' She arranged 32 cards face down in four rows of eight, and told him: 'Now you go out into the hall, close the door, and wait, while I pick up one card, think of it hard, and put it back where it lay. Then you will come back in, focus all your attention on the array of cards, and pick out the one I selected.' After he had picked up the correct card three times out of five, Peter said: 'Maybe you're just *saying* that I picked the right cards, maybe that is your little game!' She laughed confidently: 'Well, then let's turn the tables.' She went out, he picked up a card, put it back, kept concentrating on it without looking at it, as she had told him, and sure enough she picked out the right one. They did this several times after that, in between her favourite canasta, never reaching the same level of correctness as on that first day, but after a few weeks they scored 20% pretty steadily, and so easily that the game got boring. Peter is not asking anyone to believe it, because he has tried much of his adult life to ignore it himself. Just see it as an uplifting tale about the benefit of practice. Our joint intuition tells us that you are working on it already.

EVERYONE STARTS ENLIGHTENED

It is said of many enlightened beings that they were 'like children': observing without prejudice or expectation; pure consciousness encompassing the universe. Nothing escapes these little creatures, and their bliss is the goal of all inner seekers. (In short: a state when food and diapering have been taken care of, there are no demands to be met, and there is no separation between the self and the universal, *casu quo* between the self and the divine.)

All healthy young children are enlightened, in a state of full consciousness. It is only during education that endarkenment clouds their minds. Not all of them, but many. The superego, which in early youth was just a summer cloud, a puff in a blue sky, during puberty and early adulthood accumulates into a dark cumulus of demands and prejudices, attachments to sensual pleasures, guilt feelings, and opportunistic calculation. This massing cloud cover gradually moves in over the mountains, cuts a broad swath across the inner sky, and ends up obscuring the sun almost continually. As a result, consciousness gets heavily filtered, and life impoverished, however rich it may seem from the outside. Daily life becomes a slog, because that which is of true importance hardly manages to penetrate the shield. This leads to psychic under-nourishment (we need inner light as we need food and water), and a chronic sense of exhaustion.

True adulthood, in the spiritual sense, requires the opposite of that under-nourishment: a pushing back of those clouds, and regained access to the light behind them that throughout the dark ages of the mind has never kept shining. We get a promise of our powers to achieve this whenever we see the sun break through heavy cloud cover, sending out rays in all directions – one of those sunbursts that all humans revere, and which many link to the divine (almost all cultures depict deities with sunbursts behind their heads), probably because they are strikingly good illustrations of the visions reported by saints and people who had near-death experiences. Various spiritual schools link sunbursts to the inner path, as they provide such an awe-inspiring display of the universal forces, and symbolise the process of enlightenment so brilliantly.*

MARKS OF A PROPERLY FUNCTIONING THIRD EYE CHAKRA
- wisdom, insight
- a tendency to introspection, inner clarity, self-knowledge
- intuitive understanding of natural relationships
- rich imagination, flights of fantasy, creation of ideal worlds
- the capacity to perceive others' inner state
- good memory
- a capacity to transcend details, to see the big picture
- the attitude that the American author and adventurer Jack London recommended: 'Be one of those whom nothing escapes ...'
- sensitivity to extra-sensory perception, paranormal powers.

SYMPTOMS OF A BLOCKED THIRD EYE CHAKRA
- incomprehension of one's place in the world
- finding oneself continually surprised by twists of fate

---

* There is a striking parallel – more on this below – with the Kundalini Yoga concept of repressed life force, *shakti*, which needs to be awoken where it lies sleeping, curled up like a snake in the Root Chakra, and steered up the spinal column.

- difficulty grasping symbols, metaphors and evocative description
- a closed mindset, narrow-mindedness
- failing memory
- an unshakable trust in fixed values (Cartesian/Newtonian/Lutheran worldview)
- firm trust in the reliability of authoritarian sources
- subscription to axioms such as 'to know it you have to measure it'
- lack of imagination
- living in fantasy world
- going through life blinkered.

Place on earth: There can't be a better place on earth to experience the Third Eye Chakra than Polonnaruwa on Sri Lanka. In a beautiful grove we find a huge standing Buddha, hacked out of a granite boulder, in several ways a unique work of art. The first time Peter saw it, or rather him, as a young traveller, he was so deeply moved that he walked around in a kind of trance for days, and kept going back to Him at all hours. He returned when he was forty – as a professional who had taken a year off to show his wife the love of his younger years – and again was touched so deeply that he wasn't quite walking on earth. In the world, but not of it ...

What the sculpture does, assuming you have the proper sensibility, is two-fold. First, it makes you feel serene, at peace with yourself and the entire universe. A feeling so warm and so full of happiness you want to embrace the whole world. But all you need to do that, is just stand there and return his smile, feeling what he came to share with us. Love gushes forth from the folds of his robe, flowing into the surrounding fields ... After a while you may start to sense a deep compassion with the human condition.

Second, the image turns you inside out, or rather outside in. The Buddha here is fully turned inward (he is shown, see www.rovingstar. com/chakras/chakras_buddha.php, with arms crossed over the chest, very rare in Buddhist iconography), yet he has not left us alone here on earth: by gazing at him, giving him our full attention, without expectation or programme, simply being with him, we become conscious of our oneness with him, and are taken up into the atmosphere of his exalted being. All this has been done with such power of artistic expression, that showing the radiance of the Buddha's third eye did not even require the usual nub on the forehead.

Wholly apart from the artistic, and perhaps also religious or mystical experience, in places like this one strongly becomes aware of the presence of the work's principal, in this case King Pramabahu I, and its actual maker: the nameless creator who put his soul into this work, and expresses his essence in a way that even eight centuries later has lost nothing of its expressiveness and personality. By opening ourselves to such connections through space and time we are deep in the realm of the Third Eye Chakra. No further guidance or illustration is required, so we gladly leave you alone now with your own standing Buddha.

Exercise 1: Self-awareness. Having seen above how we know someone from the product of his hand, how we meet the maker in opening ourselves to what he makes – in substance and in style, in intent and in expression – now study in your inner mirror what presence other people become aware of as they open themselves to what *you* have created in this world.

Exercise 2: Steps to improve or restore intuition. It is undoable to calculate the effectiveness of intuition from historical analysis of our hunches and actual behaviour, because we have a tendency to fool ourselves, especially when something goes wrong. 'Yeah, I knew it …' we say, 'but …' But apparently we didn't *really* know, because if we did we would have been idiots to do the other thing anyway. We were simply plain wrong, thinking that things would work out okay the way we did them. And because we are attached to the notion that we actually have pretty good intuitive powers, when things go wrong we claim to have had a presentiment of failure. Whereas in fact we have just doubted, weighed, wavered, generally messed up and taken the wrong decision.

Because of this second guessing of themselves many people have much less reliable intuition than they believe they have. Do the following to make your own more acute and practical: any time you have a presentiment, write it down. Then you go do what you want to do, either following your presentiment or contravening it, and write down, as concretely as possible, what the effort brought you. People who maintain diaries sometimes do this their entire lives. Keep this up for a year and you will notice that you become much more alert to presentiments, lose your doubts about intuition as something that works for you, and find yourself using it to greater practical effect.

Balancing of the books: at year's end make a list of all the times when following your intuition really helped you. Then list all the times that your intuition was right, but you did something else. I suppose that by now you have a presentiment where this is leading ...

INTEGRATION IS OF THE ESSENCE

Here, as on all other energy levels, an exclusive focus would lead to disappointing results. The enlightened leader combines two contrasting ways of processing information: *intuiting* and *sensing*. Sensing looks at discrete, empirical facts and records observations. Intuiting looks into a whole phenomenon, interpreting its meaning and significance. In surveys we ask:

Which option best describes how you manage?

a) In solving problems I like to analyse the situation and look hard at the facts. I believe these speak for themselves, needing no window dressing.

b) In solving problems, I like to gain deep insights into the meaning of the issue. Once I have grasped this I test my supposition against all available facts.

c) In solving problems, I like to gain deep insights into the meaning of the issue. Facts are dependent on context. Once I grasp the context the facts fall into place.

d) In solving problems I like to analyse the situation and look hard at the facts, but then I start to draw inferences, until the meaning of this issue is clear.

The integrated answers are b) and d). The polarised answers are a) and c). In d), the person starts with sensed facts and develops intuitions. In b), the person starts with intuitions and tests these against the available facts.

The greatest scientific example of the sensing type was Sir Isaac Newton. He convinced three centuries of scientists, and through emulation a dozen generations of laymen, to look first at the facts and only then draw cautious inferences. Didn't he say: 'We must humbly reflect God-given realities on the pupils of our eyes and not let our beliefs or conceits stand in the way …' Frankly, we don't know if he did, and we failed to confirm any authorship of this quote even after thorough internet searches. But does it matter? The saying certainly recapitulates the ruling wisdom of that age: only after we have made sure of all the facts should we start to draw inferences, and we must disregard any notion, inkling, hunch, dream or other input not based on empirical facts.

But science moves on, and contemporary theoretical physics is a challenge of an entirely different nature, relying on intuition to disentangle its puzzling anomalies and create theorems that explain the previously inexplicable. Albert Einstein was famed for his intuitive powers, and would cut himself shaving if an exciting intuition struck him. But this does not imply that he ignored facts when they were available. Having gained his intuitions, he proceeded to validate them through empirical testing – an excellent example of harmonising one's abilities.

EGOMANIA GALORE

Ego is one of the most problematic phenomena we encounter in our consulting practice. And any ego issues tend to get magnified, sometimes acutely, during mergers and acquisitions. Of course all of us have egos and there is nothing wrong with that. Our egos are like the game plans of our lives, setting out the parameters, and our standard responses to social stimuli. They can be powerful stuff: no ego, no greatness. Alas, no greatness also without ego. One of its most harmful aspects is vanity. As the Indian sage Sri Ramakrishna said in the late 19th century, vanity is the last trait that leaves man on the path of enlightenment, just before he reaches Samadhi, the exalted state of liberation – but really only just before.

Ego is not just a bad thing, let's not forget its positive aspects. We would not be so wonderful and kind, so courageous on the battlefield, so brilliant in the arts, if it weren't for our well developed egos with their many winning aspects. As Geoffrey Miller explains in *The Mating Mind*,[111] we use our highly evolved brains, and the equally evolved egos that they helped us construct, to show off in the mating game. Nothing wrong with that either, as long as both reader and writer know what they are involved in, honing their brains the way deer hone their antlers.

What *is* wrong is imposing your game on others, wrestling others to the ground with that proud rack. What is also wrong – and psychologically damaging to the self – is letting your ego take over control for its own sake. You start doing things not because they are good, but because your cheating ego tells you that they are good for you. Pretty soon you are doing things that are bad for you, while reinforcing the ego trait that made you do them. It leads victims to persistence in views that are no longer valid, and to impose those views on others. It makes them push ideas, not for their belief in them, not out of passion either, the burning desire to achieve an end they believe in with all their hearts, but solely for the sake of proving power to exact obedience. The afflicted often fall into habitual nurturing, and fattening, of self-serving ambition.

Unfortunately this kind of ego-tripping appears to be endemic to corporate environments. We have no reliable statistics on the matter, but going by our instincts (which of course is fully sanctioned at this energy level) we would say that bad ego cases in corporate environments outnumber those in the general population by at least four to one. What is more, these bad cases tend to cluster. We see stable high densities in all metropolitan areas, and occasional eruptions in pleasant places with five star resorts. The sufferers often do well out of this and live opulently, though perhaps not always happily. Many of them, like Eliott Spitzer, the above-mentioned New York governor, develop a convoluted subconscious scheme to trip themselves up and expose themselves, usually with tragicomic effect, to be devoured by the media.

During M&A processes, when huge sums of money tend to be involved, egos are particularly prone to inflammation, swelling and eruption. All consultants and executive coaches recognise the need to treat these cases with utmost care, lest they blow up the process or make successful integration a lost dream before one has even started. One of the most pernicious, but also most effective ways of dealing with them is an appeal to inner greatness: 'Come on John, you're a greater man than that!'

Ego issues are also, as we found in a survey Trompenaars Hampden-Turner developed with the Dutch financial paper *Financieele Dagblad*, the chief limiters in organisations' quest for objectivity.[112] Second in importance was a cluster of questions around rigidity and narrow-mindedness. Both are related to the Third Eye Chakra. Taken together, ego issues and rigidity are powerful creativity blockers. You don't really need anything more in an organisation to kill all spontaneity and intuitive imagining.

Now to turn it around: when an M&A process is led by someone with a strong intuition as to where to take the newly created body, how to use its energies, how to breath life into it – the sky is the limit. We have been lucky to have been involved with a few of those, and wait for more of them with all lines open. What the world needs today are men and women who know themselves, in power and in limitation, who know what they want to do with the energy of the people entrusted to their care, and who have the energy to execute their plan. They will be helped by introspection, by an intuitive understanding of the relationship between power and responsibility, and by the cosmic forces that always favour work done with conviction – not guaranteeing success, but smoothing the path.

EGO AS THE DESTROYER OF VALUE

Five years ago we were approached for an intervention by a British logistics company, let's call it Xfer S.A., that over the last decade had acquired about a dozen companies all over Europe. The idea was to let us give a presentation on diversity to an annual gathering of managers from all across the footprint, and run a workshop to help them deal with colleagues from different cultural backgrounds – a type of programme that, in one version or another, we have been offering for years at many transnational companies.

At the briefing, George, the CEO, who had been in the job for less than a year, made a nervous impression. He was patently excited about the programme, but had difficulty focusing on the discussion, clearly distracted by some urgent preoccupations. His eyes frequently drifted off towards corners of the room, not in wandering but staring hard as if there in those corners he saw before him some fascinating scenes depicted in high definition video. Then he would abruptly cut back to our eyes, with a great, hungry intensity. As we discussed the content of our presentation,

George seemed deeply worried about what it might do to his people, and insisted on having the final version a week before the great day. He explained that, yes, the theme of our intervention would indeed be 'Diversity', so as not to give offence to certain parties, but that in reality all our efforts were to be aimed at dealing with the problems caused by one particular opco, namely the French operation.

What was wrong? Was the French firm not performing? Did its quarterly figures disappoint? Had employees been fleeing in droves? Were clients complaining about abysmal service, seeking ultimate redress at Xfer's head office? No, there was none of that, George said, in fact the French company was a stellar performer, responsible for as much as 50% of the group's profits. The problem was, quite simply, that the French were idiots. Impossible to manage: arrogant, unreliable, intransigent. All of them, from the general manager on down. They never did what he told them to do, never so much as pretended to listen, never responded to his emails marked 'high priority' or even 'urgent', and generally behaved as spoiled brats. 'Clearly,' George said, 'they feel that their disproportionate contribution to our bottom line gives them the right to do whatever they please.'

'Did you appoint any of them to the group excom?' we asked.

'Are you kidding? They'd just be making trouble.'

'Well, obviously they are doing *something* right ...'

We nearly lost the job right there and then. Maybe that would actually have been for the better, but the presentation was to be held on Madeira, which called for above average flexibility. We did the intervention, preached respect for diversity, entertained and wise-cracked, and had an excellent opportunity to get to know the various country managers, including the French, who behaved as if the whole event was their private party. They must have felt that, 'heck if we're paying for half of this ...' They clustered at their own tables, easily identifiably by the noise level, and continually invited Spaniards, Poles, Germans, Belgians, Czechs and Turks to join their boisterous, when not raucous, goings on, and kept pouring wine into them.

During one of the scarce quiet moments, we managed to take the French GM and his CFO aside for some serious questions. For instance, how would they characterise George's leadership style? 'Highly directive.' Would that be a euphemism for 'dictatorial'? 'Absolutely.' Big grins. And how would they characterise their own leadership style? The general manager: 'Dictatorial'. Bigger grins. After they allowed this to sink in the CFO said: 'The difference is, that our guys love us. His guys hate him. We drive people hard, but then, when we break another performance record we take them all out to a country inn to celebrate. George, when he gets good figures, he invites his PA into his office and has champagne with her.'

We presented George some well substantiated reasons why he should break out of his confrontational relationship with the French team, and with some other country managers that he equally perceived as idiots (albeit less threatening because they did not make quite as much profit), why he should transcend his ego and attempt reconciliation. But none of it was absorbed. The only response we got was more complaints about the character weaknesses of the many managers out there that he was dependent on for his survival.

The French, to our knowledge, were never brought on board at group level, nor any significant others for that matter. About a year after our intervention the French arranged a management buy-out. Today, a mere four years later, they have acquired half a dozen other logistics companies in Europe, two of them from plodding Xfer, which has had to shed about half the operations it once owned – and by now they are Xfer's main competitor on its home market. It appears to be a matter of years before the French will gobble up their former parent. None of this was unpreventable, but ego stood in the way of a reconciliation– while elsewhere the country inns worked their magic.

When ego stands in the way, you can argue till you are blue in the face, you can prod and cajole, and present all the arguments in the world, but unless there is some degree of self-reflection and at least a beginning willingness to accept that perhaps not all the others are idiots, there is nothing one can do but give more presentations on Madeira and keep the wine flowing.

THIRD EYE CHAKRA SHUT TIGHT: ARCHETYPE MARY Z. – CLUELESS IN WONDERLAND

For the last five years, Mary Z. has been at the front line of the battle to get more women into top corporate positions. Alas, she has done more for the cause than the cause has done for her. As long as most remember she has been stuck in the same position of modest import and remuneration. At conferences and seminars she fulminates ever more fiercely about the discrimination and disenfranchisement of women – especially at the cocktail sessions after hours, where she has been giving participants the same jeremiad for years about how she was passed over for promotion by a man, just because she is a woman, and for no other reason, and how beastly unfair this is.

Everyone who half knows Mary Z. is aware that she has a problem far greater than any related to gender, namely that whatever the subject, she will nag you about her views, intensely and for hours. The latest female CEO hounded out of office with a scandal concocted by envious men, Sarbanes-Oxley, public transport, the proper way to make a macchiato, take your pick. As soon as Mary joins a gathering, there is no more peaceful moment, even if it's a meandering discussion of golf related injuries or an office meeting about the Christmas cards.

Mary does not register how others regard her, does not regard herself, and does not really regard others either, as she is always too involved in self-expression to give a moment's attention to others. This is why she usually does not have a clue what is going on around her, and keeps being surprised by developments, both in her corporate and her private life. Friend Ben suddenly turns out to have another woman, whom he has practically been living with for half a year. The department that she applied to be transferred to is terminated the week after she switches desks. The redundant department's manager, whom she had cultivated long and assiduously, reminds her on parting that he gave her repeated hints that she should not pursue her ambitions to join him, but that she did not seem to get any of them, kept on pushing for it regardless, and …

What keeps Mary Z. afloat in the corporate ocean, her self-inflating survival harness, is her solid work in the realm of the Root Chakra. She is always on budget, and in uncertain times (when are times not uncertain?) this is a quality one likes to retain for the organisation. She will not make a smashing success of anything you ask her to undertake, because she misses the requisite vision and sense of purpose, but it's a safe bet that she is not going to lose you any money. And in uncertain times …

THIRD EYE CHAKRA WIDE OPEN:
ARCHETYPE HERMAN D. – AN EYE FOR COINCIDENCES

As told by Peter

An example from my immediate circle: a friend with whom I had discussed striking coincidences that we had experienced, suggested that I meet a friend of hers, Herman D., a young consultant who shares my interest in the work of Arthur Koestler, and specifically the subject of coincidences and what to make of them. I called him and made an appointment.

The next day I received an email from Frederick H., a classmate from grammar school whom I had not seen in almost forty years At school and for a few years after we had maintained a relationship that could only be characterised as budding friendship; a sentiment kept warm by the enjoyment of mutual friends and a shared interest in philosophy. However, in the budding stage it remained. I found him a bit otherworldly, but then perhaps I needed such critical attitude towards dreamers to keep myself somewhat grounded.

Frederick H. wrote that he had just read one of my recent books and enjoyed it immensely – testament to his wide open Third Eye Chakra! – and was struck that I mentioned as one of my teachers 'Garib Nawaz' Moinuddin Chisti, a 12th C. Indian sage, not known to the general public, to whom he had just devoted a chapter of his upcoming book on the Indian branch of Sufism. A nice coincidence, absolutely, but not far above reaching for that same bottle of Chardonnay. However ...

I made appointments with both Frederick and Herman, offering to drive over to where they lived, fairly far apart, and in my striving for efficient motoring booked them on the same day, Herman in the morning, Frederick in the afternoon. A few days before the agreed date Herman called to ask if we could move the appointment to after lunch, but I told him that alas, in the afternoon I was seeing someone else. So we stuck to the morning, and over coffee it turned out that Herman knew me from way back, having seen me a few times as a kid, and had even of course read my letters from India. When I stared at him non-plussed, not recollecting to have ever corresponded with children: 'Letters to my dad. He used to talk about you now and then, that you had been classmates, the only two with any interest in philosophy ...'

You probably guess by now. Yes, indeed, that afternoon I was to see that student of universal connectedness Frederick H., Herman's father, whom he had not seen for over a decade – nor wished to see or hear about for that matter. Inspired by his spiritual leaders and a guru he was then seeing, Frederick had run off to India in the 1980s to live in a monastery, leaving Herman's mother to care for him and his two younger sisters. He loathed his father for this abandonment, a sentiment that was heightened every time his dad returned to the home country for a visit to his family, a supposedly noble act that he presented as self-sacrifice. Dad would show up at the door dressed in robes or pyjama suits and put up an act as if he was suddenly holy or at least somewhat elevated – the selfish [expletive after expletive] ...

After the storm had raged out young Herman and I sat opposite each other as if we had been melted together in a lump. Hours later we were still trying to sort out the meaning of it all, to make sense of fate's weave. We could sense Arthur Koestler's presence at the session, quietly chuckling in his little corner of heaven: 'Told you, didn't I?'

I hoped that the coincidence, pairing him with his father, would have a conciliatory effect, but Herman crushed that hope instantly. In fact he was quite horrified of the idea that I would go see his father directly after I left him, saying that he felt almost as if he was being abducted spiritually, being brought together with the man against his will, this man whose name he had shunned, preferring to assume his mother's surname. Still, Herman had the social grace to accept fate's agenda and wished me a good afternoon with Frederick, 'not that I suppose such wishes will help ...' Half an hour after I left him he called me in the car and asked if I was going to tell Fred about our meeting this morning and about the coincidence we discovered. 'I don't know,' I said. 'If it makes you uncomfortable ... But then, the coincidence also occurs to him in a way, don't you think? And would it be fair to keep it from him?'

'Yes, that is true,' he said. 'Do what you think feels right.'

The meeting with Fred began under a cloud: there was something I might not tell him. It made it impossible to restore any of the old amity. The conversation did not help: Fred went almost straight into an expert monologue on the difference between various Sufi schools, supported by many quotes from teachers he had followed at one time or another, and which left me both cold and bored. That is the problem with mysticism:

once it has been experienced there is little left to talk about – unless of course the wording is particularly poetic.[113] It turned out that Fred had a small practice as a spiritual teacher, with a dozen people gathering every Saturday for his *darshan*, and a few individual sessions throughout the week for struggling disciples.

At one moment, as I stood with my back to him, looking out his window to a tiny garden fringed with taxus where no love had been spent, I asked him casually: 'Do coincidences have much meaning to you?'

'Oh no,' Frederick said in that soft, ever so slightly pedantic voice of his: 'We pay no attention to such ephemeral phenomena. On the path of enlightenment they have no real importance.'

Lightening up, I knew that I need not tell him. Still, I felt a small loss. I would have loved to share it with him, because it would become more realised in the telling; and also feeling vaguely that it might in some way be healing. The greater loss, of course, was that we did not really manage to connect.

In the car on the way home I called Herman, and told him how it went. 'What a relief!' he exclaimed. Clearly, the coincidence was a treasure he did not want his father to have any part of.

'So now Fred will never know,' I said.

'No great loss,' Herman said, 'he'll never know anything.'

There is more to this story that makes it even more striking, with some beautiful detailing on the seams where the lives are joined, but that is beyond the point. The point being, that at times events take place which beat the odds and reveal the hidden coherence of life's occurrences. Sure, if you insist, I shall admit that it is *possible* that there is no relevance at all in this double encounter, that it is all chance, and that we are all autonomous little packages of energy, going about our ways independently and bumping into each other at random – but does that seem *logical*?

More logical, and more in line with the findings of modern physics, is that the entire universe is intimately connected, an energy field of many dimensions in which we are fused together with everything existing both in the dimension of measurable energy and in the dimension of non-measurable energy. It is also logical to assume, as the Vedic sages of India did thousands of years ago, that we have been given the third eye to perceive this.

7. CROWN CHAKRA: UNIVERSAL CONSCIOUSNESS

Sanskrit name: Sahasrara Chakra
Aspects: universal consciousness, servant leadership
Location: the top of the skull
Colour: amethyst
Element: mental energy
Sense: cosmic sensing
Right: the right to know
Demon: attachment
Figure: thousand petaled lotus
Maslow: the transcendental aspect of levels 6 and 7, defined in his later works

Personal Aspects

Favourable development: This is the chakra of universalism and cosmic consciousness. Its realm is our sense of connectedness with 'something greater than ourselves', however we define it. It can bring tremendous strength to any endeavour that is deeply felt to have universal importance – or, if that sounds a bit too grandiose, any endeavour that contributes to happiness on earth, even if the immediate effect has limited range. It is also the chakra of our longing to transcend all duality (e.g. the cruel separation from God that is man's fate in the Judeo-Christian and Islamic traditions), and merge with the universal/divine.

Unfavourable development: As is the case in all chakras, all problems are found in either neglect or over-development.

Where there is a strong focus on one's own individuality – as promoted in our dominant, materialistic and individualistic culture – this chakra folds its thousand tiny petals inward and draws shut, effectively closing us up top-side like one of those modern football stadiums with a roof like a huge eye open to the sky that is incrementally closed in adverse weather. As a result of almost permanent closure – the weather in the corporate zone tends to be inclement nearly throughout – many business leaders have little or no sense of universal connectedness, one more reason why books like this are useful. The Crown Chakra can only open up again and bloom when a more universal, 'self-transcending' concept of self is entertained, and will then do so of and by itself.

Conversely, exaggerated focus on the Crown Chakra can lead to 'addiction' to spirituality, and neglect of the realms governed by the other chakras. The most common neglect is that of the lowest energy centre, the Root Chakra, held in contempt by some on account of its supposedly inferior earthiness, its rootedness in the dirt of survival. Such disregard results in neglect of the body, which leads to physical deterioration, possibly even dereliction, or to neglect of business basics and a slide into poverty – which, oh bitter irony, inevitably results in a forced focus on the Root Chakra in order to assure survival.

This syndrome may sound exotic, yet, alas, is far from rare. The smarter sect leaders (as a bunch highly adroit at exploiting the allure of an exclusive focus on spirituality), always make sure that their disciples transfer their worldly assets to the sect *before* they come to this stage.

Corporate aspects

Favourable development: In corporate leaders, a properly functioning Crown Chakra manifests itself in, among other traits, a conscious striving to let any effort made for the benefit of the organisation also benefit 'the world' – all stakeholders near and far. For a better understanding of this issue and stimulating input, the reader is referred to the Weatherhead School of Management's efforts under the label *Business as an Agent of World Benefit*.[114]

This conscious striving is rooted in a feeling of connectedness with all living things, and with all that which may not be living by anyone's definition, but which permeates and nurtures us, and on that account is part of us as well. Traditionally, this feeling is not strongly present in the business world, and where it did crop up it was generally trampled upon in a sustained effort to suppress it; but in the last few years we are seeing a strong resurgence, especially in Europe, which is freeing itself from American political and cultural domination – freeing itself also from a subliminal indoctrination with the teaching of holy corporate egoism, more sharply put rapaciousness with religious sanction.* After some hesitation (money markets don't like change) the European business world now appears to lead this process of liberation. This is not immediately apparent perhaps in daily corporate practice across the zone, but going by the many business leaders we meet in our work, our impression is that there are few circles in Europe where the need for the development of sustainable and therefore powerful alternatives to the old business model is felt so urgently. The smart money by now is on sustainable, socially aware, and healthy.

We see parallel processes in the psychological make up of people in the top of large organisations. The focus on the individual and his or her strictly personal freedom and strictly personal material possessions is gradually shifting – once again, more noticeably in Europe than elsewhere – to care for society and the environment. In short: *we are moving from exclusion to inclusion.* Put another way: *we are shifting from short term personal gain to sustainability.* The European constitution may have not made it the first time, in that ambitious and overly detailed form, but the fundamental attitude it represented (marked by care for the well-being of the continent's citizens) is shared and supported by a vast majority of Europeans, and will no doubt inform whatever new constitution or similar charter is agreed to in the future, as it already informs many of the new developments now taking shape in the public sphere.

Leaders with a strongly present Crown Chakra do not wait until these developments affect them, but consciously apply their talents in ways that help propel the development of society to a higher level of humanity.

Unfavourable development: An exaggerated focus on the Crown Chakra can lead to neglect of the bottom-line and endanger financial survival. Universal consciousness is wonderful, but only few manage to integrate it into an effective leadership style. Most of the few who do appear to be successful at it, are working in the spirituality industry, a fast growing line of business.

The publication of this book and our other activities in this field contribute to that growth (substantially we should hope), reason enough for

---

* Exploitation of the weak by the strong is sanctioned by many biblical Christians as being a natural result of divinely ordained differences in talent. This keeps the US minimum wage at $6.55 per hour (Fair Labor Standards Act federal minimum wage for 2008) and 12–15% of Americans living under the poverty line, millions of them in stark conditions.

us to take a critical look at that growth and our supposed contribution, because selling sweet talk is one of the world's two oldest professions. Its continued popularity through the ages should surprise no one. You get to say things which reflect very nicely on your character and ambitions, and are actually paid to do this. Now let's hope that this critical distance from our own work does not lead you to reject what we are saying, because even though the messenger may be flawed, the message may be exactly what you need to hear.

The hidden agenda behind our openness on this point is to goad you into taking an equally scorifying look at your own motives: pour onto it the mixed acids of suspicion and ruthlessness, and after the smoke lifts take stock of what you've got left. In the ideal case you see a glowing core of love, shining like gold, freed from all encrustations and pollutants. (In ourselves we see a promising, vaguely yellow nugget with lumps of baser metals caked on, which we aim to chisel away in the coming years.)

If the results disappoint, don't try to polish off the dullness, because that won't work, but go back to the primal themes. What was it again, that we are here on earth for? Exactly, [here your favourite answer]. And what is your core duty as leader of an organisation? Exactly, turn it into a goldmine. Remember therefore the ground rule of spiritual mining: the deeper you go, the better it gets.

Chief Challenge: Opening yourself to higher impulses without levitating. Seeing the light while not losing sight of the ground under your feet.

The idea is to give spirituality the proper weight in your life – not dominant and not subsidiary either, but all permeating, like the life force itself, which we do not consciously experience, but which animates us as long as we live.

THE CHAKRA OF COSMIC CONSCIOUSNESS

In the Indian tradition the Crown Chakra is represented by a thousand-petaled lotus that blossoms on the top of the head, envisaged as hovering a little above the crown. The name Sahasrara derives from Sanskrit *sahasra,*

'thousand'. This is the chakra of thinking, wisdom and universal consciousness. It represents our relationship with the universal, the timeless
all. It will be experienced more intensely by monists, people who are
convinced that everything is one, than by people who experience the world
in terms of individuality and duality, in collections of dichotomies.

When this chakra is in full bloom, it brings us wisdom, connectedness
on a spiritual level, and peace, a blissful inner state of high awareness and
high energy. It gives an affinity for practices such as meditation, and a
readiness to open oneself to cosmic forces and engage with them, both
receiving and giving. It is (in analogy to that transistor radio in the
Throat Chakra) like a satellite dish with which we receive the cosmic
forces, and, in simultaneous transmission, send our inner riches into the
world, in all its thousand facets. People who meditate or pray regularly,
and do it right,* have their Crown Chakras wide open.

EXALTED STATE OF BEING, OR CUNNING PRETENCE?

The Crown Chakra has an aspect so beautiful and elevated, that some
people like to give the impression that they are in enhanced states of
consciousness, whereas in fact their soul is in pawn to much more banal
concerns. This theatre act, when performed with talent, accrues prestige
and money too – two articles that are in near universal demand.

This means that we should be prepared to encounter people with a
dominant Root Chakra who pretend to be blessed with a blossoming
Crown Chakra, with a view to further their aims in the realm of survival
and profit-making. Having said this, we must add that this is a very difficult subject matter. Even after many years of observation in the field,
we are still left with more questions than answers, even regarding ourselves. We are see, for instance, a large number of supposedly spiritually
advanced leaders who make wonderful contributions to the world, and
enrich our lives with touching and inspiring sayings, but who demand
very high fees for their seminars and conferences, invariably held in the
most luxurious of resorts.

* This qualifier is not a symptom of pedantry, but a needed caveat. There is an abundance of
classes where one can learn to meditate on money or tighter abs or even 'Power over Others', and
contacts in heaven inform us that there is a lot of prayer for promotions.

Peter has a fitting illustration: 'Two years ago I received an invitation for an intimate VIP-course with Sri Sri Ravi Shankar (no relative of the sitar master), a world guru who styles himself "His Holiness", which, due to my acute sensitivity to degrees of holiness and unholiness, honed in years of Indian pilgrimage, triggered a silent alert, as did that repeated Sri, not unheard of in India, but still an uncommonly rich honorific even in a country with a penchant for religious pomposity. If from now on I would call myself Mister Mister ten Hoopen – would that help? Would I gain recognition to a degree that so far eluded me? Red alert.'[115]

'I do admire Sri Sri, as he is lovingly called by his disciples, for the tremendous amount of good that his organisation does for the poor, for prisoners and otherwise needy people the world over. He serves as an advisor to the United Nations, and in 2005 was nominated for the Nobel Peace Prize. But the 36 hour retreat was to be held in the Hamburg Hyatt, one of the most pricey abodes in town, and cost €1250 – the equivalent of a day's living wage for 1250 of India's poorest. I found this financially challenging, and at odds with the supposed spirituality of the session. I asked the organisation in Germany why they felt this was a wise choice of accommodation. Wouldn't a monastery or a quiet country hotel, modest but decent, have been more suitable? "No," I was told by the lady who handled the VIP-packages, "in order to change the world, we need to focus on business leaders, and they simply won't come to such simple places. So we have no choice, we need to be where they are, this is their world, and we need to be in the middle of it."'

'I was right in the middle of it a year later, when friends of my wife – Ravi Shankar disciples John and Angie, the dearest people, full of spirit and go – invited us to join them for a private audience with Sri Sri in Madrid, advertised by them as a unique opportunity to meet his Holiness in person, and ask him a few questions. The red alert immediately flashed on again, but no, it was all free and we could stay in any hotel we wanted, so we rented a Vito bus and drove 800 km from Portugal where we live to go see their Guruji. On the road my wife Ineke was a little defensive about me, explaining to John and Angie that I am allergic to gurus who live the good life and have too many Rolls Royces, while also explaining how I had incurred that affliction.'

'"Ooh, our Guruji has no Rolls Royces, he is the humblest of men! He never takes anything for himself. He gives away everything!"'

' "Okay, good," I mumbled, trying to get over my reserves and commit myself to the trip. I looked at the beloved Andalusian landscape, and gained some spiritual strength from the old cork oaks on a hillside, with their angular shapes, all bent the same way by the wind, but wilful in their expression of individual existence. I was going along to Madrid but to stay firmly rooted. (Rooted in my prejudice, John and Angie would have said.)'

'It didn't help that we arrived at the luxury hotel where the session was to be held, only seconds before Sri Sri. We were just about to enter the front door when a white Rolls Royce drove up, with a bearded and pink robed gentleman in front next to the driver. It was only when Sri Sri got out that I noticed that the car had been upholstered in what looked like fur, a lush, foxy kind of brown probably selected to go well with the walnut dash. I gave John an "I told you" look and let His Holiness pass to be welcomed by his waiting disciples. Some genuflected to kiss his feet, rather hindered by him wearing socks in his sandals. (A week later John called me about the Rolls. He had investigated: the car was not really Guruji's, but had been bought for him by a Spanish disciple, to use whenever he was in Spain.)'

'We began with a public audience in the conference room, where Sri Sri Ravi Shankar spoke a few platitudes about love and sharing, and the importance to work hard: "*Seva, seva, seva* … Devotion to labour is the answer! Only by learning to serve will you ever free yourself. Come to our ashram, there is so much beautiful work to be done." Appearing exhausted by this motivational speech, His Holiness leaned back in the low throne that had been placed on the stage, a cream faux-Louis XIV with carmine velvet upholstery, and enriched with fluffy pillows, and sat yawning and nodding through the clumsy song and dance offered by his local disciples. After a brief meditation and benediction our little group was shuffled off to a room in the catacombs where His Holiness held the private audience for core workers like John and Angie and a couple who built up presence in a new country and supposed hi-potentials such as me.'

'When my turn came I asked His Holiness how I could help corporate leaders to integrate their spiritual needs in their daily work.'

' "Tell them to take our Corporate Course. Angie can give you the website address." Other questions were answered in similar vein.'

'Next came Catarina, a lady who had travelled with us in the van. She told us about her work, and her passion. She is a social worker, based in one of the poorest parts of Portugal, the hot and dry and depopulated Alentejo, where many people actually die of hunger – if they don't kill themselves before. The region has one of the highest suicide rates in Europe, especially among elderly people whose pensions have been reduced to small change by the waves of economic development that passed them by. She explained her work to His Holiness in some detail.'

'"Guruji, what should I tell these people?"' our friend said.

'For a second I saw Sri Sri Ravi Shankar struggle, then he beamed his photogenic smile at her and spoke the unforgettable words: "Keep smiling! Tell them to keep smiling! When you smile, all good things come to you."'

'I stole a glance at Catarina to see how she would take it. Tears welled up in my eyes when I saw her crushing disappointment. On the long way back she sat silent in the back of the van. It was dark by the time we dropped her off in the village where she worked, and saw her disappear in the unlit maze of alleys, a mere shadow of the woman that we had taken to see her guru.'

One more example. Because this is a pressing issue that should concern many – or perhaps because it addresses a part of ourselves with which we are not wholly reconciled. Maybe you can help us with this reconciliation. Take the case of Deepak Chopra, who says the most beautiful things, hands out nuggets of insight and love left and right, and moreover has an impressive and pleasant stage presence. Who doesn't love Deepak Chopra? Immediately after the bombings in London in the summer of 2005 he wrote in a newsletter: 'There are causes behind every terrorist act and therefore hope that these causes can be changed, even as we continue to pursue justice. We still ignore the source of global instability: religious fundamentalism which has its roots in extreme poverty, where 50% of the world lives on $2 per day, 20% of it on less than $1 per day, a world where 8 million people die each year because they are too poor to survive.'[116]

We thought this was truth well spoken, bravely addressing something to which our governments seem largely insensitive and for many decades had actually hoped to remain oblivious. The iffy syntax suggested writing in great excitement, and a hurry to get out the message. Here speaks a man of the people, champion of the poor, a man not unlike the 13th C. Indian Sufi Saint, Moinuddin Chisti, the famous Gharib Nawaz, or Protector of the Poor, who is venerated by Hindus and Muslims alike and whose sayings Chopra must know intimately.

The newsletter linked through to Deepak Chopra's Alliance for the New Humanity – 'a network of love in action, a collective statement of the best of our human nature, meant to influence social consciousness so that we can move to a society of peace and serenity.' Prominently placed on the homepage we found a bit of promotion for the Alliance's annual conference. It was to be held on Puerto Rico, more specifically at the 'Westin Rio Mar Beach Golf Resort & Spa' and cost $1,000 – excluding accommodation and travel, though including arrival day cocktails. There were several possible upgrades, such as participation as *7th Heaven Sponsor* [no kidding]. This would get you to stay in a special suite, in the same wing as Deepak Chopra and the other speakers. The cost then increased, depending on the arrangements, to $6,722 or $7,708.

To pull in the truly spiritual, extra promotional bait is thrown in: the first 75 delegates to sign on would also get a *private sunrise group meditation* with Deepak Chopra himself. Clearly, like the Pope, who also does private audiences for dozens at a time, Chopra in his meditations transcends ordinary contradictions. The serene and loving atmosphere that the website exuded was enhanced by a quote from Maria Teresa: 'There is no greater sickness in the world today than the lack of love.' How good to know that out there in Puerto Rico a bunch of people convene who are not shy to express their love with their wallet.[117]

We've done the math, based on rough, but conservative estimates of travel expenses, mini-bar bills and the number of *7th Heaven Suckers*. If 300 delegates signed up, probably in the low end of the bandwidth for a Deepak Chopra seminar, then the participants in that Westin Rio Mar Beach Golf Resort & Spa jointly and communally spent about a million dollars on the noble cause of ennobling themselves. Enough, by Deepak's own reckoning, to one day give *one million* of the world's poorest twice as much to eat as they are used to.

Any ideas on the reconciliation of this apparent contradiction? Any nuggets of wisdom to help us accept, and perhaps even join in the applause?

SUBTLE MASSAGE IN THE SERVICE
OF EXPLOITATION?

Of course it is important that more leaders in politics, the civil services and 'the business community' become aware of interhuman connectedness, and get inspired by the idea of a new humanity, more loving and caring. Yet this change is taking place in a way which appears to benefit mostly the leaders themselves, allowing these grandees to indulge:

- their desires to get themselves pampered, body and soul;
- their desires to be irradiated with love and bathe in beautiful feelings;
- their even deeper desires, at mature age often acute, to see themselves in a more glorious light.

A few words on this from Henry S., CEO of a leading European management training institute. We've known him for years, mostly through joint work for advisory boards, and have both shared the stage with him on occasion. He is an inspiring man with an acute mind and flashes of brilliance. On one of his many unguarded, and therefore enlightening, moments he imparted to us an insight that shocked us. Not so much of the content, but because it had never occurred to us – an indictment perhaps of our intelligence. In Henry's usual tone, at the same time amusing and challenging: 'All these programs that we are offering with a somewhat spiritual, healing nature, have the effect to make participants feel good about themselves. Companies are willing to pay high prices for this kind of maintenance job, because after these managers come back all lubed and shined, they are good for another run. Even the somewhat older guys, you might think that they'd be at the end of their rope, but then they come to us for a psychological massage and ... Look, there's more service to be gotten out of them yet! So, in a very subtle manner, we are actually helping to perpetuate the process of exploitation.'[118]

Psychological analysis, Marxist analysis – how correct are they, and how honest? Corporate motives, personal motives – how noble are they, and how self-seeking? When we believe ourselves to be truly altruistic, are we not even then acting from an underlying selfish motive? To wit, that it makes us feel good? As we help the people who work for us to feel good about what they are doing, are we actually applying the corporate grip on them even more firmly? Maybe it all comes down to the intent. But who shall judge the intent? Who, having read Musil's masterwork *The Man Without Qualities*, will ever believe that a person is always clear about his or her own motives? Too many questions, too few answers... But that is nothing to worry about, because awareness was what it was all about, wasn't it? Awareness requires opening yourself, and on the rational level opening yourself starts with questioning.

The effect of all this questioning is, that we take a caustic look at all activity in this area, including our own. Other than that we primarily go by our intuition. Fortunately Fons' has been fine-tuned by decades of consultancy work all over the globe; Peter's by international journalism and years of travel in Asia – where, if you really want to, it is still possible to find truly enlightened souls, but where you certainly encounter hundreds of busy, self-advertising gurus and thousands of shameless impostors.

Now what about us? Of course we are the purest souls on earth, overflowing with universal love, which, for an appropriate fee, we gladly share with corporate audiences. So, should you ever have a couple of thou to be enlightened on the effect of perpetuating stark wealth disparity on the corporate and the human soul, you know where to find us.

Final question: why do we phrase the above so bitterly? Because we couldn't raise a million for nice to-do with *us* in the Caribbean? Or because sometimes when are transported to our comfortable hotel in Asia, Africa or Latin-America, we see people sleeping on the streets? Because we know and support priests who do not live in Golf Resorts & Spas but in the same type of hovels as the people they care for? Or are we bitter because we live in well appointed houses in safe communities, and contribute no more to care for the disadvantaged than some digital transfers and occasional sweet talk?

THE CHAKRA THAT TRANSCENDS ALL

Now some more uplifting words. Because really, at the level of the Crown Chakra none of this matters. Say to yourself: 'I am not my money, I am not my words, I am not my body, nor my thoughts, not my senses, nor my feelings, I am pure consciousness, untouched by anything that befalls me.' Take a deep breath and transcend all these differences. Or is there still someone around who wants to keep us here at the worldly level and its dialectical problems? Let us enjoy our powers at his level, and open in ourselves, what the architect Daniel Libeskind so beautifully calls our 'capacity to evoke wonder'.[119]

MARKS OF A HEALTHY CROWN CHAKRA

- universal consciousness
- a strong sense of connectedness with all that lives
- mystical experiences
- the capacity to learn from experience
- an open mind
- the power to evoke wonder.

SYMPTOMS OF A BLOCKED CROWN CHAKRA

- scepsis towards spirituality in general ('all nonsense')
- negation of spirituality as a positive factor in working life
- attempts to rationalise phenomena that fall outside the realm of reason
- addiction to spirituality
- surrender to wrongly chosen, self-seeking gurus, joining a sect
- overestimation of one's own level of saintliness
- spiritual materialism (the common 'I Am Holier Than Thou' Syndrome)
- living counter to, and fundamental non-understanding of basic rules of self-management (such as 'If you want to become happy, stop doing what makes you unhappy.')
- neglect of one's own mental capacity, mental degradation by addiction to pulp media
- slow learning
- confusion.

Place on earth: To Peter, the Crown Chakra is best found on a place in Southern Portugal that he frequently visits, the hill not far from his house that a few years ago he bought from his old gardener. In Peter's words:

'Senhor Joaquim was always on about a hill of his that I should definitely buy – it was so right for me! A little remote, but with a wonderful view. I loved views, didn't I? As it happened he needed some money for an extension to his house in the village, and he would offer it to me for a *prix d'ami*. Once he got me to go and have a look. The whole hill was overgrown with sticky rock rose, exuding so much resin in the burning sun that the leaves glistened wet. The smell was intoxicatingly sweet and invited approach, intimate contact even; but after twenty steps my clothes were not what they used to be.'

'After some fifteen minutes of plodding and wriggling through the shrub, we had made it to about half way up, a small plateau with a view of distant hills. We both looked as if we had bedded with the pigs. Shocked, I stared at Senhor Joaquim's dress pants, no doubt ironed for the occasion. They were coated in smears and globs of resin, blackening as they dried. Senhor Joaquim was the first to acknowledge that it was a mad venture. "Of course Senhor Peter should see the view from the top, which is, eh... much higher, and..." He suddenly appeared to lose all hope to reach me with words. "Well, at least now you've got some idea."'

'I went home with the impression of an impossible place, and a disappointed gardener. In the years after he kept promoting that hill covered in rock rose that he reserved for me and would never sell to anyone else without offering it to me first, but I did not want to ruin another pair of pants and never paid much attention. One day I ran into Senhor Joaquim at the windmill on the market square. He looked at me like a man holding a trump card. "You really have to go back to that hill with me," he said. "I have had a path bulldozed all the way up." I didn't have anything else to do, so we got into the jeep and rolled out of the village into the interior, following a narrow valley with a little river that was dry now but could become a wild stream in winter.'

'"Now stop right here in the bend," Senhor Joaquim said, "Look, the boundary runs from here straight along this ridge to the top. On the other side it runs down to the river bed and ..." A rocky path of freshly crushed slate veered upwards along a gentle slope. I rolled the jeep across the rubble in first gear, which afforded a pleasant feeling of control and dominance – master of my domain – and drove up in one smooth sweep.

I got out, looked around me, and staggered as if I had been blown off my feet by the wind. The hilltop turned out to have a stunning 360° view: on one side the ocean, on another the mountains, and on yet another that pastoral valley of almond trees and little farms. Unbelievable: had I let him beg me for years to come here?'

' "Now don't appear too eager!" was my first thought, revealing a deeply engrained opportunism. "Hmm," I said. "Nice, very nice ..." I tried to keep my tone flat. "How much was it again you wanted?" As I spoke the words, I thought of the years that had passed. Of land prices that had not lain dormant. Fortunately Senhor Joaquim's regard for our friendship was unchanged, as was the budget of his extension.'

' "Of course I have to consult the *senhora* first," I told him on the way home, but as I spoke these words we both knew this to be a formality. Now the *senhora* and me frequently go to the top of that hill. To meditate, walk the dog, or just stand there, preferably in the middle of the night. The effect is to make you feel united with the entire cosmos. There is a connection in the horizontal plane because your energy is free to flow in any direction, and everywhere you look there is space for miles and miles. There is a vertical connection because you are standing on the axis that runs through the middle of the hill to the core of the earth. Your head actually forms its very apex. This makes you aware of the fact that, as everywhere else for that matter, you are standing with your feet towards the centre of the earth, with your crown to the zenith. Meanwhile, the thousand leaved lotus is shown in simile by the night sky with its thousand stars, hovering above the head like a giant chakra.'

'Sometimes when we take friends up there, I prepare them by explaining that to experience the effect no meditation is necessary. Just stand there and do nothing. Experience, be aware. Be aware of what you receive – and of what you pass on. Nothing more. The effect is a powerful charge of energy, that sometimes you will free yourself from with a surprised shake of the head, because yes, it is too wonderful, too much almost, but then again you can't stand there forever.'

'On that hill I am starting to understand the wisdom of Ashtavakra, which I freely paraphrase as: Countless are those who attempt to advance themselves by practicing austerities and exercises, one more strenuous than the other, and there is meditation without end. But only the rare enlightened soul strives for nothing and lives in peace with himself.'

RECONCILIATION ACROSS A WIDE SPECTRUM

The great challenge for business leaders and consultants in this era is to reconcile, not just short term versus long term, global versus local, bottom-line versus society, discipline versus inspiration, customer versus employee, brand versus identity – but to reconcile each and all of those. The ability, the propensity rather, to synchronously reconcile multiple dimensions will be the chief characteristic of what we will term great leaders. They create not structures, but flowing patterns of energy. They are masters not of the material but of energy use. Not of displacement but of focus shift. Not of staying the course, but of continual correction.

As Norbert Wiener[120] said, the visionary scientist who coined the term 'cybernetics' for our complex steering systems: You can't ride a bike in a straight line. What we call going straight is actually achieved by continuous corrections of oversteer. Ooh, gone too far to the left, oops! Go to right... Oops too far! Go left quickly, oops... Cyclists in Vienna and other towns blessed with streetcars discover the truth young: you can't cycle on tram rails. As soon as your front wheel gets stuck in the straight track, you fall. The only way to cycle is to continuously swerve left and right with minute corrections. Great leaders in this respect are like riders: using their finely honed cybernetic gifts, in their reconciliations they now favour this side of the scale a little, then that, to keep energy flowing on all levels. Each chakra well developed, but not overdeveloped at the expense of other levels. No choking or bloating, but an even, smooth running energy economy. Running on All Seven.

This fine inner balance resembles the inner balance that yogis strive for in meditation. The traditional depiction of chakras in Indian miniatures shows the energy centres as a series of glowing orbs, one above the other along the straight line of the spine. Importantly, the spine is seen as a conduit of energy, to be raised from the lowest chakra where it lies dormant, through the other chakras, to the highest, where its great power and radiance will become manifest. Even when looking at it with the eye of someone who does not know whether chakras actually exist, or are just convenient symbols of a mental state – borrowed here for art and convenience – it strikes one that, separate from any attributions one might or might not grant them, the symbolism is very powerful. It shows how the great operate, their inner workings.

This ability to practice full spectrum reconciling across a series of dimensions is partly innate – in the sense that it requires at least an average level of sensibility to start with – but can be developed through practice. The more often you manage to frame your life's issues as dilemmas to be reconciled, the more likely it becomes that you will find a good way to live with yourself. Reconciliation is partly ideal, partly emotional, but part of it is also technique, the acquisition of a mindset. What needs to be created is a habitual approach to issues that is non-linear (thinking in opposites creates a lot of misery) and non-confrontational, not given to compromise nor stooped in submission, but that builds on the conviction that yes, in many cases, you *can* have it both ways.

Recently in a workshop with hi-po young managers we gave an impromptu illustration of what constitutes a typical dilemma: 'There is always the "On the one hand", and "On the other hand". For instance (we tried to keep it simple on account of their age), "On the one hand you want to make money, on the other hand you want to stay in bed."' 'Oh, but that's easy to reconcile,' one young man answered, evoking an eruption of laughter. The example was not reused in further workshops. A shame really, as the boy's uncalled for answer actually made it a memorable illustration of the concept.

IS THERE LIFE BEYOND MASLOW?

We often ask mature audiences where they are on the scale of Maslow. First, are your survival needs met? Now these are all successful people otherwise they would not be there. So all hands go up. How about your safety needs? All hands go up. Most are living in suburbs or towns with decent security. Social needs then? Networking is part of the event, and they are good at it. Esteem needs? All enjoy the respect of their peers, their staff, or at least think they do, so most hands go up again. Self realisation? These are people who have made something of what they were given, and usually proud of it. All hands go up. Next question: 'Now that you have attained all this, even the highest level of the pyramid, what else is there?'

This is always followed by a deep silence. You can feel them all trapped there in the top of that pyramid. We elaborate the question: 'Where are you going from here, or *is this all there is?* Ask yourself, what great drive can you still muster? Where do you see a way to achieve substantial further growth?' Then we draw a triangle representing Maslow's pyramid, and extend the sides upwards beyond the top, creating an ever widening new space (see illustration).

'Now what might there be in that new space? And what does it take to get there?' We always hope that someone in the audience says it before we do. 'Yes indeed, brilliant!' The answer of course, in all its simplicity, is *transcending your own needs*. Maslow's hierarchy of needs was strictly limited to description of the individual's own needs. But as soon as you start devoting yourself to something, whatever it is, that transcends your own interests, you have created a whole new ambition, and a whole new world in which to manifest leadership.

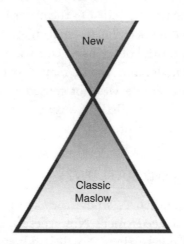

The first level of this new inverted pyramid we call Inner Nobility. It is the true domain of the Enlightened Leader. But it is so far out of our own reach that we shall not say a word more about it. It is up to you to channel your vital energy as you see fit. We can only hope that this book will help you do it more consciously.

CROWN CHAKRA DOMINANT:
ARCHETYPE TREVOR M. – SANCTITY FIRST

Trevor M. was born and raised in gritty Liverpool, son of a dock worker. A tough lad, and a fighter, he managed to overcome the drawbacks of his humble beginnings, and by his thirtieth was general manager of a paint factory. Everything went well – because he was a good leader, whose relentless dedication inspired his employees to similar application – until he met the graceful and mysterious Claudine, a psychologist of upper middle-class background with strongly felt spiritual interests. She took him to gatherings and workshops with Guru Maharaj Ji, who convinced them that love was the answer, and within months, all spare time was spent in the guru's ashram outside London, much of it in each other's arms.

It did not take long for the running of a paint factory to become a chore, only performed to scrape together money – most of it now earmarked for ever more generous donations to the ashram, and rising prestige in the guru's immediate circle. After a few years of ever higher initiations and journeys to India, Trevor realised that he had a mission in life beyond the manufacture of paint, and that his leadership qualities had been given to him for a destiny in the spiritual realm. He quit his job, and devoted himself full-time to evangelising, in short the promotion of holiness.

The family moved to the countryside, to be near the ashram. When it became apparent that some household money would still need to be made, Trevor found occasional employ through temp job agencies, or did odd jobs in construction. His father, who had been deeply proud of his son, factory director, was not just disappointed, but deeply saddened. Trevor saw him as – and called him – a spiritually handicapped old chap who devoted his whole life to making money and never developed himself beyond playing darts with his mates. Soon he cut the relationship with his father, explaining that it became a stumbling block on his spiritual path.

The children grew up in changing environments, because when the guru moved his seat elsewhere, to establish an ashram in say Tuscany or California, the M. family moved along with him, as part of the court. The boys were not lavished with attention, because their needs were of a distressingly worldly, uninspiring nature – such as shoes, schooling, clean clothes, dental checkups, help with homework ... Thanks to her strongly spinning Root Chakra, Claudine still managed to keep the household going, and neat as a pin, but she too would rather sit and meditate than play cops and robbers with the boys or talk about sports and cars, let alone girls.

Trevor became ever more elevated in his demeanour, and no longer spoke a word to people who were not devoted to the spiritual – and with those that were only if they explicitly or implicitly recognised his superiority in this area. In fact he saw every meeting as a *satsang* where the others got to enjoy his glorious *darshan* for free. If Claudine managed to tag him along to a party he would sit the evening out in silence, a beatic smile on his face, helped in the maintenance of this pose by the drinking of enough beer to anaesthetise him to the surrounding stupidity.

When their intelligent sons graduated from grammar school, and it became time to send them on to the university, it soon became obvious that there was not enough money. Claudine suggested that maybe Trevor should go back to work, but her husband was so far above this by now, that he would not hear a second word about it. She herself took on jobs caring for people in their last days, to come up with household money and a little support for the boys. But after two years of lonely plodding she called it quits, went back to London and found work in her old profession. Trevor, too, went back to the city. He now lives in Liverpool and lives off odd jobs in the docks.

CROWN CHAKRA BLOSSOMING:
ARCHETYPE Y.H. – THE ENLIGHTENED LEADER

Yes, it would be wonderful to have a case from corporate life here as well, but this is a category so rare that you don't run into specimens daily. They are somewhat more common outside the fortresses of hard core capitalism. The recently deceased French priest Pierre Abbée comes to mind. A man with all chakras wide open, rooted like a tree in the worldly tissue of poverty, deeply beloved by his constituency, endowed with a willpower that changed a nation's look at its poorest classes, so full of heart that he devoted his life to people that others had rejected, vocal to the point of being loud when the case called for a voice raised in anger, connected with all living beings, and obviously open to divine inspiration.*

Yes, there exist some who appear to be pretty close to the ideal, teachers of universal peace and love and harmony, and a new energy ... But many of them have egos inflated to bursting point, so that we actually help them by not giving them any further exposure.

It's not easy. The widely revered Bengali saint Sri Ramakrishna, referred to earlier, a man from the common people with an intellectual following, lived a life of utter simplicity, and often spoke from an ecstasy so intense that he needed to be supported by disciples. Even he, this man of the people who transmitted his wisdoms not in sermons but in enlightening little stories about daily life, had to admit that vanity is not easily conquered, that it is the last of the dragons to be slain.

So let's not enthrone here any supreme gurus or leaders of all leaders, let's enthrone you, Your Honour. Because it is *you* who will have to make a difference. Let's face it, if there is anyone who can bring enlightenment, it is you. To begin with within, in your inner being. Then, consequentially, in the outside world as well.

'Your Honour' feels inside a deep longing for a more spiritual way of life, reinforces it by reading books such as this, and for some time now has been contemplating how that longing for a higher self could be reconciled with a professional career – or is in fact well into this process of reconciliation already. You (if we may revert to the familiar) have exposed yourself to other cultures, such as the Indian, in which the spiritual is woven into the very fabric of daily life, into the finest sarees, and the coarsest *khadi*. You understand the language of the Sufi poets who sing about a beloved they miss so dearly that it hurts, knowing that the true beloved is the divine, the universal, and that to them there is no greater grief than missing that sense of unity with the universal force that permeates everything, keeps everything together, and animates our life.

---

* Those who object to the terminology shall please substitute 'divine' with any word of their approved vocabulary that describes a sense of union with the entire universe.

In your work as a leader you try to put the enormous forces that are generated in your organisation to work for the well-being of all involved. Your vision and engagement are on a global level, and you are never short of people who respect your commitment and follow you intuitively, with great dedication. As long as you make sure that all the chakras below this one are running freely as well, you have it in you to become a truly great leader. We expect much from you, and in the coming years will follow your career closely.

Balanced Energy Economy

HOW HALLOWED IS THE HIGHEST?

If the Crown Chakra represents so much that is noble and beautiful, shouldn't we then set our sights on it exclusively, go all out for cosmic consciousness? Isn't this the hallowed state that leaders should ultimately strive for? And, the Root Chakra being so worldly, so rooted in the muck of primal struggle for survival and the making of profit, should we not attempt to rise miles and miles above it? (To that 7th *Heaven* for instance?)

If only things were that simple, or that cheap. Of course that would be heavenly, to just sit there and be visionary all day and let your warm feelings flow into the world. Union with the universal with your eyes closed. But if that is the attraction, you are better off sitting in a cave in the Himalayas – mail Peter for suggestions when the appeal gets too strong to ignore – or on Gomera with a few chickens and a cabbage patch.

In a corporate environment this undivided focus on the higher realms of consciousness is impracticable; both in the sense of impossible to maintain (because other people will bring you down) and in the sense of unworkable. It is barely possible even for anyone with nothing else to do. But then, this isn't the goal anyway. In Yoga philosophy, which has inspired the Chakras of Leadership, it is definitely not considered ideal to be in your Sahasrara all day.

The goal, in Kundalini Yoga, and in all tantric traditions, is the awakening of a force that is lying dormant within the Root Chakra, traditionally depicted as curled up like a snake. That force is the higher consciousness. Comparable to the total consciousness that we had as children, and which has been suppressed, smothered and distorted by upbringing, education, 'the struggle for life', and most effectively of all through the autocratic management by the ego. The goal is to wake this slumbering consciousness, and then, in consecutive stages, bring it up through the chain of chakras to the crown.* The ideal situation has been reached when *all seven* chakras are wide open, glowing, receiving and radiating energy.

The same goes for leadership in a corporate environment: enlightened leadership can be truly successful only in a healthy energy economy, in which all seven realms receive balanced attention.

- If the Root Chakra is neglected, that humble energy centre of survival and profit and independence, not enough money flows in; and before you know it, it is time to close the business. A prime example is Amsterdam's world famous Oibibio, a multi-storey spiritual centre in the heart of Amsterdam near Central Station, a colossal old mansion redecorated with great artistry and expense. It was an instant hit with locals and had people flying in from all over the world, but was loss-making from day one. It had been founded by Gerrit Jan Heijn, a son of the founder of the Ahold conglomerate, who kept throwing money at his dream, gave thousands of people a great time, and in the end sank most of his patrimony in the venture because there was no attention to the bottom-line, or any line for that matter. In Dutch business-speak it became a cliché for neglect of the financial aspects of an organisation: 'Hey come on, we're not at Oibibio!'
- If the Sacral Chakra is underperforming, this is likely to manifest itself in uncomfortable relationships with superiors, colleagues, clients, the community, or all of the above. This is frequently observable in companies that have been misled by their consultants into believing that Customer Relations Management is a matter of service level agreements and clever programming. For them, customers, clients, suppliers, are there to be exploited, and the less time spent on the process, the better for the bottom line. If the Sacral Chakra *is* performing, but with negative effect, we speak of *perverted* relational energy, a result of unfavourable development of the energy centre. A common type,

---

* A much reduced version, by now stripped of apparent spiritual intent, is found in the ancient European fairytale of Snow White. In the prehistoric ages when the fairytales were created, they all conveyed messages of a spiritual nature, since lost as Christianity and Rationality took over. Originally Snow White's awakening must have been widely recognised as a tale of spiritual awakening – we all have to wake the sleeping princess within.

ripe for the textbooks, is the sales manager who spends a fortune on wining and dining his contacts, trying to lure them into golden deals he concocts, with margins for himself that are the boast of his toast. As now and then he manages to pull off one of those rip-deals, he thinks himself real smart; but true success eludes him, as he has a conversion ratio (sales/quotes) to make a CFO sob. His reaction, typically, is a dip into the sweet-and-sour sauce of self-pity. Isn't there anyone who loves me? Doesn't anyone like me enough to let me rip him off in full consciousness? An archetype of perversion of the chakra in the lower belly.

- If the Solar Plexus Chakra is weak, you can have the most beautiful product and the greatest network in the world, but the drive will be lacking to really score. A sluggish energy centre at this level enfeebles the will to conquer market share or land a particular commission, the will that would be needed for the ultimate realisation of the organisation's potential. High-tech companies can be so afflicted, including many of the nerds that people them *à titre personnel*: sky high on what they can accomplish, but failing to go beyond, because that thrill of success in creation is enough for their rush, making them neglect to seriously bring it to market. Many are developing new improved versions before they have any cash flow from the first. They are the horror of investors.

- If the Heart Chakra is weak, the heart is weak. Either that or there is no heart. A weak heart function at the spiritual level blocks further growth beyond lower instincts, and leads to imbalance. This is the level of inner turnaround – both on a personal and a corporate level. Heart makes the difference.

- If the Throat Chakra is underdeveloped or blocked, communication is deficient: you can have the most wonderful ideas and bring many wonders into the world, and no one will know. This was the case with pre-Kleisterlee Philips: making wonderful products, but styling and advertising them so middle of the road and boring that only dullards would buy them. Think of what that does to your margins. Wonderbra said it best in their Hall of Fame 1960s slogan 'If you've got it, flaunt it.' Speak out, bring your wonderful content to people's attention. Keep in mind though, this is also the chakra of purity. Perverted development of this chakra leads to speaking of untruth, an objectionable practice that unfortunately is so common in daily business practice world-wide that millions of lawyers are driving in Jaguars.

- If the Third Eye Chakra is closed, or peering through lazily lowered lids, there is a lack of connection with the inner self. You plod on through life like a plough horse; year in, year out, from client to client and from deal to deal, without a clear vision of where the world is going, the market is going, the business is going, life is going. Success follows bungling, bungling success. The same applies to an organisation: there is no clear vision, no well-defined purpose, no shared ambition, hence no energy. Worst of all: there is no clear *self-image*. How can you expect the world to have a correct image of who you are as an organisation, if you don't know yourself? Conversely, if you know yourself well, know who you are and what you stand for, you can speak with a strong voice and command the world's attention. Almost half of the work we do at Trompenaars Hampden-Turner is aimed at giving organisations a clearer self-image; when they go through cultural upheaval, and when market forces call for an increase of fitness.

- If the Crown Chakra has fallen asleep, a common condition in 90 per cent of all commercial organisations, the effect may be noticeable only to those attuned to certain inner conditions. They might observe, for instance, a lack of visionary gifts, the ability to feel what is coming before the trend watchers send out their alerts. Or they might see a denial of human connectedness (manifested in exploitation of any kind), an uninspiring working environment, an inability to attract and keep truly great people. And worst of all in our minds a lack of Libeskind's 'capacity to evoke wonder'.

To get an impression of your own chakra line-up, take the Chakra Test that was developed especially as a companion to this book: www.chakratest. org. The results page depicts your energy distribution, with its favourable and unfavourable developments, in a clear and unique manner.

RUNNING ON ALL SEVEN

A leader who is 'Running on All Seven' has a healthy energy economy. This gives him or her the visionary qualities, self-knowledge, communicative strength, courage, will power, relational warmth and groundedness truly great leaders need. She leads the organisation to success by paying attention to financial solidity and continuity, builds relationships with all stakeholders, uses her willpower to push issues that she believes in, uses her heart force to connect on a deeper level and maintain harmony in the organisation, communicates with an authentic voice, ringing with inner conviction and respect, is alert to what happens in the world, not just on the material plane, but also in the global psyche, has a clear view of her role in the organisation and the organisation's role in the world, and shoulders the yoke that universal consciousness lays on her shoulders.

Part III

Enlightenment in Practice

Work is love made visible.

Kahlil Gibran

The moment you live something, you are teaching it,
whether you want to or not.

Dadi Janki

A Higher Reality in Sight

If we wish to practice enlightened leadership, the first thing required is at least a ray of light into our souls, if only through a crack. And then we need to look up through that crack into the wider, lighter world beyond and let our gaze expand in wonder. Because having an inspiring vision gives much energy, and direction as well. Omraam Aivanhov, introduced above:

> We cannot improve anything in this world when we don't have higher visions, other forms of being that can serve us as illustration and example. You cannot create anything better and more beautiful if you have not somehow contemplated a reality that surpasses the current. And this precisely is the work of the initiated. In their meditations, their contemplations, their ecstasies, they contrive to receive this higher perfection. And after that they try to recreate all this on earth.
>
> Most people are not capable of stretching themselves, to dwell upon a higher world, and make no progress. [...] But thanks to the masters and initiates who stand up and strain, overcoming all obstacles, to bring us concepts that are closer to heaven [an obvious reference to enlightened leaders like you, Your Honour], the work of mankind's improvement makes progress.

LIBERATION FROM INNER TYRANNY

You cannot bring into the world concepts that are closer to heaven by living contrary to your own values. The first thing required is authenticity: acting in concordance with your inner being. This is the true integrity: the inner person and its manifestation in the outside world are in complete harmony, mirror images of each other.

But don't turn this rule into a matter of life and death, because then your Crown Chakra seizes up – it is all energy, keep it flowing. In the inner world no law must be adhered to strictly, and even this law may be safely broken. Taken down to the level of daily life: the general rule is, that straight after meditation you are not going to head-butt yourself with caffeine. On the other hand, should you, in one of your meditative meanderings, happen to pass by a sidewalk café that serves a decent macchiato, for heaven's sake don't deny yourself the pleasure. If saints had to be perfect there wouldn't be any.

Alas, it took me most of a life to learn this. 'God, how often hast Thou not punished me for my misdeeds by making me feel guilty and miserable. Still I am struggling to free myself from this harness, and love myself like You are supposed to love me. But a critical, reviewing, weighing, judging and condemning attitude was hammered in from above in Your name, Lord, from pulpit and dinner table. It became so chiselled in and interiorised that I am still spending half my time trying to get this ogre of disapproval off my neck.' Recognise any of this? We certainly come across it often enough in our work, particularly during intensives or workshops with an emphasis on coaching where deeper matter comes to the surface. Peter likes to quote Buddha, who once said something on the topic of discipline that resonates deeply with this erstwhile sitar student: 'How does the sitar player tune his strings so that they sound just right? Not too loose, and not too tight.'

The problem is, that our ego is always pushing for extremely loose or extremely tight. The ego would prefer that we do not listen to our inner voice at all and only pay heed to him, this inner tyrant to whom we have voluntarily submitted ourselves. When this submission is no longer guaranteed because we are undergoing spiritual growth, the ego attempts to take over the process, in order to carry on its despotic rule in another fashion. Do a little yoga and meditation and watch what you eat, and before you know you find yourself laced up in a straitjacket again. Didn't do your Sun Salutation today? Oh you are a lousy yogi, shame on you! (Cf. the dietary prescriptions and prohibitions that are popular in alternative circles, the faddish orthorexia of organic turnips and surrogate chocolate.)

The ego loves orthodoxy of any kind. These are the laws that have been promulgated. Note them and beware of infraction. Cup of coffee? Oh, watch it buddy! After queuing patiently forever suddenly grabbing an opportunity to move up in the line? Lashings with thorn bush twigs! Salacious thoughts when a girl born for sin steps into the bus? Baaaaad boy! Three days on bread and water! A sudden urge to rear-end that lane-hugger in front? Electroshocks to the private parts! That is why it is so terribly difficult to escape from the ego, and why we so often see people who are supposedly enlightened grow egos the size of a house. Some with five-car garages. Everything they say sounds like an offering from on high to the lowly disciples. Beware, *megalomania is the demon of sainthood*. Often, the first indications are affectation in speech, and the wearing of robes or silky designer casuals.

As the Indian guru Ashtavakra taught his king Janaka at the beginning of time:

> Those who strive for worldly pleasures, and those who strive for enlightenment, are found in great numbers. But rare is the elevated soul who strives neither for enjoyment nor for liberation. Let go of all desire and be happy.[121]

WHAT IS WISDOM?

Wisdom is an important element of enlightenment and its inevitable result. It is hard to be seen as enlightened while at the same time being judged as not very wise. Conversely, you cannot be considered wise if you have not reached a certain degree of enlightenment. But what is wisdom? Every self-respecting thinker has given his definition, so we shall not hesitate to add one more to the collection:

> **Wisdom** is the ability to live in peace with life's contradictions.

In other terms you could say: wisdom is laying new connections that resolve tensions, inner and outer, and re-establish peace. Wisdom is reconciliation. Anyone who attains even a fair degree of it saves energy that would otherwise have gone to waste in the struggle to live with life's unending contradictions. He or she lives more happily, and spreads happiness without even trying.

HOW IS WISDOM ATTAINED?

Wisdom is most readily attained through life experience – assuming you have the ability to learn from experience. It will teach you that not everything is as black or white as it seems, that it is hard to draw a straight line anywhere, that objective, quantifiable truths do not occur freely in nature, that greatness may hide smallness and the reverse, that the poor can be rich and the rich poor, that charity may be heartless and neglect a favour, that excess tends to convert to its opposite, that in scarcity the greatest luxuries are found, that bathing in luxury may masque a transcendence of attachment to renunciation, that striving too hard for enlightenment can lead to endarkenment, and that true beauty is found only where the inner being and the social being fully support each other.

Well, that's quite something, right? But how do you attain more wisdom quickly when you are young, and/or have no time to go out into the wide world experiencing? For starters you should try not to get excited about everything ephemeral, unless it be something that really arouses your passion. Passions count as not highly spiritual – because people who are deeply spiritual are above striving for result – but if you want to be authentic *and* have a career in a corporate environment, *it is essential to follow your passions*. Nothing else will do. Passions ensure that you bring into play your whole personality, Running on All Seven.

Above all, do not get drawn into the excitement of the day. Bomb blasts in Baghdad, bodies and blood. Tribal war in Africa, child soldiers, chopped off hands…Horrible. An emotional onslaught bringing wounds that will not heal. Because, excepting deeds of exceptional heroism, what is there to do beyond sending the occasional tax-deductible donation? Ask yourself: why should you allow such onslaught on your soul on a daily basis? And it goes on, plodding through the swamps of repeat performance, fake crises and pretend change. President of the Philippines more corrupt than predecessor – booh! Yes, today's youth behaves scandalously, ruining its own future, but isn't that its time-honoured duty? Then there are the World Cups, elections, royal weddings, shocking revelations, mega mergers, market crashes and bubbles, and cats that were miraculously saved from drowning. Again, why should you allow the media to inundate your soul with images of misery and mass mindlessness – even with that occasional rescued baby thrown into the format for emotional relief?

Before the industrial revolution, *Homo sapiens* lived largely in villages, and in small towns, where one largely went on foot. Information spread slowly, and in a distorted, faded, shredded and embellished form. Most people had reliable information only on their relatives and neighbours. If anything dramatic occurred, they were around to help – instantly if need be. This laid a link between emotion and the possibility to react in an adequate manner. The people were rarely touched by stories of disaster far away that might weigh on their souls, but that they were not in a position to change. This provided them a degree of inner peace that most of us have lost. It is a great loss, and worth attempting to recover. So, if you are not personally or professionally involved in the story, ignore it. Skip the pandemics, skip the hypes. As any skipper will tell you, don't pay attention to the ripples and waves so much, but gauge the swell.

For a large part, wisdom consists of ignoring information. Don't act on it. Delete to trash like so much spam. Wiser still is *avoiding information*. The truly wise have been withdrawing from the crowds for as long as men remember, seeking the solitude of deserts, caves and hermitages. No satellite with unlimited channels, no billboards and broadcasting, no mobile phones and websites, no claptrap and gossip and market update, no books about endarkenment and enlightenment...

The most important piece of wisdom, achievable at any age, is not to take yourself too seriously. Strip it all off. See yourself in the spatial perspective of a trillion light-years, and in a chronological perspective of at least the hundreds of thousands of years that humans and proto-humans have lived on earth, and then reflect on how truly important your position is, your status, your assets, your conflicts, your pain and excitement, and your striving for enlightenment. And after all this stripping away, note what remains. This reflection in itself is liberating and enlightening. It makes the young wise before their years, and rejuvenates the elderly.

The Wisdom of the Sea Urchin

We have said this before, while announcing a return to the subject: *the softer you get, the tougher you need to get.* This is not a call for super-assertive, leave alone aggressive behaviour, but a recognition of the fact that a greater degree of emotional sharing, of what the philosopher Don Beck broadly calls 'compassion', has been making headway in our society for centuries; incrementally, but steadily, like a pilgrimage. For a society to realise such growing longing for compassionate and humanitarian arrangements of daily life, to integrate this longing for love – *excusez le mot* – in daily life, everyone who has a part in the process needs to live on a shared emotional platform, and share a communal sense of purpose.

In such an environment of cultural growth, individuals who cannot or will not contribute are so many pathogenic cells in a larger organism,[122] that need to be removed or made harmless for the desired inner growth to take place. Ideally they are turned around by reintegration, co-optation, transformation, boot camp, or the traditional kick in the hind parts. Individuals who resist attempts at humanisation have to be dealt with sternly, because a society built on connectedness, solidarity and loyalty is very soft in its core – and inherently more vulnerable than the power based societies that have been the rule everywhere for thousands of years, except in some very small and isolated communities of loving people. And look how vulnerable they proved to be...

Look also at the animal world (or rather the rest of the animal world), and you'll see how a soft organism protects itself: by the construction of a very hard and painfully sharp or otherwise repellent exterior. The sea-urchin is the perfect model: as enticing as an apricot, so soft inside that it just begs to be eaten, but don't pick it up like you'd pick up an egg or the spikes enter your fingers to the bone.

It is far from us to preach a world of softness and cuddling. All this talk of enlightenment is not aimed at seducing more people in high positions to become softies. To the contrary, all this talk aims to show more people in leading positions that an enlightened type of leadership is a serious and necessary matter, that we all have to work for together. For humans with their genetically encoded fight-or-flight behaviour, being good for any but your closest relatives is evolutionarily recent. To many of us it is counter-intuitive, and there are battles to be fought, all of them inside.

Love is tough. The wusses can stay at home. (We don't even mind paying them to do it, never seemed to hurt the economy.) And the true leaders now go to work.

CLARITY IS ACHIEVED BY ELIMINATING DISTRACTIONS

Of course the work does not begin at the office, but at home: breathing in deeply in front of the mirror, or gazing out over the land, shrouded in drifts of morning mist. Here I am, but who am I? What do I receive, what do I radiate? What am I taking, what giving back? And who is this 'I' who is doing that? Where does he begin, where does he end? At the skin, at the garden's hedge, or the end of the sphere of influence? Who is the thinker, the feeler, the doer? Who lives and who dies?

Or work begins in the car, when you have been moving in a dense pack at unvarying distance and unvarying speed for what seems forever, the cars appearing like products on an assembly line, moving on, moving on… And suddenly you see yourself sitting there in that nicely upholstered box, a human body steering in a chosen direction. And where is it *you* aim to go? Where are you going in that little toot-toot! bumper car on the well laid track? Sometimes I can't read the inner road signs anymore or they are just blank: huge blue shields without any indication. Yes, I am on my way, still on my way – but where to for heaven's sake?

At such moments of emptiness and loneliness and longing for inner healing, if you are lucky these words of Swami Satchidananda will come back to you: 'Actually, you don't have to do anything to heal the body and mind. If you don't interfere, the body and mind will heal themselves. There is a healer within everybody. We don't have to do anything to get the positive things. When we stop doing the negative things, the good happens by itself. We disturb and drain the body and mind too much. We waste so much energy-overdoing, oversleeping, overeating, over-talking. That drains you completely, so you lose your immunity. The mind over-thinks and that leads to anxiety, worry, fear. Learn to relax. That is the yogic way, nature's way. Not to overindulge in anything. That way, you can heal yourself well.'[123]

Peter: 'At such moments of truth I turn into a service station, buy a packet of Ritter Sport dark with hazelnuts and eat it in one go. Which puts me right back to basics. So, what was I doing? I was busy making the world a slightly better place, and making money while I am at it – enough for a nice car and a good chunk of chocolate. Something like that. Hard to think of anything else but chocolate at the moment. But when the energy boost arrives, sometimes moments of great lucidity occur and then I try to mentally store the insights, so that I may profit from them in coming days. The phenomenon also occurs independent of the con-sumption of chocolate, though less frequently. Perhaps there is a begin-ning dependency.'

We all have lucid moments, those moments when the cohesion of our life suddenly is seen with crystalline clarity, when we are charged with a higher energy than we experience in day to day life – and the trick is, to recognise those moments for what they are, these Golden Moments, Moments of Truth, and to hang on to what they give you. By becoming aware of the cohesion, you become more aware of who you are in a larger context, what your stronger and weaker aspects are, and how they operate on each other to make you who you are.

So, it is an advantage to have lucid moments frequently. Ideally, one should have complete lucidity all day. But how often do we have moments when we truly see the light? Some have them more than others, that seems established. Which leads us to ask: how can you obtain this advantage? You can't just call them up, can you? By lighting a candle or burnishing a magic lamp? Aren't these moments like shooting stars, unpredictable in their passage? Indeed they are, but you increase your chances of seeing one by looking at the night sky more often. And seeing more of the sky largely comes down to taking things away. Things that cloud the inner sky. Attention slurping, distracting matters, the massed cumulus of worries…It also doesn't help to have the radio on all the time, because it was invented to prevent us from being aware of what we are doing.*

When you tune into a popular music station, then all life is reduced to Super Hits and Mega Parties, a kind of life with the consistency of cotton candy with red dripping sauce. Finger lickin' good, but you know you'll be sick in the end. When you switch to Business Radio or some such, before ten minutes are over it's hard to tell that there exists a world beyond stocks and making deals. Indexes up and down, CEOs signing on or off, rumours and revelations, the whole shabang.

We know it is absurd for people who work in a corporate environment, but listening to these channels (leave alone *watching* Bloomberg) sometimes make us deeply uncomfortable, because they remove us from our essence. They block any notion that maybe life is not about stocks but about people and their feelings, their loved ones, and passions. That it really is about my life, right here and now, this moment of the century, the month, the day, the hour. Leading to questions such as: what do I do with my energy, which I expend in this world? What does my being here on earth accomplish? Something akin to those spokespersons answering the press on Business Radio? Stocks that due to me are sent higher or lower? Or does my life have a higher purpose, beyond survival, the amassing of fortune and sensual indulgence?

Fortunately most European nations have one or two classical stations with decent coverage, which sometimes play music compatible with contemplation, introspection or exploration of deeper emotional levels. But by far the largest part of all that we absorb through the media is wallpaper at best. Another large part consists of the needle of fear that is stuck into us every time again, always made just bearable by a reassuring balsam of commentary. A smaller but still significant part is flat out poisonous: an instrument of addiction to adrenaline which spreads coarsening of conduct, and creates insensitivity for all but the most intense stimuli. Opium for the people. Dopey people are happy people. In Huxley's dystopia *Brave New World*, the masses all walked around like

---

* Not literally of course, but that particular function goes a long way to explain its surging popularity – which applies equally to most of the rest of the media. In many communities where wisdom is cultivated, media are shunned or simply not available. Direct experience rules. It is a thousand times more enriching to have someone sing for you, than to hear the same song on a radio.

that, kept stupid and amused, and allowed a nice little buzz – so that they would question nothing and just keep doing what they were supposed to.

The powers that be, whatever their kind, are always intent to keep us a) in fear and b) amused. Because by producing fear in us they create a longing for protection, for a saving, fixing and managing force – to wit those selfsame powers. Amusement prevents people from seeing how they are being played – by those selfsame powers – and how they are deployed like any other assets. Human resources burnt up in uninspiring, uncreative lives, all going up in the fire of fear and whipped up emotions. All this so that they will submit themselves to what, as early as 1550, Étienne de la Boétie recognised as *The Voluntary Servitude.*[124]

Why do people willingly consent to their own enslavement? For De la Boétie, the collective obedience of society came from 'a vice for which no term can be found vile enough, which nature herself disavows and our tongues refuse to name.' Indeed, he had to invent a new term to even have a referent to the phenomenon, common as it is. To escape from the hell of self-imposed slavery is not easy, but if people really want to, they can do it, and if they're talented, it'll probably do wonders for them. There are two ways of doing it: quitting, and staying on to work on the inside. In the sixties and seventies we saw much of the former, now we see a growing tendency to stay inside the system – which is more attractive now than it was before, because you're no longer alone.

Clearing things up means taking stuff away: the obstacles that keep you from seeing things in a clear light. The things are clear of and by themselves, and it is only because of our own manipulation of the impressions, filtered for usefulness in terms of animal survival and refracted by the preferences of the ego, that we do not see them as such. Chögyam Trungpa, the great Buddhist master of the West, wrote in *Cutting Through Spiritual Materialism*: '... it is not a matter of building up the awakened state of mind, but rather of burning out the confusions which obstruct it.'[125]

For that reason, clearing things up means honesty, openness – especially towards yourself, but also towards others: 'I experience this exactly so, see it so, feel it so, want it so, do it so.' Not easy, because the world is full of prejudices and prefabricated opinions and there are vast sets of norms for socially desirable behaviour, speech, thought, and even, ridiculous as it may seem given its largely uncontrollable nature, emotion. If you really want to be yourself, like most of us you'll have to fight pretty hard to get there.

OBSTACLES ON SOCIETY'S GROWTH PATH

Once again: the softer you get, the harder you need to get. If you are working to increase your sensitivity to subtle impressions, you will have to shield yourself from rough approaches. This is an issue that we have not resolved for ourselves, and which to many of us will certainly form one of the greatest challenges of the coming decades – also on the level of state and country. We foresee more living in closed communities of like-minded individuals, so-called shared interest communities (according to Jeremy Rifkin, as many as 16 percent of all US citizens already live in such SICs), and unfortunately also in gated communities. The US and Europe also have a growing number of communities of people who get together around a particular spiritual concept or teaching. Findhorn is one of the prototypes, but new ones are created all the time.

Peter keeps painting to friends and colleagues the picture of a rural estate somewhere in the midst of untouched nature, say the west coast of Portugal, with ten or fifteen houses scattered over the land, grouped together for minimum impact, yet far enough apart so you can be just by yourself any time you want. Meals are often taken communally, but equally often at home alone with loved ones. The chief criterion for admission is sensitivity – and the resultant need to help create an environment that is somewhat shielded, *abrigado*, through a degree of isolation, so that the sea-urchin can safely expose himself, the cherished sensitivity can be expressed and realised in daily life. A place where you can drop your armour because no insensitive people are likely to arrive. Many other people are starting to entertain dreams of this nature.

What is happening on this private scale, is reflected on the national and global levels. A large section of our western society (Europe, Canada, Australia, New Zealand, and the more progressive US states) has matured to a point where it appears ready to make another growth spurt towards a higher degree of humanity, fraternisation and embrace – whereas lodged within it is a sizeable demographic entity which is in a wholly different stage of development. 'Wholly different' meaning: comparable to our own culture not just before the Age of Enlightenment, but *centuries before*. The period of inquisition and 'one faith for all', immutable and without heresies. Imposed, if not by persuasion then by the sword. This component of 12th century culture with its single-truth thinking, disregard for women, ardent desires to kill non-believers and crude concepts of justice, makes it very hard for us to achieve the kind of growth in consciousness that the majority feel they are getting ready for.

How we deal with this component in the next decades will have more impact on our lives than whether the stock markets fall or rise, and what the yuan is doing. How can we allow ourselves greater gentleness and openness at a time when we are threatened in our own land? Looking back does not help. Maybe we have not embraced the newcomers lovingly enough, or maybe they did not come to be embraced. Whatever the cause, we are in the middle of a cultural conflict, temporarily depressing our chances to create a better world. Remember how trusting most countries used to receive you? How you dropped your bags at the curb and showed your ticket and boarded to wherever? We were so nicely on our way...

Hopefully in Europe, too, leaders like Obama will stand up, who create more connectedness between the original culture and the imported, otherwise rejection is the predictable, ominous reaction of the social organism. Only half a century ago we saw in all its degrees of horror what rejection may ultimately entail, and how far average people will go without much prodding – to tattooed lamp shades and soap manufacture. Is mankind that much better today? Has the unthinkable become thinkable? Let us hope so, yet also be on our guard, and protect our soft side with great care. If we lose our ability to be human, we lose it all.

The Courage to Stand Up

The greatest courage required of you as a leader, is to stand up and take on the world.

We cannot speak of leadership today without weighing its content and intent. In the past, in fact till fairly recently, management literature used to deal with leadership as something mostly technical. An ability that you mastered in order to get done what you wanted. But this concept is rapidly losing effectiveness. You can't possibly see leadership separate any more from societal consequences for instance. Even charisma and charm don't effectively cover up wrongdoing anymore – what is the world coming to?

The notions of what constitutes good leadership are subject of intense discussion, critical revision and soul-searching. The only thing truly apparent, is that the leaders of a number of very large companies have failed miserably and spectacularly. As a result of some top executives' ruthless intent on personal gain, thousands of shareholders were cheated, thousands lost their jobs, thousands their pensions, their lives. Doubtless, more skeletons are waiting to fall out of closets, and the fear is justified that new skeletons continue to be created behind our backs, though more craftily than before. What risks to fellow human beings are taken today in some board rooms to increase profits, shareholder value, personal wealth?

No skeleton yet, but dying: the Third World, particularly Africa. It is still being plundered and raped as it was in colonial times, but the good news is, that the negative social effects and economic idiocy of it all are becoming obvious to more people every day, particularly in Europe, the neighbouring continent. (To those who might find some of this strong language we would like to bring to mind our dumping of hazardous waste, occasionally erupting into acts of corporate manslaughter and mass poisoning; our production of luxury articles at slave wages and under inhuman conditions, including forced labour and indenture; our sex tourism aimed at children held in the most abject form of slavery by deep poverty; our export of government subsidised agrarian over-production, which drives overseas producer communities into communal destitution, which we then worsen by our import levies on their agrarian products, so that we need to help them with oh, so humanitarian food aid, *et cetera ad infinitum.*)

All this forces us to reflect on what kind of society we want for this century. A society in the Anglo-Saxon and especially American mould with high income disparity, a social safety net with holes so large that many people fall right through, a feast of deregulation and a harsh business culture, bristling with lawyers? Do we want a *principle based society*, such as Europe has had for ages, or a *rule based society* such as the United States with its 'three strikes you're out' mentality and marginalised millions?[126] Do we want to live by the gospel of Sarbanes-Oxley (expect security updates as often as with Microsoft Windows, to be installed by lawyers) and sue each other more often? Are we going for The Number* – to hell with anyone standing in the way? Or do we want a society rooted in 'the old world' culture, with its respect for human values, and more deeply held belief in corporate social responsibility?

A DESIRABLE SHIFT OF FOCUS

There is a growing consensus – contradict us if you disagree – that we are in need of a fundamental transformation of the way we do business. Dissatisfaction with the way large corporations function in our global society has become a major, and hotly debated theme in public discourse. One could object that times of instability always bring out the whiners; which is true, and shame on them. But this goes beyond whining, because inspiring alternatives are being discussed. Moreover, the complaints are not heard on the shop floors so much as in boardrooms and brain shops and conference break-out rooms, which is also where most of the alternatives are born.

* Wall Street slang: 'The amount of money needed never to have to worry about money again.'

So, the continental plates are shifting, but how far exactly, and which way? Central themes in these reflections are Europe's emergence as a recognisable entity in the world – an economic powerhouse from birth with nearly half a billion inhabitants – and Europeans of so many different nationalities merging into this larger body, this larger concept of identity. The discussions are enlivened by the injection of an enormous dose of urgency. Because, if Europeans all become part of a larger whole, what kind of whole will that become? What norms and values are held dear in this community? Will it become a Europe of ever larger corporations, led by ever more greedy CEOs, protected by ever more lawyers? A Europe of financial constructions so clever that bankers end up buying and selling each other's rubbish for good money? A Europe where employers can deal with employees as an expense, and ultimately expendable? A true 'world class combatant', matching the US tooth for tooth?

It is important to know what we want, otherwise we cannot direct the process. In our view, we should direct our main energy focus away from money, and towards happiness. Any degree of shift is helpful. It would make us happier, and probably richer as well, simply because happy people are more productive than unhappy people. (This was the underlying, true cause for slavery's abolition. Productivity was atrocious. If it had been fantastic, slavery would *never* have been abolished, just as sweat shop production, which everyone claims to hate but which produces the goods for pennies on the dollar, is not abolished. Whatever union leaders like to think, most humanitarian improvements since the onset of the industrial revolutions were really exacted from employers by the need to increase productivity.)

For that reason, organisations have to learn to say 'no' to work that they do not really feel like doing, so that they can concentrate with total dedication on the things that they *do* like. That is enlightenment, that is good business sense, and that is what we try to practice in our own organisation.

It is high time we realised that the same principle applies to society as a whole. How do we direct the life force of all these people? And what kind of example do we set? How do we leaders, advisors, managers, consultants and writers deal with our own power? Are we deploying it exclusively to further our narrowly defined personal ends, or do we use some or even most of it to make the world a slightly better place than we found it at birth?

Thinking about these matters takes courage for people in the higher echelons of corporate life, especially in quoted corporations, because such thinking could well be seen as heresy. More courage is required to discuss them with colleagues, because it might be seen as subversion. This is because it deviates from an unspoken rule which in commercial circles has been adhered to for centuries, namely that 'thou shalt not engage with the world other than to enrich thyself'.

CORPORATE SOCIAL RESPONSIBILITY – A COSMETIC EXERCISE?

Many people still question if corporate social responsibility is even *desirable*. Because they are convinced of the truth of Milton Friedman's view, hammered in over decades, of the role of corporations in society. To quote once more from that by now famous/notorious article in the *New York Times*, cited above: 'The businessmen believe that they are defending free enterprise when they declaim that business is not concerned "merely" with profit but also with promoting desirable "social" ends; that business has a "social conscience" and takes seriously its responsibilities for providing employment, eliminating discrimination, avoiding pollution and whatever else may be the catchwords of the contemporary crop of reformers. In fact they are – or would be if they or anyone else took them seriously – preaching pure and unadulterated socialism. Businessmen who talk this way are unwitting puppets of the intellectual forces that have been undermining the basis of a free society these past decades.'

Yes, watch out, you leader on his or her way to enlightenment, because you may not be aware how you are played like a puppet, or how subversive your thoughts are! Where are the thought police when you need them? It is a miracle that things are still going as well as they do in enterprise – at least when compared with decades ago – because Friedman wrote this in 1970, and since then the advocates of socially responsible corporate conduct have certainly not become less vocal or influential.

The *Economist*, that old stalwart of capitalism *pur sang*, still has its doubts about all that socially responsible thinking. *Vide* its January 2005 special titled *The Good Company*, headed: 'The movement for corporate social responsibility has won the battle of ideas. That is a pity.'

That 'pity' sets the tone: 'In public-relations terms, their victory is total. In fact, their opponents never turned up. Unopposed, the CSR movement has distilled a widespread suspicion of capitalism into a set of demands for action. As its champions would say, they have held companies to account, by embarrassing the ones that especially offend against the principles of CSR, and by mobilising public sentiment and an almost universally sympathetic press against them. Intellectually, at least, the corporate world has surrendered and gone over to the other side.'

It all boils down to their view that there are a handful of misguided people who are making everyone crazy with their notion that companies have a societal duty beyond making money and bringing prosperity through the injection of wages into society. The cynical tone betrays the sore loser. The end of the piece reads: 'Better that CSR be undertaken as a cosmetic exercise than as serious surgery to fix what doesn't need fixing.' Right, let's digest this a second ... So if you really, really must, because everyone around you is on about social responsibility and stuff all the time, then limit it to a cosmetic exercise – gentlemen, could you *be* more cynical?

Pieces like these are written from fear, well phrased by Daniel Primozic in his article 'Corporate Social Responsibility: Must There Be Any?',[127] that the social responsibility of corporations could ultimately translate into personal responsibility of chief executives; 'mere' moral responsibility to begin with, but potentially judicial as well. This is not well taken by everyone in the room. And then of course there is the fear, felt somewhere deep in the wallet – demonstrably baseless and proven erroneous, that 'doing good', going beyond blind focus on profit and shareholder value will yield less than the familiar amoral style of doing business, which alas so easily slid into an immoral style but brought in the bacon.

From the mountains of research on the subject of corporate social responsibility let us pick just one recent example, found on the Source-Watch site of the Center for Media and Democracy: 'People's consumption patterns are influenced by corporate social responsibility efforts, according to a 2004 survey of more than 400 "opinion elites" (members of the top 10 percent of society, with regard to media consumption, civic engagement, and interest in public policy issues) in 10 countries, by

APCO Worldwide. "Positive CSR information has led 72% of the respon-
dents to purchase a company's product or services and 61% to recommend
the company to others. Conversely, negative CSR news has led 60% to
boycott a company's products and services".'[128] These kinds of figures
should make many an aficionado of corporate poker scratch him or herself
behind the ears.

The magazine *Financial Director*, not exactly a mouthpiece of socialism
and subversion, in a critical piece on the *Economist's* stance, quoted Mallen
Baker, development director of Business in the Community, who had this
to say, no doubt in his soft-spoken and plain speaking manner: 'The
people who really get CSR are the business leaders who have been the
most engaged in looking at how they can create wealth in a sustainable
way rather than at how they can give away a portion of the wealth they
create.'[129]

The unfounded fear that 'doing good' will lead to loss of turnover or
profitability, or create a social need to give away money sooner or later
(sometimes long postponed, but then in a surge, as seen in Bill Gates) is
one of the many false dichotomies that we keep alive – pairs of conditions
that are erroneously seen as mutually exclusive. Notions that are wrong,
but were never found out to be so, as they were handed down as received
wisdom by generation after generation, and rarely if ever questioned. All
these false dichotomies, usually antique if not archaic, make an urgent
appeal on leaders of inner strength to show them for what they are – void
– and clear the road towards a better world.

Much more courage than mere thinking, speaking, writing and consulting about enlightened leadership – we are acutely aware of this –
takes integrating it into corporate policy, and implementation in an often
fiercely competitive, and merciless market environment. We can only
hope that thinking, speaking and writing will fortify that courage.

BUSINESS AS AGENT FOR WORLD BENEFIT

Fortunately, a few insights have been acquired along the way that may
help us, in an unobtrusive way, almost subliminally, but quite effectively.
When asked about our own way of working, we sometimes say that what
we try is not to direct people, to knead them into shape or seduce them,
or run them through cultural fitness classes, but to get them interested

in a particular self-image of the organisation, and then make them fall in love with it.

A few years ago we stumbled on a website of the Weatherhead School of Management, headlined 'Business as Agent for World Benefit', that we have since often revisited, if only to copy the URL and pass it on to others. The concept that the site explicates, in all its stunning simplicity, boils down to this:

A. *Companies have great, practical power in our society.*
B. *Power equates responsibility.*
C. *Responsibility means that this power should not be applied just to enrich the shareholders, but also make the world a somewhat better place.*

Position A. by now is near impossible to refute, though the more docilely conservative financial media still try with some regularity, out of misplaced loyalty to large corporations (large advertisers), and a vain attempt so save their buddies from the onerous yoke of responsibility for what they do to the world. Most ordinary citizens these days are quite convinced of the global power of large organisations.

Few say it as beautifully as Dee Hock in *Birth of the Chaordic Age*: 'Global corporations now have implicit sovereignty over people throughout the world, since they are beyond the reach of any nation-state. They hold government and its instrumentalities to ransom for use of land, for reprieve from taxation, for access to natural resources far below cost, for direct monetary subsidization, and for use of land, air, and water as a repository for refuse; all by the simple expedient of bargaining one government against another for the claimed economic benefit of their presence. *Global corporations are creating a market for government in which they are the sole buyers* [our italics].'[130]

Position B. is an ancient moral principle. If you reject the notion that morality has any role in business, as many have done following guru Albert Carr, and are still doing today, you can skip Point C., because it won't thrill you.

Position C. begins to become a basic assumption for ever more people, and is the driving force behind the work of thousands of individuals and organisations the world over. As an example: a growing number of consultants from all continents, including these authors, are putting into practice a methodology called Appreciative Inquiry (AI), developed at this same Weatherhead School, by David Cooperrider and colleagues. AI is by now embraced by hundreds if not thousands of organisations that develop cutting edge leadership programs, including the US Navy. AI is the answer of positivists to the traditional consulting approach that 'something is wrong, let's fix it'. The Appreciative Inquiry practitioner says: 'in almost every organisation some things are doing fine, let's focus on those and reinforce them. It gives more energy and more happiness, and more result quickly'.

In 2002 the AI Commons started a worldwide interview project to chart the reactions of businessmen to the concept of 'Business as Agent for World Benefit'. Volunteers interview executives and managers following an established protocol in which one single theme is viewed from many angles, requiring participants to think hard about their answers. The answers are tested, bluntly where necessary, against espoused values of the participants. The interviewer goes on point after point, following the protocol – which as the interview proceeds tends to generate greater and greater interest in the subject. This technique is informed by a brilliant discovery that is one of the cornerstones of AI: everything that you inquire about gets reinforced.

This way to bring executives to a more noble attitude has something excitingly cunning, a cleverly conceived grass roots campaign. It also has a kind of almost comic smartness, which perhaps we see reflected in our own contribution to the world wide project: by talking about the issues and making people think about them, half the work is done. But that other half is still going to require hard work, with much personal dedication and courage.

THE WORK AHEAD

In this effort we may learn from, and be inspired by some emerging-market multinationals, who are new to the game of globalisation, and are in a position to reinvent the rules and the spirit in which it is played, so as to speed up the process of integration. As the *Economist* noted in 2008: 'Encouragingly, firms from emerging markets are finding that a globally integrated company needs a single culture, and that the best way to foster this is to make the highest ethics anywhere in the firm the norm for everyone, wherever they are working. Anything less tends to corrupt the culture.'[131]

This is in line with our own consulting experience: ever more globally operating organisations are discovering that the greatest work that they have ahead of them, lies within. That they need to create a winning corporate culture. Winning in both senses of the word: in terms of doing well materially, and in being attractive, engaging, easy to love. This discovery is not always lived by – concern for short term results may get in the way – but we see it lived more often now than in the past decades.

We are witnessing a historical acceleration of social development. Through the coincidence of suddenly, almost magically, increased transparency with the cataclysmic failure of greed-based financial systems, the world these organisations operate in is changing very rapidly in a direction of openness, fairness, and better stewardship. No one will be unaffected by this tide, not even behind what may now still seem impenetrable firewalls of government protection in certain areas.

More than ever before, people all over the world are sick of the excesses of organised greed. They want to see the world's material and human energy used in a way that benefits the many, not the few. They want business organisations to become aware of their power as change agents and assume leadership roles in society. And they are crying out for enlightened leaders to show them the way to a brighter future. You are one of those, we are sure.

Appendix

CHAKRA TEST ONLINE – IN DAILY USE WORLDWIDE

The web-based Chakra Test developed as an adjunct to this book rapidly became an established web presence. There is not a huge amount of traffic, but a good percentage actually completes the test. The scores are parsed for spurious submissions (e.g. unconscionably lazy choices) and tracked in an anonymised tally, giving an average for all participants, displayed on the site. The average by now, after thousands of participants, appears pretty much settled, though we would not be surprised if 'discovery' of the Chakra Test in a certain geographical area, or by a certain school would bring changes over time.

So what is the picture like? Striking, in this age of communication, is the relatively meagre score for the related chakra. Perhaps most people endure and produce rather *too much* communication. Willpower and respect come out strong, intuition and introspection could be more developed, and cosmic consciousness is at a level that provides hope for a better future – and much potential yet to be developed.

The contact details transmitted to the site for email feedback inevitably give us some inkling of the types of users that find their way to the site. About half of them appear to be consultants, trainers, academics and students, yoga teachers and coaches. They also show that sometimes a group of people from the same company decide to do the test together – an excellent idea, which is the cornerstone of the consulting practice described below.

CHAKRA TEST ONLINE – CONSULTING AND COACHING TOOLS

Many leadership thinkers see the organisation no longer as a mechanism, but as an organism – an organism which tends to take on human form.

In an era like this with its apparent trend towards a more humane global society, such an anthropomorphic view of organisations has much appeal. Which is why it makes sense to apply the instruments that we use to chart aspects of personality equally to organisations, with some adaptation, but essentially identical. For use in corporate consulting, a special site is set up for the group to be charted, so that participants can not just compare individual scores, but also their own scores compared with the group average, and discuss these in workshops.

The Chakra Test for Organisations gives insight into the favourably and unfavourably developed personality aspects of an organisation: is it mostly concerned with survival or profit-making, or about making a valuable contribution to society? Does it have a heart, or is it emotionally cold? Is it directed mainly by willpower or by vision? Is its customer relations management inspired by opportunism or true loyalty? And how well balanced is the organisation's energy economy?

The web-based survey takes about twenty minutes to complete. Compilation of the input of all participants creates an overall image that graphically reveals the *current personality* of the organisation. A second round of questions charts the *desired personality*. Juxtaposition of the results, statistically clear and visually attractive, makes clear to all involved where pain and discomfort is experienced, where the greatest potential lies for growth, what aspirations people have, and which aspects of the corporate personality require extra attention.

Because of the scripted processing of the survey input, the cost of employing the Chakra Test for Organisations is modest – certainly in comparison with most traditional ways to scan organisations. Moreover, the investment required is independent of the number of participants. Essentially there is no difference between charting the energy distribution of fifty people or fifty thousand. However, very large groups are best charted in a more comprehensive survey with several cuts, e.g. along functional or regional lines, to show more clearly cultural differences among them. Organisations serving the common good may apply for a reduced fee.

Interested parties can contact the authors through Trompenaars Hampden-Turner in Amsterdam, at www.thtconsulting.com.

Endnotes

1 Peter ten Hoopen, *De Trancekaravaan ('Trance Caravan')*, Contact, 1996.
2 Charles Handy, *The Hungry Spirit, Beyond Capitalism: A Quest for Purpose in the Modern World*, Broadway Books, 1998.
3 Canadian management-thinker Harry Mintzberg in an off-the-cuff session after the formal part of his presentation at a seminar in De Doelen, Rotterdam, March 26, 2004: 'It's disastrous, 70% of all American workers now live in mortal fear of being fired'. And this was in good times.
4 Sue Howard & David Welbourn, *The Spirit at Work Phenomenon*, Azure, 2004.
5 James MacGregor Burns, *Leadership*, 1978. Many translations and later editions.
6 Thanks for this analogy to Kirsten Jørgensen, Danish architect, private conversation.
7 Robert Goffee & Gareth Jones, 'Why Should Anyone Be Led by You?', *Harvard Business Review*, Sept/Oct 2000.
8 James MacGregor Burns, *Transforming Leadership*, Atlantic Monthly Press, 2003.
9 Abraham Zaleznik, 'Managers and Leaders: Are They Different?', *Harvard Business Review*, 1977, reissued as HBR Classic, 2004.
10 Simon Head, *The New Ruthless Economy: Work and Power in the Digital Age*, Oxford, 2003. For a partly contrasting view see Daniel Cohen, *Our Modern Times: The Nature of Capitalism, in the Information Age*, MIT Press, 2004.
11 Elias Canetti, *Masse und Macht*, Claassen Verlag, 1960. Translated as *Crowds and Power*, Victor Gollancz, 1962. Many other editions, among them Penguin.
12 Danah Zohar & Ian Marshall, *Spiritual Capital*, Bloomsbury, 2004. See also Peter's speech honouring the authors in *Enriching ourselves with Spiritual Capital*. URL: www.rovingstar.com/soul/soul_artikel_5_zohar.html.
13 This at least is the traditional view. Recently some Egyptologists have contested this view, saying that the quality of the workmanship makes use of forced labour unlikely. We beg to differ and stay on the side of traditionalists. In all civilisations examples abound of compulsory workmanship,

including slave labour and child labour, that produced works of stunning quality. As the great designer (and successful businessman) William Morris observed in the early 20th C.: 'In most sober earnest, when we hear it said, as it often is said, that extra money payment is necessary under all circumstances to produce great works of art, and that men of special talent will not use those talents without being bribed by mere gross material advantages, we, I say, shall know what to reply. We can appeal to the witness of those lovely works still left us, whose unknown, unnamed creators were content to give them to the world, with little more extra wages than what their pleasure in their work and their sense of usefulness in it might bestow on them.' William Morris, *Architecture and History*. URL: www.marxists.org/ archive/morris/works/1884/spab10.htm

[14] Few cruder forms of exploitation are seen in the world today, than the bonded labour still practiced in Bihar, Orissa, Madhya Pradesh and other states, by friends of local party bosses, and those bosses themselves. The phenomenon has been on our watch list for decades, because it is so unspeakably crass – in its effects on the enslaved people, and on the physiognomy of the usurpers, regularly exposed by India Today. URL for case referred to: www.swamiagnivesh.com/gwalior1.html

[15] Frederick Winslow Taylor, *The Principles of Scientific Management*, Harper & Brothers, 1911. Reprint: Dover, 1998. URL: http://melbecon.unimelb.edu. au/het/taylor/sciman.htm

[16] Alan G. Carter & Colston Sanger, *Thinking about Thinking, 1997*. URL: http://www.reciprocality.org/Reciprocality/r0/Day1.html

[17] Albert Z. Carr, 'Is Business Bluffing Ethical?', *Harvard Business Review*, January–February 1968. URL: http://falcon.tamucc.edu/~sencerz/Carr_ Business_Bluffing.htm

[18] Sinclair Lewis, *Babbitt*, Harcourt Brace Jovanovich, 1922.

[19] Joep Schrijvers, *The Way of the Rat: A Survival Guide to Office Politics*, Cyan Communications, 2004.

[20] Milton Friedman, 'The Social Responsibility of Business is to Increase Profits', *New York Times*, September 13, 1970. URL: http://www.colorado. edu/studentgroups/libertarians/issues/friedman-soc-resp-business.html

[21] Not an exact figure, but an estimate. The actual figure is probably closer to 100%.

[22] Robert E. Kelley, 'In Praise of Followers', *Harvard Business Review*, August 26, 2006.

[23] Ira Chaleff, *The Courageous Follower: Standing Up to and for Our Leaders*, Berrett-Koehler, 2nd edn, 2004.

[24] Dee Hock, 'The Art of Chaordic Leadership', *Leader to Leader*, No. 15, 2000. URL: http://www.leadertoleader.org/knowledgecenter/journal.aspx? ArticleID=62

[25] Rasmusssen Reports, June, 2006. URL: www.rasmussenreports.com/2006/ July%20Dailies/churchAttendance.htm. See also: Walter Russell Mead,

'God's Country?', *Foreign Affairs*, September/October 2006, URL: www. foreignaffairs.org/20060901faessay85504/walter-russell-mead/god-s-country.html

[26] Kevin Philips, *American Theocracy: The Peril and Politics of Radical Religion, Oil, and Borrowed Money in the 21st Century*, Viking, 2006.

[27] Or perhaps as a result of the moral progress that Vanderbilt professor of philosophy John Lachs links to economic progress in *A Community of Individuals*, Routledge, 2002.

[28] Jack London has endowed many of his heroes with this very attribute. About the protagonist of his famous story *Building a Fire*: 'Empty as the man's mind was of thoughts, he was keenly observant.'

[29] Ed Oakley & Doug Krug, *Enlightened Leadership: Getting to the Heart of Change*, Simon & Schuster, 1994.

[30] Credit for the last riposte to Krauthammer CEO Ronald Meijers, shooting from the hip at participants gathering of Foundation for European Leadership, 2005.

[31] Robert G. Eccles c.s., *The Value Reporting Revolution, Moving Beyond the Earnings Game*, John Wiley & Sons, 2001.

[32] Former Enron CEO Jeffrey Skilling was sentenced to 24 years in prison. Source: MSNBC. URL: www.msnbc.msn.com/id/15389150/

[33] Former WorldCom CEO Bernard Ebbers was sentenced to 25 years in prison for his role in orchestrating the biggest corporate fraud in US history. Source: CNN. URL: http://money.cnn.com/2005/07/13/news/newsmakers/ebbers_sentence/

[34] Former Tyco CEO and CFO both convicted of grand larceny, conspiracy, securities fraud, and eight counts of falsifying business records. Source: *Washington Post*. URL: www.washingtonpost.com/wp-dyn/content/article/2005/06/17/AR2005061701003.html

[35] Former Sunbeam CEO Al Dunlap agreed to pay a $500,000 fine to the SEC, plus another $15 million to defrauded investors who filed a class-action suit. According to news accounts, Dunlap never admitted wrongdoing. Source: Knowledge W. Carey. URL: http://knowledge.wpcarey.asu.edu/article.cfm?articleid=1656

[36] Former Qwest Communications CEO Joe Nacchio was sentenced to six years in prison for making $52 million in illegal stock sales while helping to bring the company to the brink of bankruptcy. Source: MSNBC. URL: www.msnbc.msn.com/id/19996449/

[37] Former Samsung CEO Lee Kun-hee was convicted of tax evasion charges and fined the equivalent of US $109 million. His three-year prison sentence was suspended. Source: Directorship, Boardroom Intelligence. URL: http://www.directorship.com/lee-fined–avoids-prison

[38] Former Adelphia CEO John Rigas was sentenced to 20 years in prison for his part in multibillion dollar fraud. Source: CNN. URL: http://money.cnn.com/2005/06/20/news/newsmakers/rigas_sentencing/

[39] A slang term referring to securities that are unattractive due to certain underlying provisions or risks making them generally illiquid with poor pricing schemes and transparency. Mainly used in reference to CMOs, toxic waste represents the small portion of these products that are byproducts created as a result of providing the majority of CMOs with minimal risk. In effect, this small portion of byproducts is used as outlets for transferring a substantial portion of the underlying risks involved in making the obligations and then marketed to investors. Source: Free Dictionary, URL: http://financial-dictionary.thefreedictionary.com/Toxic+Waste

[40] A newsletter from the Integral Yoga Foundation, containing this quote from their guru Sri Swami Satchidananda, appears to continue where we left off: 'That's why I say, every Yogi should be a surfer. If you know how to balance, you'll like big waves. You're not even happy with small waves. The world is an ocean – *samsara sagaram*. It has a lot of waves. And if you know how to surf, you will never get caught in the waves. You will be above the waves enjoying the flow. You don't need to dissolve all the waves to make the ocean peaceful. That would be a bore. Leave it as it is. Instead, find the balance and then have fun.' *IY Magazine*, e-newsletter, October 2006.

[41] Bill George on his own website. URL: http://www.authenticleaders.org/articles/crisiscorporateethics.htm

[42] Bill George in interview, *Harvard Business School Alumni Magazine* On-line. URL: http://www.alumni.hbs.edu/bulletin/2003/december/qanda.html

[43] Bill George on his own website, *ibid*.

[44] See Hock, above.

[45] Robert E. Staub, 'Leading wholeheartedly', *Journal for Quality and Participation*, January, 2001. Web: http://www.findarticles.com/p/articles/mi_qa3616/is_200110/ai_n8961302

[46] Andrew Cohen, 'Enlightenment for the 21st Century', in *What Is Enlightenment?* March-May 2005. Quote of the Week #119 on his website. URL: www.andrewcohen.org/quote/?quote=119

[47] Aviv Shahar, executive coach, former Israeli air force pilot, on the website of his vehicle Amber Coaching. Not a celebrity like the other quoted leadership coaches, Aviv was chosen because his voice sounds wholly sincere, and because his words have an idealism and at the same time a down-to-earthness that resonate with us on a deep level. URL: http://www.ambercoaching.com/whole_person_development.html

[48] Jim Dreaver writes and teaches about the art of awakening the leader within. He graciously allowed quotation of this excerpt from his book, *End Your Story, Begin Your Life*, available at www.endyourstory.com.

[49] Richard Barrett, *Liberating the Corporate Soul*, Butterworth/Heinemann, 1998.

[50] Abraham H. Maslow, *Motivation and Personality*, 2nd ed., New York, Harper & Row, 1970.

51 It is remarkable that Maslow's hierarchy of five vital needs is widely taught, discussed and used, but that few mention his later addition of the higher levels. Perhaps the transcendental is insufficiently understood in the academic world to be expounded in scientific magazines, handbooks and works about popular psychology. What may also play a part, is that few people develop consciousness at this level, so that its omission is not widely experienced as a lack. See: Abraham Maslow, *The Farther Reaches of Human Nature*, Viking, 1971. Various later editions, including Penguin, published under the auspices of the Esalen Institute.

52 Selvarajan Yesudian & Elisabeth Haich, *Yoga and Health*, Allen & Unwin, 1957. Various later editions.

53 B.K.S. Iyengar, *Light on Yoga*, Schocken Books, 1966. Various later editions.

54 Paramhansa Yogananda, *Autobiography of a Yogi*, 1946, location unknown. Various later editions. URL: http://wikisource.org/wiki/Autobiography_of_a_Yogi and http://www.crystalclarity.com/yogananda.

55 *The Yoga Sutras of Patanjali*, translation and commentary by Sri Swami Satchidananda, Integral Yoga Publications, 1978.

56 Peter's earliest and best meditation teacher, who taught Kundalini Yoga in silence, offering only his own meditation and hand signals for instruction, Hardwar, India, 1969.

57 Abraham Maslow, *Toward a Psychology of Being*, 3rd ed. (the most commonly used, much revised edition), Wiley, 1998. And: *The Farther Reaches of Human Nature*, Viking, 1971.

58 Richard Barrett, *Liberating the Corporate Soul*, Butterworth-Heinemann, 1998.

59 Stephen Covey, *The 8th Habit: From Effectiveness to Greatness*, Simon & Schuster, 2004.

60 Jim Collins, *Good to Great, Why Some Companies Make the Leap. ... And Others Don't*, Harper Business, 2001.

61 Studied, though some only cursorily: the 3 Levels of Leadership of John Paul Lederach, the 4 Levels of Strategos, the 5 Levels of Jim Collins and the 5 of Steven Geigle, the 7 Levels of Leadership of Richard Barrett, the 8 Levels of Leadership of Baxter Bean and a few with so many levels that in real life they are no use.

62 Jeremy Rifkin, *The European Dream*, Tarcher, 2004.

63 Anodea Judith, *Eastern Body, Western Mind: Psychology and the Chakra System as a Path to the Self*, Celestial Arts, 1996.

64 'Why did Bhagwan Shree Rajneesh own 90 Rolls Royces? Why did Saddam Hussein own dozens of luxurious palaces? Those desires were products of the base animal mind of two men who grew up surrounded by poverty. Enlightenment does not care about symbols of power and potency. Looking for hidden esoteric explanations for obsessive behavior is pointless. Is there a

secret spiritual reason that Rajneesh had a collection of dozens of expensive ladies' watches? The universal cosmic consciousness is completely neutral and without any need to possess, impress, or dominate. It also cannot drive or tell time.' Christopher Calder, *Osho, Bhagwan Rajneesh, and the Lost Truth*, web publication. URL: http://home.att.net/~meditation/Osho.html

[65] Kenneth Ahern and J. Fred Weston, *Mergers and Acquisitions in 2007*, Social Science Electronic Publishing, 2008. URL: http://papers.ssrn.com/sol3/papers.cfm?abstract_id=1087111

[66] Gary Clyde Hufbauer and Paul L.E. Grieco, 'The Payoff from Globalisation', *Washington Post*, June 7, 2005. URL: http://www.washingtonpost.com/wp-dyn/content/article/2005/06/06/AR2005060601508.html.

[67] Source: Reuters. URL: www.reuters.com/article/mergersNews/idUSN2837929220070628

[68] *Economist*, 9 January 1999.

[69] Selden, Larry Selden and Geoffrey Colvin, Geoffrey, 'M&A needn't be a loser's game', *Harvard Business Review* 81/6, 2003.

[70] Matthias M. Bekier, Anna J. Bogardus and Timothy Oldham, *Mastering Revenue Growth in M&A*, McKinsey, 2001. Quoted by Institute of Mergers, Acquisitions and Alliances, URL: http://www.manda-institute.org/en/links+mergers+acquisitions+m&a.htm.

[71] New York University website. URL: http://w4.stern.nyu.edu/news/news.cfm?doc_id=3741.

[72] Nikos Mourkogiannis, *Purpose, The Starting Point of Great Companies*, Palgrave Macmillan, 2006.

[73] Places of such purity, that connect us to the earth strongly, are best kept hidden from the masses, as in western cultures purity and public use rarely coexist.

[74] Various sources, among them International Labour Organization. URL: http://www.ilo.org/global/About_the_ILO/Media_and_public_information/Press_releases/lang–en/WCMS_075504/index.htm http://itrs.scu.edu/faculty/mbousquet/en2spr6/wkwok/printable%20version.htm

[75] Various sources, among them US Department of Labor. URL: http://www.dol.gov/ILAB/media/reports/iclp/sweat2/bonded.htm. See also: Ravi S. Srivastava, *Bonded Labor in India, Its Incidence and Pattern*. International Labour Organization, 2005. URL: http://digitalcommons.ilr.cornell.edu/cgi/viewcontent.cgi?article=1017&context=forcedlabor

[76] Various sources, among them *The Telegraph*, issued in Kolkatta, India.URL: http://www.telegraphindia.com/1061108/asp/jamshedpur/story_6973193.asp

[77] In different chakra systems, the Svadisthana is variously called Sacral Chakra, Sex Chakra or Navel Chakra – the latter term being very confusing, given the location of the energy centre much lower in the body. Then there are systems that reserve the name Navel Chakra for the next chakra up, what

we call the Solar Plexus Chakra. Given the belly button's location at the same height as the Solar Plexus this name is at least somewhat logical, though still erroneous because the chakra lies deep in the body, in front of the spine. We prefer to cut through the confusion by not using the term Navel Chakra at all, being quite satisfied that the terms Sacral Chakra and Solar Plexus Chakra are both traditionally sanctioned and clear, leaving no doubt as to the location.

[78] Omraam Mikhael Aivanhov. Quote from website, a selection of his sayings. Translation PtH. URL: www.aivanhov.de, one of several websites devoted to Aivanhov.

[79] Source: Wikipedia. URL: http://en.wikipedia.org/wiki/Sodomy_law. See also Sodomy Laws website. URL: www.sodomylaws.org.

[80] Thanks to French 'aspiration consultant' Marc Bourgery for that observation. We missed that issue.

[81] *Ashtavakra Gita* or *Ashtavakra Samhita*. Translation by John Richards available on-line. URL: http://realization.org/page/doc0/doc0004.htm.

[82] Adam Brandenburger and Barry Nalebuff, *Co-Opetition: A Revolution Mindset That Combines Competition and Cooperation*, Doubleday, 1997. See also accompanying website, URL: http://mayet.som.yale.edu/coopetition.

[83] One might ask: Why bring up someone like George Clooney in this context? What does he have in common with business leaders? Well, could it be the private jet? The cash flow management? Distribution channels and rights? Merchandising? Joint ventures? Production and traffic? Public relations management? Long and short term investments? Tax issues? The whole raft of representatives, assistants, advisors, producers, project managers, stylists and sundry other suppliers? Not to mention *the community*? Could it be all of the above? The running of an enterprise is similar across industries and dimensions, because great leadership has appeal everywhere, and mediocre leadership leads to the same uninspired plodding in each type of organisation. Network organisations, such as George Clooney's, are cutting edge these days. They are the hardest to lead, but once you get them going they can rapidly create great momentum. All they need is leadership by truly inspiring individuals, hugely energetic and infectious, who connect well with others and come over for pasta.

[84] Everything we ever experience is stored in all its details. We have suspected this from childhood, but recently, while flicking channels in a hotel room, saw it confirmed in the work of a Japanese prodigious savant who can take one look from the top of a skyscraper, and in several days of seclusion render the whole view in a drawing so detailed that the numbers of windows in the most distant façades match. An older case is that of a English savant, who, after a 12 minute helicopter ride over London, completed in three hours an impeccably accurate sketch which encompasses 4 square miles, 12 major landmarks and 200 other buildings all drawn to scale and perspective.

Apparently all visual imagery is stored; as, we feel sure, are all other experiences. We are sitting on huge hard disks of data, but clearly, we have unlinked much of the stuff from the index, to be lost in limbo forever – till we stumble upon the orphan clusters in dreams, psychoses or creative crazes. See: Darold Treffert, *The Savant Syndrome in Autistic Disorder*. URL: http://www.awares.org/conferences/show_paper.asp?section=000100010001 &conferenceCode=000200010007&id=31&full_paper=1 (A URL fitting for savants.)

[85] One of us read this as a teenager. Unfortunately, we cannot retrieve the source.

[86] This is not empirical fact, but a considered estimate based on observation of human behaviour in numerous developed and less developed cultures over several decades. Analysis of thousands of results of the Chakra Test confirm this. It must also be said that most of the truly stellar returns are, or appear to be, from men.

[87] Robert K. Greenleaf, *The Servant as Leader*, Greenleaf Center for Servant Leadership, continuously reprinted.

[88] Jim Collins, *Ibid*.

[89] Tom Wolfe, *The Painted Word*, Farrar, Straus and Giroux, 1975.

[90] This trend has been obvious for several years now, yet HR-directors the world over, while ringing their alarm bells, appear incapable of convincing their CEOs and CFOs of what is coming, so that in many companies – never mind the mission statements – the human factor remains low on the list of priorities. This creates a huge hidden liability for such companies in a time when talent can move freely worldwide, and the entire baby-boom generation is preparing to retire.

[91] *A Survey of Talent*, Economist Special Report, October 7–13, 2006.

[92] Richard Branson, *Losing My Virginity: How I've Survived, Had Fun, and Made a Fortune Doing Business My Way*, Three Rivers Press, 1999.

[93] One might wonder if we should have been there at all. The dilemma was obvious: on the one hand we did not want to do anything that might help the regime, on the other hand we wanted to assist our client, whom we began by trusting – and on the third hand we wanted to learn. Curiosity being one of our main drivers, we are more likely than the average consultant to encounter such dilemmas. As luck would have it, as authors and speakers, we can always claim the higher purpose of fact finding and learning in the service of knowledge transmission.

[94] Baghwan Shri Rajneesh (Osho), quoted on website of his organisation. URL: http://sannyas.org/quotes/chakra07.htm

[95] Johnson & Johnson's Credo. URL: www.jnj.com/connect/about-jnj/jnj-credo.

[96] Interface Inc., corporate website. URL: http://www.interfaceinc.com/who/founder.html

97 Henri Bergson, *L'Energie Spirituelle*, in *Oeuvres*, Presses Universitaires de France, Paris, 1959.

98 Not to equate God with Santa Claus, but in the USA, where according to research by the Pew Institute, 30% of the population call themselves evangelical Christians, and 42% believe in the historical truth of the Bible, plotting the creation of the world at about 6,000 AD. But then again, as the *New York Times* reported, 20% of the US population believe that the Sun revolves around the Earth. Sources: Pew Research Centre, URL: http://people-press.org/reports/display.php3?PageID=757; Article 'Teaching of Creationism is Endorsed in New Survey', *New York Times*, August 30, 2005. URL: http://select.nytimes.com/gst/abstract.html?res=F20616F63D550C728FDDA10894DD404482 (requires login). Also see: Walter Russell Mead, 'God's Country?', *Foreign Affairs Quarterly*, September/October, 2006. URL: www.foreignaffairs.org/20060901faessay85504-p20/walter-russell-mead/god-s-country.html

99 An oft quoted pronouncement (with remarkably strong presence on universities like Harvard and Stanford), taken from his foreword to Daniel Goleman, *Destructive Emotions: How Can We Overcome Them?*, Bantam, 2003.

100 Malcolm Gladwell, *Blink, The Power of Thinking Without Thinking*, Little Brown, 2005.

101 Talula Cartwright, *Developing Your Intuition: A Guide to Reflective Practice*, CCL Press, 2004.

102 Gay Hendricks, Ph.D., & Kate Ludeman, Ph.D., *The Corporate Mystic: A Guidebook for Visionaries with Their Feet on the Ground*, Bantam, 1996.

103 A classic text of the Tantric tradition, found in several early and modern translations. Paraphrase by Peter ten Hoopen, based on various sources, among them Peter Fenner, 'Spiritual Inquiry in Buddhism', *Revision*, Vol. 17, No. 2, 1944. URL: http://ccbs.ntu.edu.tw/FULLTEXT/JR-ADM/peter.htm.

104 Sheikh Ansari (1006–1089), *Kashf al-Asrar*, Vol. 7, Maqulat-o Andarz-ha – Sayings and Advice, translated by A.G. Farhadi. Web: http://wahiduddin.net/sufi_poetry.htm#Sheikh Ansari Jabir ibn Abdullah al-Ansari. We have felt impelled to replace the translator's prosaic 'the hereafter' with the more poetic 'heaven', which serves the intent of the poem, and is in line with classical Sufi translations such as those by Arthur J. Arberry.

105 Arthur Koestler, *The Roots of Coincidence*, Random House, 1972. *Note by Peter:* On the flyleaf of my copy I jotted down an example of coincidence that Koestler would have loved: 'In my hotel room [in adored Chichilliane, but that may be circumstantial, although the name does evoke the crepitating of insect wings] I had just read an astonishing case of Carl Jung's involving a scarab beetle, when I went down for dinner. As I sat down at the long rustic table, my head still tingling from the reading, the lady sitting opposite (a person wholly unknown to me), said something to her neighbour

about a scarab. She used the Italian word *scarabeo*, which was promptly translated into French by the gentleman next to her for the benefit of yet another person at the table, almost as if to make sure that, whatever my language skills, I would be in no doubt which word had just been uttered. The coincidence, involving a word rarely used in everyday conversation, was so striking that a chill ran down my spine. When I came home a few days later I called a woman whom I had not seen or spoken to in twenty years to verify some memory about the mutual friend who had recommended *The Roots of Coincidence* to me, and had recently deceased. She was on the phone after the first ring, and seemed not at all surprised to hear my voice, starting to tell me straight out, as if it had been she who had dialled, that she wanted to speak to me about a tiny antique scarab that, after it had been missing for some twenty years, just turned up as she cleaned up her apartment. I was quite astonished to hear of this find, remembering well the tiny blue piece of ceramic that her son once found in the early sixties, as he clambered into a pyramid's corridor with the same gentleman who had so highly recommended *The Roots of Coincidence*.'

[106] The scientific studies are highly specialised, hardly accessible to the general reader, but thrilling because of their proof that something like a 'third eye' has a biological basis. See: I.R. Schwab and G.R. O'Connor, 'The Lonely Eye', *British Journal of Ophthalmology* 2005, Vol. 89. Also: Richard L. Puzdrowski and R. Glenn Northcutt, 'Central projections of the pineal complex in the silver lamprey Ichthyomyzon unicuspis', *Biomedical and Life Sciences and Medicine* Vol. 255, Number 2, January, 1989. A fine example from the mystical angle is John Van Mater, Jr, *The Third Eye and Human Evolution*. Web: http://www.theosophy-nw.org/theosnw/evol/ev-jvmj2.htm

[107] Steve Jobs, *You've got to find what you love*, Commencement address Stanford University, in Stanford Report, June 14, 2005. Web: http://news-service.stanford.edu/news/2005/june15/jobs-061505.html

[108] Joseph W. McMoneagle, *Mind Trek*, Hampton Roads Publishing, revised edition1997.

[109] H. E. Puthoff, Ph.D., *CIA-Initiated Remote Viewing at Stanford Research Institute*. Web: http://www.militaryremoteviewers.com/cia_remote_viewing_sri.htm

[110] Brenda J. Dunne en Robert G. Jahn, 'Information and Uncertainty in Remote Perception Research', *Journal of Scientic Exploration*, Vol.17, No.2, 2003. Web: http://www.scientificexploration.org/jse/articles/pdf/17.2_dunne_jahn.pdf

[111] Geoffrey Miller, *The Mating Mind*, Anchor, 2001.

[112] An English version is running on http://www.creativityresearch.net/ Readers are kindly requested to participate. Results will be collated over a two year period, and published in cooperation with a media partner yet to be announced.

113 There is nothing particular to quote here, but who could write a sentence like that without thinking of Jalaluddin Rumi? Those who missed him might want to start with his *Masnavi I Ma'navi*, translated by E.H. Whinfield, Kegan Paul, Trench, Trübner, Second Edition, 1898. Full text on-line at URL: http://www.intratext.com/X/ENG0134.HTM.

114 The first place to start would be at the BAWB Global Forum. URL: http://www.bawbglobalforum.org/

115 Actually there are gurus who go Sri Sri Ravi Shankar one better. One is Sri Sri Sri Guru Viswasphoorthi, whose radiant countenance may be admired at his website. URL: www.srisrisriguruviswasphoorthi.com/ Another triple Sri is His Holiness Bhadwan Sri Sri Sri Vishwayogi Vishwamji Maharaj, whose radiant, and bejeweled 'lotus feet' may be admired at his website. URL: http://www.viswaguru.com/

116 Deepak Chopra, *The Answer Is Still Peace*, newsletter, mailed out via Be the Change (www.bethechange.org) on July 8, 2005 at 01:01 AM

117 You can get some cute peeks into the world of spiritual business by Googling for +spiritual +business. It will take you to a whole bevy of less veiled sites like www.coachingfromspirit.com, that radiate unmitigated focus on making money — first of all yours. All vibrant examples of the topic of this chapter: activities directed by the Root Chakra that are presented as the work of the Crown Chakra.

118 This was said in private, confidentiality not asked but assumed, which is why we have masked his identity.

119 Daniel Libeskind in CNN feature about his extension of the Denver Art Museum, the Frederic C. Hamilton building, Nov 12. 2006.

120 Norbert Wiener, *Cybernetics: Or the Control and Communication in the Animal and the Machine*, MIT Press 1948 and *The Human Use of Human Beings*. Da Capo Press, 1950.

121 *The Heart of Awareness, A Translation of the Ashtavakra Gita*, translated by Thomas Byrom, Shambhala, 2001. Many other translations, e.g. *Ashtavakra Gita*, translated by John Richards, on website of Realization, Classics. URL: http://www.realization.org/page/doc0/doc0004.htm and http://www.clas.ufl.edu/users/gthursby/ind/ashtgita.htm. The classic remains *Ashtavakra Samhita*, translated by Swami Nityaswarupananda, Advaita Ashrama, Calcutta, 3rd ed., 1969.

122 We are aware that this evokes horrible memories of the Nazis' use of the term *Fremdkörper* ('foreign bodies') to indicate the Jewish part of the population. They too spoke in pathological terms. Yes, dangerous territory. So, with all idealist forces, stay on the alert for proto-fascist potential. Yet it is common experience that groups which strive for more connectedness, need to exclude elements that will not or cannot connect, in order to allow them to realise their desired development. We see this most markedly in pioneer communities, communes and other utopian environments, in the major

Indian ashrams, who are very selective in who they allow permanent residence, in clubs like Lloyds, and many mission driven organisations, and of course in secret brotherhoods like the Rosicrucians, the Masons and the Hell's Angels.

[123] Quote from Swami Satchidananda in *Integral Yoga Magazine*, electronic newsletter, Feb. 18, 2007.

[124] Étienne de la Boétie, *Discourse on Voluntary Servitude*, originally published in 1550. Excellent translation by Harry Kurz, Columbia University Press, 1942. URL: www.constitution.org/la_boetie/serv_vol.htm. Original French text in PDF on: www.forget-me.net/LaBoetie/servitude.pdf. Given De la Boétie's harsh indictment of the phenomenon in the book, a better term for what he describes would have been 'slavery', but purists would have condemned the translator to work among the galleys. De la Boétie may well have avoided the word in his title himself to avoid provoking the censors.

[125] Chögyam Trungpa, *Cutting Through Spiritual Materialism*, Shambhala, 1973.

[126] A fascinating 2004 report in the *Gotham Gazette* on the distribution of lawyers in the New York metropolitan area, showed densities of 10–15% of the population in some parts of Manhattan and Westchester county. The total tally came to 118,810 lawyers, not counting the many thousands of paralegal secretaries. Andrew Beveridge, 'New York Lawyers: A Profile', in *Gotham Gazette*, December, 2004 URL: www.gothamgazette.com/article/ demographics/20041228/5/1231. In the years since 2004 the number of litigations, and presumably the number of lawyers, has gone up steeply.

[127] Daniel Primozic, 'Corporate Social Responsibility: Must There Be Any?', *Discernment*, Wheaton College, Vol. 6, No. 3, 1999. Summary on URL: http://www.wheaton.edu/CACE/resources/discernment/adobe/vol06no3.pdf

[128] Center for Media & Democracy's Sourcewatch. Web: http://www. sourcewatch.org/index.php?title=Corporate_Social_Responsibility

[129] Anthony Harrington, 'In Good Company', cover story of *Financial Director* (published by VNU), 20 July 2005. URL: http://www.financialdirector.co. uk/financial-director/features/2140109/good-company

[130] Dee Hock, *Birth of the Chaordic Age*, Berrett Koehler, 1999.

[131] From 'In praise of the stateless multinational', *Economist*, September 20, 2008.

Index